Kit Hausa

Phonological Acquisition
and Phonological Theory

Phonological Acquisition
and Phonological Theory

edited by

John Archibald
The University of Calgary

LEA LAWRENCE ERLBAUM ASSOCIATES, PUBLISHERS
1995   Hillsdale, New Jersey   Hove, UK

Lawrence Erlbaum Associates, Inc., Publishers
365 Broadway
Hillsdale, New Jersey 07642

Cover design by Cheryl Minden

Library of Congress Cataloging-in-Publication Data

Phonological acquisition and phonological theory / edited by John
Archibald.
   p.   cm.
Includes bibliographical references and index.
ISBN 0-8058-1352-7
   1. Language acquisition. 2. Grammar, Comparative and general—
Phonology. I. Archibald, John.
P118.P47 1994
401'.93—dc20   94-10386
                                                CIP

Printed in the United States of America
10 9 8 7 6 5 4 3 2 1

*For Samantha and Jessica,
who made the acquisition of phonology
interesting and entertaining*

Contents

List of Contributors

John Archibald
Department of Linguistics
University of Calgary

Peter Avery
Department of Linguistics
University of Toronto

Ellen Broselow
Department of Linguistics
SUNY at Stony Brook

Steven B. Chin
Department of Linguistics
Indiana University

Katherine Demuth
Department of Cognitive and
  Linguistic Sciences
Brown University

Daniel A. Dinnsen
Department of Linguistics
Indiana University

B. Elan Dresher
Department of Linguistics
University of Toronto

E. Jane Fee
School of Human Communication
  Disorders
Dalhousie University

David Ingram
Department of Linguistics
University of British Columbia

Hye-Bae Park
Department of Linguistics
Suwon University

Keren Rice
Department of Linguistics
University of Toronto

Thomas Scovel
Department of Linguistics
San Francisco State University

Harry van der Hulst
Department of Linguistics
Leiden University

Preface

Much of the current work on language learnability has focused on the acquisition of syntax. There has been much less on the acquisition of phonology within this theoretical framework. Most research on the acquisition of sound systems could practically be viewed as developmental phonetics, not phonology.

As someone who is interested in both language learnability and phonology, I thought it was time to put together a collection that showed the range of work going on that utilizes a sophisticated phonological framework. Most of us in this field have spent our share of time in the small rooms of the phonology sessions of acquisition conferences, dreaming of the auditorium. One conference organizer confessed to me, "We scheduled the phonology session just before the party, so people would stay."

I would like to thank all of the contributors to this volume for doing their bit to get us out of conference basements by showing a wider audience what it is we do. Maybe one day we'll even run out of handouts.

John Archibald

Introduction:
Phonological Competence

John Archibald
University of Calgary

What do we know when we know phonology? That is the question that I would like to address in opening this volume. This is, in fact, an acquisition question, as can be seen when we look at Chomsky's familiar goals for linguistic theory:

1. To account for the knowledge of a native speaker.
2. To account for the acquisition of that knowledge.
3. To account for the implementation of that knowledge.

The approach to language acquisition that has come to be known as *language learnability* is concerned with the first two goals. I begin by determining an adequate description of the final-state grammar and then try to determine how the learner could have arrived at such a system of knowledge. Although I do not deny that language learners move through developmental stages, the end of the journey is always kept in mind. In order to be able to describe the developmental stages that the learner moves through, we must refer to the kinds of linguistic structures that the learner is trying to represent. Thus, the study of acquisition cannot be divorced from considerations of the final state (see Dresher & van der Hulst, this volume, chap. 1).

Although there may be differences between child and adult learners (see Scovel, this volume, chap. 9), I maintain that this is a useful paradigm for discussing both first (child) and second (adult) language acquisition. Both varieties of acquisition are addressed in this collection. Whether the learner is a child or an adult, the goal is the same: to acquire the final-state grammar. Therefore I take the term *learner* to refer to either the first- or the second-language learner.

The first step is to consider what the final state of phonological knowledge is. What does phonological competence look like? In this overview, I do not provide exhaustive (or, at times, any) arguments for the existence of particular structures. The purpose of this chapter is to lay the groundwork for the consideration of the acquisition studies that follow. As is traditional in an overview of phonology, I begin somewhere in the middle.

1. THE SEGMENT

Probably the most salient level of phonological structure is the segment. We assume that a word like *dog* can somehow be represented as a sequence of segments that looks something like [dɑg]. And although this may be a convenient phonetic shorthand, the segment plays a part in phonological representation. The learner has to acquire the segments of the language being learned (see Rice & Avery, this volume, chap. 2).

But a question that has often arisen in the history of phonology is whether there is a level of structure beneath the segment. I outline the proposal regarding a unit known as a *feature*.

2. THE FEATURE

In many models of phonology, the segment is taken not as a primitive of phonological structure but rather as a convenient shorthand to represent a collection of features. Probably best known are the features proposed by Chomsky and Halle (1968) in *The Sound Pattern of English* (henceforth SPE). Using this kind of feature system, it was assumed that a segment was composed from a set of primitive features. So the sequence [dɑg] could also be represented as in (1):

(1)

[d]	[ɑ]	[g]
+consonantal	−consonantal	+consonantal
−syllabic	+syllabic	−syllabic
−sonorant	+sonorant	−sonorant
+anterior	−high	−anterior
+coronal	−round	−coronal
+voice	+back	−coronal
		+voice

The segments were represented as *bundles* of features. Later proposals (Clements, 1985; Sagey, 1986; etc.) have suggested that the features are not grouped into unordered matrices but, in fact, have an internal hierarchical structure. Clements proposed the kind of internal segment structure shown in (2):

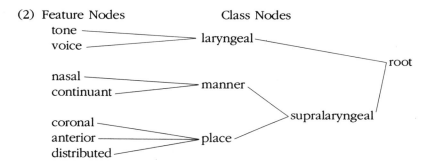

(2) Feature Nodes   Class Nodes

tone — voice — laryngeal

nasal — continuant — manner

coronal — anterior — place — supralaryngeal

root

I assume, then, that the final state includes some kind of representation of segment structure. The learner has to acquire the features of the language being learned (see Dinnsen & Chin, this volume, chap. 7; Rice & Avery, this volume, chap. 2).

Related to the issue of feature values is the notion of underspecification. Underspecification theory assumes that redundant information is not represented in the lexical entry. For example, radical underspecification proposes that most phonological features are redundant and can be specified by a set of universal redundancy rules or markedness conditions. As Ingram (this volume, chap. 4) points out, some redundancies are absolutes; for instance, a vowel that is [+high] will be redundantly [−low]. Others are determined by markedness; for instance, liquids and nasals are redundantly [+voice]. Underlying representations are specified only for the marked features, and the redundant features are specified by redundancy rules. For children, we must ask how they acquire this underspecified representation.

Now, let us consider units larger than the segment.

3. THE SYLLABLE

Current phonological theory also includes a unit of structure that groups segments together into a larger constituent known as a *syllable*. Intuitively, we know quite a bit about the syllables of our native language. For example, we are pretty good at deciding how many syllables are in a word like *Samantha*. And we are pretty good at knowing whether something is a well-formed syllable in our language (we probably would not argue that the last syllable of *Samantha* is *-ntha*). So we know something about the internal structure of syllables, too. And if we have a system of knowledge in this domain, we need some way of representing it. Again, I do not argue for a particular model of the syllable but merely present a widely used model. Selkirk (1982) proposed the syllable structure shown in (3):

(3)   Syllable (σ)
          /   \
     Onset   Rhyme
               /   \
         Nucleus   Coda

In the word [dɑg], the [d] would be in the *onset*, the [ɑ] would be in the *nucleus*, and the [g] would be in the *coda*.

Now, languages vary as to the degree of complexity allowed in each of these syllabic positions. When describing a language we need to ask whether the onset, nucleus, and coda can branch. As an example, consider languages that allow only CV syllables and not CCV syllables (i.e., no consonant clusters in the onset). We could say that the language that allows only CV syllables does not allow a branching onset, whereas the language that allows CCV syllables does. Cross-linguistically, we find that variation can be described with reference to the branching allowed in each position:

Can the onset branch? (yes/no)

Can the nucleus branch? (yes/no)

Can the coda branch? (yes/no)

If the onset or coda branches, we have consonant clusters. If the nucleus branches, we have long vowels or diphthongs. If we syllabified the word *drives* we would produce the structure shown in (4):

(4)   σ
              /   \
         Onset   Rhyme
         / | /   \
        / | Nucleus   Coda
       / | / \   / \
      d   r   a   y   v   z

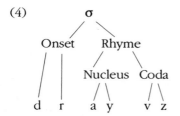

Note that all of the nodes branch. The learner must acquire the syllable structure of the language being learned (see Fee, this volume, chap. 3).

A concern with syllable structure also leads us to the question whether a branching nucleus or rhyme has a different theoretical status, or behaves differently in any way, from a nonbranching structure. Often it is claimed that branching and nonbranching structures do behave differently. This has led to the suggestion that there is an intermediate level of structure between the segment and the syllable known as the *mora*.

4. THE MORA

The mora is proposed to account for phenomena related to syllable *weight*. In many languages, difference in syllable type may affect phenomena like stress assignment. For example, in a quantity-sensitive language, a heavy syllable would attract stress but a light syllable would not. Heavy syllables are syllables that have either a branching nucleus (long vowel: CVV) or a branching rhyme (closed syllable: CVC). Light syllables are generally CV (open syllables). Languages vary as to which syllable types count as heavy or light. For example, in Latin CVC is considered heavy, whereas in Lardil CVC is treated as a light syllable. As always, if we see that certain forms are behaving differently, we would like to assign some structural difference to them. Hayes (1989) represented such structures as in (5) (where μ stands for mora):

(5)

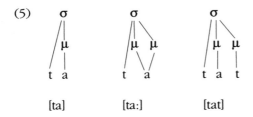

Thus, we can maintain the generalization that, in quantity-sensitive systems, bimoraic syllables attract stress and monomoraic syllables do not. The learner would have to discover the moraic structure of the language being learned (see Broselow & Park, this volume, chap. 8).

5. OTHER PHONOLOGICAL PLANES

I have already mentioned that syllable (or moraic) structure can influence phenomena like stress assignment, where heavy syllables attract stress in some languages. Let us now look at some issues in stress assignment. It is widely assumed that the metrical structure of a word is projected from the syllable structure. In Idsardi's (1992) terms, a grid mark is projected for each element that can bear stress. So in English a word would project a grid mark for each syllabic nucleus. The words *edit* and *collapse* would be represented as in (6):[1]

(6) x x   x x

    édit   collápse

They have two syllables and project two elements onto the metrical grid. If we recast this in terms of moraic phonology we can account for the phenomenon of quantity sensitivity. Consider the moraic structure of these words:

$$
\begin{array}{lll}
(7) & \sigma\ \ \sigma & \sigma\ \ \ \ \sigma \\
    & |\ \ \ | & |\ \ \ \ /\backslash \\
    & \mu\ \ \mu & \mu\ \ \mu\,\mu
\end{array}
$$

    é d i t   c o ll á p se

These elements are then grouped into a larger constituent called a *foot*. The foot may be strong on either the left (a trochee) or the right (an iamb). If the foot is strong on the left then additional prominence is added to the element on the left. The bimoraic syllable is labeled strong and forms a foot of its own. If there are no bimoraic syllables, a trochaic foot is built. The following structures are produced:

$$
\begin{array}{lll}
(8) & \quad F & F\quad\ \ F \\
    & \ /\ \backslash & |\quad\ \ | \\
    & \ s\quad w & .\quad\ \ s \\[6pt]
    & \sigma\ \ \sigma & \sigma\ \ \ \ \sigma \\
    & |\ \ \ | & |\ \ \ \ /\backslash \\
    & \mu\ \ \mu & \mu\ \ \mu\,\mu
\end{array}
$$

    é d i t   c o ll á p se

Then the feet are gathered into a constituent known as the *word tree*, which can be strong on either the left or the right. In English the word tree is strong on the right. This final step would produce the structures in (9):

---

[1] I use standard orthography, which, I trust, will not be confusing.

(9)   W
     W   / \
     | w   s

     F   F   F
    / \ | |
   s   w   .   s

   σ   σ   σ   σ
   | | | /\
   μ   μ   μ   μ μ

   é d i t   c o ll á p se

Learners will have to acquire the relations between syllabic phonology and
the metrical grid, as well as the principles governing stress placement for
the language being learned. That is to say, they will have to learn, for
instance, whether the feet are trochaic or iambic, and whether bimoraic
syllables receive added prominence (see Archibald, this volume, chap. 5).

The notion that there is another phonological plane for metrical structures
leads us to the last element of phonological competence that I want to
discuss.

6. AUTOSEGMENTAL PHONOLOGY

Just as a consideration of metrical phenomena has led us to a nonlinear
model of phonological representation, so, too, does a consideration of tone.
In fact, the analysis of tone was probably the driving force behind the
proposal of autosegmental phonology. In languages where the pitch contour
on a word can influence the meaning of the word, it emerged that the tones
and the segments were best viewed independently. Goldsmith (1976) proposed that a word with tones assigned to it was best construed not with
tone as an integral part of the vowel (e.g., *búlù*)[2] but rather as a nonlinear
representation along the following lines:

(10) Tonal Tier   H   L[3]

     Segmental Tier   b u l u

---

[2]ú stands for a high tone, and ù stands for a low tone
[3]H stands for a high tone, and L stands for a low tone.

Certain association (or linking) conventions connect the two tiers to produce a representation like (11):

(11)   H L
       | |
       b u l u

In this way, tones would be assigned to vowels (or other tone-bearing elements). The first vowel would have a high tone associated with it, and the second vowel would have a low tone associated with it. This model of representation implies that phonological processes should be able to apply independently to the different tiers, and they do. Note the following hypothetical examples of what might happen if either tone were deleted (as in (12a)) or a vowel were deleted (as in (12b)):

(12) a.   H
          | \
          b u l u
     b.   H L
          | /
          b u l

In the first case we note that the remaining tone spreads to existing vowels, resulting in a high tone on both vowels. In the second case, we note that there is only one vowel for both tones to associate with. As a result, the sole vowel bears a falling tone.

The learner must acquire the linking and spreading conventions of the language being learned (see Demuth, this volume, chap. 6).

7. SUMMARY

These, then, are some of the aspects of phonological competence that must be acquired. We can view phonological structure as a system of interconnected levels of representation: the feature, the segment, the mora, the syllable, the foot, the word, the metrical system, and the tonal system. Phonological competence also includes the processes that map one type of representation onto another. Traditionally, generative phonology has made use of the notion of *derivation* to link linguistic levels. A phonological rule would apply to an underlying (or intermediate) form. The learner must reconstruct the underlying form from the input (see Dresher & van der Hulst, this volume, chap. 1).

The goal for the language learner is to acquire phonological competence. This competence is a system of knowledge that includes both representations and processes.

Let us now consider the acquisition of this competence.

ACKNOWLEDGMENTS

I would like to thank E.-D. Cook for his comments on an earlier draft of this chapter.

CHAPTER ONE

Global Determinacy and Learnability in Phonology

B. Elan Dresher
University of Toronto

Harry van der Hulst
Leiden University/HIL

Most current theories of phonology allow for the possibility of different phonological representations for a particular phonetic unit (e.g., a segment type). Here we take the expression *phonetic unit* to refer to a unit in the phonological representation that forms the input to the phonetic interpretation component, that is, the surface phonological representation. A schematic representation of a two-to-one (in principle, many-to-one) relation between an underlying representation and a surface representation is given in (1):

(1) Many-to-one mapping of phonological representations to phonetics

Representation 1 (R1)   Representation 2 (R2)
$$\bigvee$$
Phonetics (i.e., surface phonology)

It need not be the case that both R1 and R2 are lexical or underlying representations. Depending on the theory, multiple sources for a surface representation may arise in the course of a phonological derivation. We therefore take underlying to refer to nonsurface (lexical or intermediate) levels of representation.

Positing multiple underlying sources for a single surface unit may be the result of theories that are as yet too loosely constructed or imprecise, but typically that is not the case. Rather than resulting from theoretical insecurity, this variability is introduced deliberately in order to explain differences in

1

processes that involve these units. In such cases, the phonological representation is underdetermined by the local phonetic properties of the relevant unit and can be established only by taking into account a wider range of data. In older versions of generative grammar the additional data would typically involve processes that affect this unit. We say that grammars in which such cases arise have the property of *global determinacy.*

In this chapter we examine a number of cases of this type and speculate on the consequences of global determinacy for the theory of language acquisition. We do not attempt to present a systematic overview. Our goal is more modest, in that we merely wish to point out that global determinacy is not a problem associated only with older versions of generative phonology, where it was recognized as a problem of (excessive) abstractness of lexical representations. Perhaps the contrary is true. Recent advances in phonology have led to an enormous increase in representational possibilities for identical phonetic events. Even though specific possibilities are usually pervasively grounded in analyses of a set of facts that may not be analyzable otherwise, the addition of every possibility introduces further ambiguity into the analysis of other sets of data that may be compatible with more than one available account.

The fact that a choice must be made between R1 and R2 raises a learnability question. The logical problem of language acquisition is the following: Construct a theory so that, for all languages, it is possible to establish a grammar on the basis of a relevant set of data, which, as is usually added, underdetermines the grammar to be attained. Given global determinacy, crucial information for certain parts of the grammar is unavailable in the local context to which those parts directly pertain. Hence, with strict reference to the local context, several grammars could be selected. In that case, there must be a reasonable way of bringing nonlocal factors into the decision space, through cues in the data that lead the language learner to the correct grammar, rather than to other grammars that are possible in general but happen to be incorrect in the given case. To arrive at a theory that explains how a grammar can be acquired, we must be able to specify what Lightfoot (1989) called a *learning path*; that is, it must be possible to specify exactly which cues determine the choice of one analysis over the other. In Lightfoot's terms, we must identify the child's *trigger experience.*

In our case, this means that there must be a reasonable way for the language-learning child to determine which representation corresponding to a particular phonetic surface form is called for if this is not locally determined. It is not sufficient to show that a unique analysis can be chosen once all the evidence is known (either because all others are wrong, or because it is the best one, according to some evaluation metric). Though consideration of large data sets and complicated lines of argumentation may in practice lead the investigator to decide which representation is correct, we must assume that children fix parameters without knowing all the evidence, or even a lot of evidence, unless we admit that our model does not aim at accounting for the fact that children fix parameters on the basis of very limited evidence.

In a broad sense, the issue of global determinacy is central to what phonology is all about. Phonology would be a trivial discipline if there were a strictly local mapping from the continuous speech signal (or surface phonology) onto the discrete mental representations that we have reason to believe form part of linguistic capacity. Much research in phonology suggests that theories limited to local determination (a strict form of biuniqueness) are descriptively inadequate. It is also clear, however, that too much flexibility leads to an unconstrained theory that allows us to construct too many representations, most of which are never called for.

Our goal, then, is to indicate some of the major causes of global determinacy that arise in variants of generative phonology, including current multilinear approaches. Of course, we are not suggesting that all the cases we discuss form part of a single coherent model. Which cases are relevant depends on the specific ideas one has regarding such issues as underspecification, unary features, feature geometry, dependency relations, system-dependent or relative interpretation of features, abstract underlying representations, rule ordering, and deletion. Nevertheless, we hope to show that the problem of global determinacy arises in every nontrivial theory of phonology and has certain recurring characteristics, no matter what guise it comes in. On the moralistic side, we note that current phonological theorizing may suffer from a lack of consideration for learnability issues raised by the explosive increase of representational possibilities, especially those involving underspecification and geometrical feature arrangements.

1. STRUCTURALIST PHONEMICS

In structuralist phonemics, the task implied in (1) would be framed as one of assigning a phonetic speech sound to its proper phoneme. Suppose, for example, that the phonetic segment in question is the vowel [a], as in (2), and that in the language under consideration the sound [a] is an allophone of two different phonemes, the phoneme /a/ and the phoneme /e/ (we are assuming here a liberal structuralist theory in which phonemes may overlap in this way):

(2) Structuralist phonemics: Overlapping phonemes

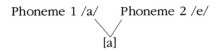

Phoneme 1 /a/   Phoneme 2 /e/

[a]

This variability in phonemic membership could be posited in order to explain differences in processes that involve this segment. For example, suppose that [a] that belongs to phoneme /e/ is associated with palatalization of preceding velars, whereas [a] from /a/ is not. In such cases, the phonological representation is underdetermined by the local phonetic properties of the segment and can be established only by taking into account a wider range of data. These data could be phonological, involving, for instance, palatalization or other relevant processes that distinguish the two representations, or morphological, as when [a] alternates with [e] in some cases but not in others.

Because global determinacy raises learnability problems, there have been recurring attempts to limit the theory of grammar to local determinacy. In structuralist phonemics, this was accomplished by imposing a number of constraints on phonemic representations. One was the constraint against mixing of levels, ruling out recourse to morphological information in identifying phoneme membership. Another was what later became known as the requirement of biuniqueness (Chomsky, 1964), which ruled out overlapping phonemes in identical contexts and required that an allophone in a given context could belong to only one phoneme. These constraints were motivated precisely by a desire to impose local determinacy for purposes of acquisition. Thus, Bloch (1941) argued that schwa must be a phoneme in English, because otherwise a child would not be able to identify which phoneme any given schwa belongs to on the basis of local cues.

This is one way of making the acquisition problem more tractable, but the price is too high. Much research in phonology suggests that theories limited to local determination are descriptively inadequate, essentially because such theories must give up the idea that the relation between allomorphs is expressed in terms of a common unique underlying representation. So it appears that we have to deal with global determinacy not by ruling it out, but by other means.

2. SOURCES OF GLOBAL DETERMINACY IN UNILINEAR GENERATIVE GRAMMAR

The theory of SPE (Chomsky & Halle, 1968), which posited fully specified, two-dimensional (unilinear) phonological representations, did away with the constraints imposed by many structuralist theories, opening the way to more descriptively adequate grammars. In the process, the problem of global determinacy made an impressive comeback. SPE allowed for derivations as in (3):

(3) Abstractness in linear generative phonology (counterbleeding order)

Underlying	/. . . k e . . ./	/. . . k a . . ./
Palatalization	c e	-
Lowering	c a	-
Surface	[. . . c a . . .]	[. . . k a . . .]

As in the example in (2), suppose we find that a language has a rule of palatalization that changes /k/ to /c/ before the front vowels /i/ and /e/. Suppose further that we also find this change occurring before some instances of [a], even though there is no trace at the surface of the phonetic element that usually causes palatalization. The SPE theory nonetheless allowed for the possibility of specifying these cases of [a] with a palatal feature, to trigger the process of palatalization. Then, before phonetic interpretation takes place, this feature is changed, in this case as a result of lowering, leading to a merger with [a] derived from underlying /a/, which lacks the palatalizing feature in the first place.

The key to this kind of abstractness is that palatalizing [a] behaves as if it has the palatalizing feature. The fact that it has this feature underlyingly cannot be determined by the local phonetic properties of [a]. It is only because [a] behaves as if it has this feature with respect to a process that refers to it that we can learn that it must have the feature underlyingly. Crucial to this type of analysis is the counterbleeding relation between palatalization and lowering, because if lowering were to apply first, palatalization could not apply.

A classical and much debated case of this kind was presented in Hyman's analysis of Nupe (Hyman, 1970). In Nupe, consonants are labialized (C^w) before the round vowels /u/ and /o/, and palatalized (C^y) before the front vowels /i/ and /e/. Before the low vowel /a/ (which is neither round nor front), we find labialized, palatalized, and plain consonants. Hyman argued that there are three underlying sources for /a/, that is, /E/, /O/, and /a/. The first two cause preceding consonants to be palatalized and labialized, respectively, and then merge with /a/. For a child to choose /E/ and /O/ as the underlying source of /a/, it must be determined that there is a rule palatalizing and labializing consonants in completely different contexts. Then the child must decide that the contrast between C, C^w, and C^y is not phonemic, which implies that the latter two must be the result of spreading from the local context, even when occurring before /a/. This is a clear case of what we mean by global determinacy.

More generally, this type of situation can be represented schematically as in (4):

(4) Apparent overapplication of P: Trigger S merges with nontrigger S′

a.
$$
\begin{array}{ccccccc}
 & & P & & N & & \\
T & S & \rightarrow & T' & S & \rightarrow & T' & S' \\
| & | & & | & | & & | & | \\
-F & +F & & +F & +F & & +F & -F
\end{array}
$$

b.
$$
\begin{array}{cccc}
 & & P & \\
T & S' & \rightarrow & \text{N/A} \\
| & | & & \\
-F & -F & &
\end{array}
$$

(Here, even though we are talking about the unilinear youth of generative phonology, we adopt a quasi-autosegmental notation. We do not exploit the autosegmental potential until we reach section 3, however.)

In (4a), a segment type S causes a process P that involves the spreading of some feature [+F] to another segment T. S, however, appears on the surface as S′, which is not [+F] (i.e., the phonetic interpretation of this S′ shows no trace of the phonetic contribution that [+F] generally makes). The SPE theory, nonetheless, allowed for the possibility of specifying what appears as surface [S′] with the feature [+F] (i.e., as underlying /S/), so that it can trigger the process P. Then, before phonetic interpretation takes place, [+F] associated with S is changed to [−F] by rule N. Rule N leads to the merger of S with S′; S′ is specified [−F] in the first place and so does not trigger P, as shown in (4b).

Sometimes, S actually surfaces in other occurrences of the same morphemes, so that we can infer the presence of S throughout the whole paradigm, given the principle that allomorphy is reduced to a unique underlying morpheme shape. SPE, however, did not impose alternation as a condition on this kind of abstractness. Hence, the term *abstractness* came to refer mainly to the possibility of positing underlying phonological (i.e., featural) information in a morpheme that does not appear on the surface anywhere in the paradigm. To have this kind of abstractness, SPE had to allow extrinsic rule ordering (in (4), a counterbleeding relation), that is, ordering between rules that cannot be derived from properties, phonological or otherwise, of the rules in question. Abstractness and extrinsic rule ordering make it possible to relate very distantly related surface forms (e.g., *father* and *paternal*). In principle, the underlying form of [kæt] could be any string of phonological material, including the empty string.

The learning problems entailed by this kind of global determinacy led to suggestions to abandon or restrict either abstractness or extrinsic rule ordering, or both. Kiparsky's (1968/1982a) seminal paper argued that abstractness that is not supported by alternation is either ruled out (the strong Alternation Condition) or limited to circumstances in which at least two processes make reference to S (the weak Alternation Condition). Other phonologists went further in attempting to limit abstractness, returning to theories with local determinacy. Such a position was taken by proponents of Natural Generative Phonology (NGP) (Hooper, 1976; Vennemann, 1973), leading to the result that all rules that were not surface true were excluded from the phonology (with wide-ranging consequences for the treatment of allomorphy). Grammars adhering to the constraint that all rules must be surface true do not allow abstract underlying forms and do not need extrinsic rule ordering. (Recently the NGP surface-true constraint has been revived in Declarative Phonology; see Scobbie, 1992).

It is clear, however, that from the point of view of learnability, the issue of abstractness cannot be resolved by considering only the distance between underlying and surface representations, the need for extrinsic rule ordering, or the relation between rules and surface phonotactics. Indeed, the question cannot even be raised unless this is done against the background of a particular theory of UG. We now show that the learnability problems that are raised by the type of abstractness discussed here need not be too serious, given certain assumptions regarding principles of UG.

First, we observe that the nonlocal factors that enter into the lexical assignment of nonsurfacing features to segments are rather limited in the sense that the cues are, partly at least, present in the immediate context of the segments in question. If, then, UG imposes strong constraints on the form of phonological rules, abstractness could emerge as a natural consequence, posing no learnability problems. To return to our earlier examples, suppose that it were a principle of UG that a segment could be palatalized only by an adjacent segment characterized by the features [−back, −low]. Then, if it can be established that /k/ is palatalized adjacent to [a], it follows that the learner must assign these features to the representation of [a], automatically converting it to /e/, whether that appears on the surface or not. With reference to (4), if the feature [+F] can be spread by P only from an adjacent segment that is characterized by [+F], then, if it can be established that [+F] has been spread by P to T′ from S′, the learner must assign [+F] to S′, converting it to /S/. Where there is no option, there is no learnability problem.

Our Nupe example has shown, however, that in order to decide that T′ has picked up [+F] from a neighboring segment, a global decision must be made that T′ is not itself underlying. In Nupe, there are no alternations between T and T′, so global consideration of the segment inventory is required. In other cases, where T′ alternates with T, the alternation could provide evidence, as long as the learner knows about the allomorph with T and can decide that T, not T′, is underlying; these decisions also involve global considerations.

In the cases discussed here, a segment spreads a property that it lacks on the surface. The reverse was also allowed in SPE: A segment bearing

[+F] on the surface fails to participate in a process spreading [+F]. One typical case is shown schematically in (5):

(5) Apparent underapplication of P: Nontrigger S' merges with trigger S

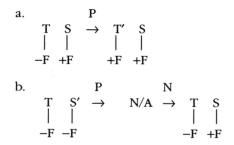

In SPE, the distinction between changing and adding information could not be made because forms had to be fully specified at all levels of a derivation. In theories allowing underspecification (cf. section 4) or unary features (cf. section 4.4), however, this distinction becomes viable. (We show later that exploitation of the autosegmental machinery blurs this distinction again because overapplication can also be handled without changing information.) The kind of abstractness exemplified in (5) does not crucially depend on specifying segments with information that is changed or deleted before reaching the surface, as was the case in (4), where [+F] must be changed to the opposite value (if F is a binary feature) or deleted (if F is a unary feature). The example in (5) can be recast as in (6), for example, where a segment is provided with additional information after a rule that refers to this kind of information has applied:

(6) Apparent underapplication of P: Feature-adding account

```
a.          P
      T  S   →   T'  S
         |        |  |
        +F       +F +F

b.          P        N
      T  S'  →  N/A  →   T  S
                           |
                          +F
```

This type of case typically arises with respect to redundant properties. Suppose there is a process of vowel rounding triggered by front rounded vowels, but not by back rounded vowels; suppose also that there are no back unrounded vowels. One way to explain why back vowels do not trigger rounding would be to propose that rounding, being nondistinctive for back vowels, is not specified on back vowels. Our rule N, then, would be a redundancy rule filling in rounding on back vowels at the end of the derivation. A similar situation exists when voiced obstruents trigger voicing assimilation, whereas sonorants (redundantly voiced in most models) do not. The relation between P and N is counterfeeding, because if N were to apply first, P would apply as well.

Vowel harmony systems provide us with many examples of this kind. In Hungarian, no contrast exists between [i] and [ɨ]—we find only the former. This segment, however, does not trigger palatal harmony in a certain set of cases. This fact can be accounted for by assuming that [−back] is not specified on high, nonround vowels. Harmony applies, and only then is [−back] filled in (cf. van der Hulst, 1987).

Cases (5) and (6), like case (4), involve a counterrelation in terms of rule ordering as well as a rule P that is not surface true. Again, as in the case in (4), assumptions regarding UG influence the extent to which this kind of variability (i.e., S′ is underlying /S/ or faithful to the surface form) is held to pose a challenge to learning. Suppose we say that redundant values are always filled in late; then this kind of underapplication becomes a consequence of a principle of UG. But again it requires global consideration of the segmental inventory to arrive at the correct grammar.

It turns out, however, that such a position cannot be maintained. In fact, it has been argued (for example, in Archangeli & Pulleyblank, 1986) that the opposite is closer to the truth; redundant values are inserted at the moment a phonological rule makes reference to them. A clear case of this type would be that of sonorants triggering voicing assimilation on neighboring obstruents. Here, as in the case of overapplication, one could propose a UG constraint on the form of phonological rules that produces underapplication as a natural consequence, thus posing no learnability problems. In this case, the principle of UG would be that a segment not triggering the spreading of some feature F cannot have F if the language shows signs of F spreading in other cases.

In unilinear generative phonology, cases of over- and underapplication of rules involve underlying representations that cannot be locally determined but require consideration of how processes apply, as well as inventories and/or related allomorphs, even if certain UG constraints on the form of phonological rules are assumed.

3. AUTOSEGMENTAL THEORY

The rise of multilinear theories distracted attention from issues of abstractness, and it is probably fair to say that most phonologists proceeded on the assumption that a reasonable degree of abstractness appears to be required by the evidence. For the sake of comparison, let us translate the case in (4) in terms of nonlinear phonological representations:

(7) Spreading and delinking in autosegmental phonology

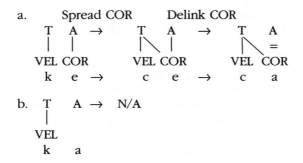

Let capital T be shorthand for a voiceless stop unmarked for place, so T linked to VELAR is a /k/. Let A be a nonhigh vowel; and, for the sake of discussion, let us say that linking a vowel to CORONAL makes it front and nonlow, that is, /e/. Suppose also that the rule of palatalization involves the spreading of the CORONAL place node onto a preceding velar, causing it to become /c/. Following this, CORONAL is delinked from the vowel, which becomes [a], merging with underlying /a/, which does not cause palatalization.

The change from linear to nonlinear representations involves an enrichment of the descriptive apparatus of phonological theory. One possible benefit of these increased representational resources is that we may be able to put constraints on derivations without giving up descriptive adequacy. For example, the derivation in (7) can still be construed as requiring a crucial extrinsic ordering between spreading and delinking, an ordering that would have to be learned. However, we can exploit the geometry of representations to give us further possible solutions not previously available. In this case, we could propose, as in (8), that only CORONAL nodes that are multiply linked may be delinked from a vowel; this, one could argue, could follow from a principle saying that one-to-one association represents the default case and is in fact forced if no loss of information results:

(8) A formulation of delinking that allows for intrinsic ordering in (7): Delink multiply linked COR from a vowel if COR appears elsewhere in the local context (due to spreading).

Given (8), delinking cannot apply until after spreading, so we could allow these rules to apply freely whenever their structural descriptions are met, an option that was not open to us before. If all cases of overapplication could be analyzed in this way, extrinsic counterbleeding orders would no longer be necessary. Apart from the fact that this principle would not eliminate extrinsic ordering in general (it would still be necessary for cases of underapplication), it is probably not the case that delinking can be derived as an automatic consequence in all cases. In the Nupe case, for example, /E/ and /O/ are arguably no more complex than /e/ and /o/. Both /E/ and /e/ combine frontness with lowness. Both involve spreading of [−back] (or [front]), but only the former must then undergo delinking.

A particular form of underspecification is available in autosegmental phonology that makes it possible to obtain overapplication effects in new ways. It is well known that autosegmental theory allows one to specify segments only with respect to a single tier. For example, to take an extreme case, when vowel-initial words behave as if they begin with a consonant, we can posit an (unsyllabified) empty skeletal position that is identified merely as consonantal (by some feature): There may be no need to posit an abstract fully specified consonant. This, of course, is possible only in cases where the abstract entity surfaces as zero. Assuming that an unsyllabified skeletal point will not be phonetically interpreted, there is no need for a neutralization rule. (In geometrical versions of autosegmental theory, postulating floating material that receives no phonetic interpretation has become even easier, given the possibility of floating root nodes.)

Another type of case where autosegmental phonology has removed the need to posit abstract segments and neutralization rules involves the device of floating features. Consider the following example. Suppose that stems containing back vowels trigger fronting on affixal vowels. Before autosegmental phonology, one could posit abstract front vowels in the stem. Now, it is possible to posit a floating feature [−back] in the stem that will not be linked to the stem vowels but will spread to affixal vowels. When the stem occurs without an affix, one would again assume that unassociated features receive no phonetic interpretation. An analysis of this type has been proposed in van der Hulst (1987) for Hungarian, but this type of approach is common in analyses of tonal downstep that involve floating tones (Clements & Ford, 1979).

The question to be asked is how such strategies can be constrained. In any event, it is clear that floating material replaces (or adds to) old forms of abstractness without resolving issues of global determinacy.

4. UNDERSPECIFICATION THEORY

In a theory such as that of SPE, abstractness introduced by feature-changing derivations is the main source of local indeterminacy. Once we allow for underspecification, a different type of approach becomes possible in cases of underapplication, as we already saw in the cases of (5) and (6). In this section, we discuss underspecification in more detail.

In (6), the underlying representations R1 (S′) and R2 (S) differ in that R2 contains more information than R1; the derivations in (6) are incremental or, put differently, have the property of monotonicity. Such a position is inherent in underspecification approaches: In cases like (6), for example, we might propose (as we suggested in our example) that R1 (S′) is an underspecified version of R2 (S), and that the filling in of omitted feature specifications is part of a phonological derivation.

This type of case involves the underspecification of a potential trigger. Underspecification also plays a role in the representation of targets and material intervening between trigger and target. In many of these cases, a single situation allows for more than one analysis, although, in principle, there is a unique analysis once we have seen all the evidence. Again, it turns out that the decision in favor of the correct analysis usually rests not on local considerations but rather on properties of the overall analysis.

For example, a segment /i/ can be totally unspecified underlyingly in one language, whereas it may be specified as [+high, −back] in another. Or in one language all occurrences of the specification [+ATR] ([+Advanced Tongue Root]) are left out, whereas in another language all specifications [−ATR] are so treated. In both cases the choice is dependent on two factors, typically. On the one hand, underspecification rests on contrast: Noncontrastive features can be left unspecified (contrastive underspecification, Steriade, 1987). On the other hand, one must carefully consider how phonological processes apply. It is crucial to know whether segments intervening between potential triggers and targets interfere with (i.e., block) spreading. Although such factors are partially local with respect to a determination of the underspecification of segments that are directly involved in a process (as trigger, target, or intervener), these factors also have consequences for the representation of segments that are not involved in the relevant process at all. For example, it may be the case that /u/ is unspecified for [high] because /i/ must be unspecified for [high], because the behavior of /i/ indicates that it does not have specifications at all. The assumption here would be that only one value of each feature can be lexically unspecified (radical underspecification, Archangeli & Pulleyblank, 1986). Hence if /i/ is not specified as [+high], /u/ cannot be so specified either.

Another example, not involving radical underspecification, is this. Suppose that in language L_1, /k/ changes to [c] before /i/, whereas it does not do so in the same environment in language L_2. A traditional analysis would assume that L_1 has a rule that L_2 lacks. It is also possible, though, that the /k/ in L_1—call it /k/$_1$—is underspecified for some property F that /i/ can then spread to it. By contrast, /k/$_2$ in L_2 is specified for F and so cannot be influenced in this regard by /i/:

(9) a. L_1: Rule k>c applies

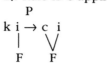

b. L_2: Rule k>c does not apply

Like (6), (9b) is a case of apparent underapplication of a rule, but this time it is the target of the rule that is misleading. In neutral contexts (i.e., where there is no rule that refers to F), a /k/ specified [−F] (a nontarget) looks the same on the surface as a /k/ not specified for F.

Alternatively, it could be proposed that $/k/_1$ has some property G that is a prerequisite for receiving F from /i/ (e.g., a docking site), whereas $/k/_2$ lacks G. Approaches like these are suggested by the strategy of setting up phonological representations in such a way that processes simply follow from general well-formedness conditions. In geometrical theories, versions of this approach involve the presence or absence of nodes/features on which the spreading feature is dependent.

Similar strategies can be followed with respect to intervening material. An intervener, I, may block interaction with respect to F between S1 and S2 in one language, but not in another language. This distinction could be made by specifying I in the former as [−F], and leaving I unspecified for F in the latter, assuming that I's value for F is predictable.

Segment structure in geometrical models can also vary from one language (or context) to another in ways that involve underspecification (perhaps better called nonspecification) that is inherent in systems of feature geometry. If a segment always lacks a node, then of course there is no learning problem. But it has been proposed that the presence or absence of a node specification for a given segment may be variable. For example, much research (e.g., the collection of works in Paradis & Prunet, 1991) suggests that the coronal node is absent in some languages, in that it is transparent to various spreading rules and OCP (Obligatory Contour Principle) effects, but not in other languages, which display a different range of behavior. If this is true, then it is an open question whether the variation is simply parametric, meaning that languages can vary freely in having certain nodes specified or not, or whether there is some principle that determines what nodes must be specified. Avery and Rice (1989) proposed that the presence or absence of a node depends on whether or not there are contrasts under that node.

Another example involves the representation of laryngeals. As extensively documented in McCarthy (1991), laryngeal consonants [h] and [ʔ] classify with pharyngeals and uvulars in a large number of Semitic languages. This calls for an explanation. One solution would be to specify laryngeals with a pharyngeal articulator node in addition to the laryngeal features. Steriade (1987) discussed other cases, however, in which laryngeals must lack all place information in order to explain why laryngeals and no other conso-nantal segments are transparent to the spreading of the vocalic place node. Further, alternations such as /t/ ~ /ʔ/ and /s/ ~ /h/ have been treated as arising from the delinking of a place node. Taken together, these facts suggest that the representation of laryngeals may differ from one language to another in ways that do not seem to affect their phonetic interpretation too much, if at all. Sandler (1990) argued that laryngeals in Hebrew show both kinds of behavior simultaneously.

Cases in which R1 is simply less specified than R2 need not involve a phonological derivation that changes R1 into R2 before phonetic interpre-tation takes place. We might leave R1 as it is, which implies that the phonetic interpretations of R1 and R2, [[R1]] and [[R2]] respectively, are different in the sense that [[R2]] is narrower or more precise than [[R1]]. For example, a segment specified as [–back] has a more or less well-defined phonetic de-scription, whereas a segment unspecified for this feature shows the effect of interpolating the two closest neighboring specifications of the feature [back]. Such a difference has been suggested in work by Keating (1988). The question is how a child decides in favor of this kind of phonetic un-derspecification in such cases.

The issue raised by the possibility of phonetic underspecification is not unrelated to the issue of using unary instead of binary features. Phonological theories making use of unary features reduce indeterminacy significantly, but not entirely. Whether redundant voicing in sonorants is specified or not is arguably a problem for such theories if [voice] is the specified pole of the phonetic opposition voiced/voiceless. A further example involves the prop-erty of voicing in the context of Government-based phonology. It is claimed that some voiced obstruents are represented as lacking the element *tense*, whereas others are positively characterized by possessing the element *low tone*. The difference is largely one of phonological behavior, although pho-netic effects are claimed to exist (cf. Harris, 1990). Underspecification of unary features may be eliminated in theories that make use of variable dependency relations. We return to this point in the next section.

In many other cases, however, unary feature theories do not allow the option, available in binary feature theories, of specifying the default value, that is, the value that is not specified lexically. In this sense unary theories are more restricted, thus raising fewer learnability problems (cf. van der Hulst, 1989).

5. COMPETING STRUCTURES

The richer phonological representations posited by various versions of three-dimensional nonlinear phonology introduce further possibilities of indeterminacy. Thus, R1 and R2 in (1) might simply be distinct competing representations that receive the same phonetic interpretation without the intervention of any derivation at all. Here we distinguish two types of cases, which we refer to as *variable grouping* and *variable dependency*.

The first type, variable grouping, is found in proposals for variable or multiple dependency of nodes or features, in which some phonetic properties of sounds can be represented in different ways. This situation is illustrated schematically in (10), where the feature or node F may depend on either G or H, though the phonetic outcome is the same:

(10) Variable dependency of a node or feature

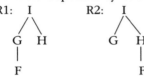

Piggott (1992), for example, proposed that the feature [nasal] is dominated either by a node he called spontaneous voicing or by the soft palate node. This difference plays a role, Piggott argued, in systems that have nasal harmony. The choice between the two landing sites for the feature [nasal] determines which types of segments can be transparent to nasal spreading. In other words, a decision regarding the location of the feature [nasal] in the feature tree is nonlocal in the sense that it depends not on any phonetic property of the nasal sounds themselves, but rather on the way other segments behave vis-à-vis the harmony process.

Another case of this type was suggested by Yip (1990). In this case it is the feature [lateral] that is dominated either by the spontaneous voicing node or by the articulator [CORONAL]. She referred to this situation as *double dependency*. It is interesting to note in this connection that in Dependency Phonology, properties like nasality and laterality are represented twice, once within the categorial component (in terms of the components |C| and |V|) and once as separate components |N| and |L|. Van der Hulst (in press), however, developed a variant of Dependency Phonology that does not have this kind of variability.

The second type of case of competing structures, variable dependency, does not involve variability in the geometrical locus of features. In various forms of Dependency Phonology (cf. Anderson & Ewen, 1987) or Government Phonology (Kaye, Lowenstamm, & Vergnaud, 1985), two components can be combined in two different ways:

(11) Variable dependency/government relations
  a. a → i   component |a| governs component |i|
  b. i → a   component |i| governs component |a|

Both (11a) and (11b) are complete and distinct. If used contrastively, these representations receive different interpretations: (11a) is a lower and (11b) is a higher mid vowel. If a language lacks the relevant contrast, however, we potentially have (at least) two ways of representing identical phonetic events. We might then adopt one of two strategies: Either we choose one of the two, depending on phonological behavior, but irrespective of what exactly the phonetic height is (perhaps we will sometimes even be unable to choose on phonetic grounds); or we could leave the government relation unspecified. The former case raises issues of competing structures, as well as the issue of system-dependent or relative interpretation of phonological constructs. The latter case raises issues of phonological or phonetic under-specification, depending on whether we fill in the dependency relation in the phonology at all.

Another example concerns the representation of uvulars. It is typically not the case that all uvulars group with consonants articulated lower in the throat, which raises the possibility that there may be two different representations for this place of articulation: roughly, velarized pharyngeals or pharyngealized velars (often for fricatives and stops, respectively). The distinction could be expressed in terms of a dependency difference, again raising the issues of double representation.

Variable dependency may obviate the need for underspecification of unary features. We can take advantage of the fact that a feature may be present in two ways—as a head or as a dependent—and propose that the mere presence of a feature does not in itself entail that it can be called upon by a spreading process. Rather, a spreading rule can be made to refer only to heads, or only to dependents. Thus, a feature may be phonetically present but fail to spread as a result of its status as either a head or a dependent. Demirdache (1988) argued along these lines that the vowel /i/ in Hungarian cannot spread its frontness if the relevant component is a head rather than a dependent.

6. SUMMARY

We have reviewed six kinds of cases in which different underlying phonological representations eventually receive a nondistinct phonetic interpretation:

(12) Six sources of global determinacy
- ia. Old-style abstractness (over- and underapplication):
  R1 could receive a phonetic interpretation [[R1]] but is changed into R2 so that we arrive at [[R2]].
- ib. Floating material:
  R1 and R2 are distinct, but certain information in R1 does not receive a phonetic interpretation.
- iia. Phonological underspecification:
  R1 is incomplete and nondistinct from R2. [[R1]] is undefined. Hence R1 must be changed into R2, which can be interpreted as [[R2]].
- iib. Phonetic underspecification:
  R1 is incomplete and nondistinct from R2. [[R1]] is defined and broader than [[R2]].
- iiia. Variable grouping:
  R1 and R2 are distinct, but [[R1]]=[[R2]].
- iiib. Variable dependency:
  R1 and R2 are distinct, but [[R1]]=[[R2]].

All these cases raise serious questions regarding learnability, because a lot must be known about the phonology of specific languages in order to determine which representation is adequate. In other words, the phonological representation of many phonetic events cannot be determined by local considerations.

It is of course not the case that all current phonological theories allow all these kinds of global determinacy. Some theories, in fact, allow very little. For example, dependency and government approaches have been described as very concrete in the sense that underlying representations can differ only incrementally from those that become phonetically interpreted, and then only in very limited cases. In section 1 we also noted that recent theories have reinstalled this kind of monotonicity in a form as extreme as in Natural Generative Phonology (NGP). Scobbie's (1992) Declarative Phonology introduces the notion of unification into phonology. Essentially, all expressions (including underlying forms) obey constraints that are surface true. Surface representations are the result of adding up relevant constraints. Abstractness is not allowed in a model of this kind, which, like NGP, appears to entail a purely suppletive approach to feature-changing allomorphy. The child learning in accordance with Declarative Phonology is more interested in getting the facts right than in arriving at generalizations.

The learnability aspects of old-style abstractness (type (i) in (12)) are discussed in Dresher (1981a, 1981b). We do not take a stand here on the degree of abstractness that we would like to allow, nor, in the case of type (ii), the degree and type of underspecification that phonological theory should incorporate. Learnability issues surrounding type (iii), as we indicated, will be heavily influenced by the position one takes regarding the arity of features. In theories making use of unary features (specifically, theories from the "AIU" family; Anderson & Ewen, 1987; Kaye, Lowenstamm, & Vergnaud, 1985; van der Hulst, 1989, in press), underspecification plays a very modest role. Variability involving empty class nodes would be eliminated if we deny class nodes, or structural information in general, an independent ontological status. Variability due to flexible feature geometries could be removed by developing a more constrained version of feature grouping. Noting that variable dependency requires the language learner to take into account global information, we believe that this concept is so well founded that it seems better to try to solve the learning-path problem than to remove it from the theory.

7. SOME QUESTIONS OF LEARNABILITY

Although phonological theory is changing rapidly, and the various proposals are tentative and in flux, it is nevertheless not too early to inquire more systematically into the learnability of these various approaches. We believe that an attempt to make explicit the learning paths required by whichever proposals one prefers is bound to yield fruitful insights into the degree to which phonological theory is indeed approaching the goal of explanatory adequacy. An inquiry along these lines would ask certain questions.

The first question for any particular proposal is (Q1): Does the analysis posit a principle or a parameter? A principle of UG is innate, and independent of experience. A parameter must be fixed on the basis of experience, though the range of possible settings may be given in advance. Not all variation is parametric. Suppose that a principle of UG states that if a language has property I, then it must also have J; otherwise, if it lacks I, it must have K. The choice of I or not I may be parametric, in that a language may freely have I or not. But once that choice has been determined, the choice of J or K comes from UG, and not from experience. Thus, in the case of the laryngeals or coronals, which may or may not have place nodes, the variation is principled if it depends on other aspects of grammar, such as the nature of underlying contrasts in the segment inventory. It is parametric if there is no such determining principle; in such a case, the learner must look for evidence bearing on the setting of the parameter. A similar question can be raised with respect to the other cases discussed earlier. (It should be noted, however, that it is not always easy to distinguish cause and effect in such matters.)

If we are dealing with a parameter, a second question must be addressed (Q2): What is the default (unmarked) parameter setting? And we must also answer a third question (Q3): What are the cues that trigger a change to the marked setting?

Let us consider the case in which the variability lies in whether or not a segment is specified for a node. If a segment (e.g., S in (13)) lacks a node G, it will be transparent to a process, P, which spreads F on the G tier; if a segment possesses G (e.g., T), it will be affected by P:

(13) Transparency in spreading

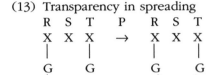

Two learning paths are possible in this case. We may take spreading to be the crucial evidence in determining whether or not S or T has G. If the existence of transparency effects is a positive cue, we might assume as default that the node G is present until we see that a segment is transparent to P. Whether G is lacking or not is parametric.

A second route assumes that the geometry of a segment is filled out only as much as is required by contrast, following an algorithm that must be made explicit. In that case, we are really dealing with a principle. Segments are assigned increasingly rich representations as more and more contrasts are learned. At the end of this process, the segments S and T will either have a G node or not; the learning model will never have to look for evidence bearing on this assignment.

The fourth relevant question we see is (Q4): Do cross-parameter dependencies exist? Informal accounts of how a parameter may be set often presuppose that certain parts of the grammar have already been learned. For example, we might say that segment S will be assigned node G if and only if there is an underlying contrast between E and F, dependents of G. But it may not be trivial to determine if the crucial contrast is underlying or derived. Or the spreading process P that supplies the crucial cue as to whether S has G may itself be ambiguous as to which node it is spreading, G or F; the evidence for this may also involve transparency effects, leading to circularity in the learning model.

8. CONCLUSION

We conclude these remarks by considering the implications for learnability of a principle that is currently widely held, to the effect that the main burden of explanation in phonology rests with representations, not rules. We first heard this view expressed some years ago by J. Kaye and J. Lowenstamm, who spoke in terms of projecting the phonology from the segmental inventory. On this view, the fundamental character of a phonology is determined by its inventory, and the properties of the rules, to the extent there are any, should follow relatively simply from the representations they apply to.

Thinking in terms of acquisition, this view leads naturally, though not inevitably, to a model that is widely assumed, though not often made explicit, and goes something like this: Suppose that a learner begins by learning the segmental inventory, making contrasts only as required. In terms of a feature geometry approach, for example, we might suppose that nodes are added as needed, so as to distinguish contrasting segments. We might call this incremental development. The rules and processes of the phonology apply to the representations so acquired, and facts such as transparency and opacity of segments with respect to processes follow from the representations.

Central to this view are a number of hypotheses that are also often tacit but influential all the same. One is that representations can be established before any rules have been learned, using only the evidence of the inventory (i.e., contrast). A counterexample to this claim would be a case where the representations themselves can be established only on the basis of rules. Such a case can arise, for example, if we have variable representations that must be fixed on the basis of experience. If the relevant experience includes knowing how rules work, then we have to conclude that the representations follow from the rules, and not vice versa.

A related hypothesis is that representations are made increasingly rich in the course of acquisition by adding contrasts, and that one does not go in the other direction, making a contrast that turns out not to be needed and then getting rid of it. Here again the notion of contrast plays a central role. It has not been shown, however, that the notion of contrast that is relevant in any given case can be established in a principled way.

We believe that the preceding remarks demonstrate that modern multilinear phonological theories raise all the same questions regarding learnability as did older SPE-style models (notably, surrounding abstractness) and, in addition, many new ones. Too often, new feature geometries or alternative applications of existing ones are proposed without serious consideration of the learnability issues that are implicitly raised. The main idea behind these comments has been to draw attention to this situation. If the goal of the construction of theories of the language faculty is to explain how it is possible for children to learn grammars on the basis of evidence that largely underdetermines the solution they must come up with, we must be careful about advancing analyses that crucially appeal to global determinacy without specifying a learning path.

ACKNOWLEDGMENTS

These remarks were written as a discussion paper for the GLOW 1991 Workshop on Phonological Acquisition (Leiden, April 1991). The collaboration leading to this paper formed part of the NIAS project on Language

Acquisition (Wassenaar, 1990–1991, coordinated by Teun Hoekstra and Harry van der Hulst), with which Elan Dresher was associated as an external participant. The present chapter is a slightly modifed version of the original discussion paper. Elan Dresher would also like to acknowledge the support of grant 410-92-0885 from the Social Sciences and Humanities Research Council of Canada.

CHAPTER TWO

Variability in a Deterministic Model of Language Acquisition: A Theory of Segmental Elaboration

Keren Rice
Peter Avery
University of Toronto

Generative phonology in the 1980s saw a shift in focus from rule systems to the nature of phonological representations. One of the major breakthroughs in the theory of representations was the development of a theory of segment structure. Whereas segments had been viewed as unordered feature bundles (Chomsky & Halle, 1968), the study of the internal structure of segments and the grouping of features into segmental subconstituents came to dominate work on segmental representations (Clements, 1985; McCarthy, 1988; Sagey, 1986). In tandem with this research program the theory of distinctive features has also been the subject of intensive investigation. The principal result of this work has been a move toward unary features. For example, Mester and Itô (1989) argued that [voice] is a privative feature, Sagey (1986) argued that place of articulation is best captured by unary features, and Piggott (1992) proposed that [nasal] is a privative feature as well. This has meant a reworking of the rule subcomponent of the phonology as well as a rethinking of the notion of underspecification (Archangeli, 1988; Avery & Rice, 1989; Steriade, 1987).

The new theory of phonology means that much of the work on the acquisition of phonology needs to be reevaluated in light of the fresh insights that have been provided. In line with most current work in generative grammar (Chomsky, 1981), generative phonologists have taken the fundamental problem for phonology to be the construction of a theory that can account for the acquisition of the representation of a given phonological system. In this way, current models of linguistic knowledge directly address the issue of acquisition. A basic assumption of such an approach is that the child is guided in the construction of linguistic representations by invariant principles of UG, as well as by a set of tightly constrained open parameters that are fixed by experience. Acquisition data are potentially of great importance to theory, as the theory is meant to provide an account of the acquisition process.

In this chapter we look at the acquisition of inventories and consider the consequences of the theories of segment structure and underspecification for research on the acquisition of inventories. We come at this task from what Menn (1980) referred to as the *centre*; that is, we extend a theory of phonology to the area of child language acquisition. We do not present new data, but instead we show the predictions that our theory makes for acquisition and test it against data in the literature. Unlike previous scholars working from the center, we do not consider language acquisition to be at the periphery. As our theories are constructed with issues such as learnability in mind, we take an account of acquisition to be a central component of the theory.

We distinguish two approaches to the acquisition of segmental representations. These may be termed the *full specification* approach and the *minimal specification* approach. Under the full specification approach, it would be claimed that segments are initially acquired as units. For instance, a sound such as /p/ has a universal representation that is fully specified when the child acquires the sound. Whatever representation the theory proposes for a particular sound, this is the representation the child begins with. Then, as the child acquires more and more segments in the inventory of the ambient language, these representations may be modified through the deletion of redundant features as the contrasts are acquired. Under this view the acquisition of phonology is seen as the zeroing out of redundant information from the initial fully specified representation.

Opposed to the full specification approach is the minimal specification approach. Under this approach, one would claim that at any time the child has only enough specification to keep a given segment distinct from the other contrastive segments in the inventory. Thus, if the child consistently used a sound such as /p/, we would know little about the child's representation of that sound without knowing what other segments were in the inventory.

In this chapter, we take the minimal specification approach, viewing the acquisition of representations as the elaboration of segment structure along a predetermined pathway. The addition of contrasts leads to elaboration of the segment structure. We claim that one expects to find a good deal of variation in the realization of sounds when the segment structure is relatively unelaborated. As the child acquires more contrasts, the segment structure is enriched and the phonetic realization of the sounds becomes less variable. In the early stages of acquisition, before the segmental structure has been fully elaborated, we expect variability in the realization of particular targets, variability that can be the result of linguistic context (i.e., early allophonic rules), or the result of free variation. With the acquisition of more contrasts, variation in the realization of segments decreases with the patterned allophonic variation typical of adult grammars dominating.

In previous work we have proposed a theory of segment structure that makes specific predictions about the ordering of acquisition of segments. In this chapter, we explore this model of segment structure from the minimalist perspective of acquisition, showing that it can account for both some of the regularities and some of the variability found in the acquisition of phonological inventories.

The outline of the chapter is as follows. In section 1 we review the literature on theoretical approaches to the acquisition of segmental contrasts, comparing the universalist approach associated with Jakobson to the cognitive approach associated with Ferguson. In section 2 we show how a cross-linguistic study of inventory shapes sheds light on an account of acquisition in terms of elaboration. In section 3 we outline our theory of segment structure as well as our approach to specification and contrast, and in section 4 we attempt to show from published data how our approach is able to sort out some of the problems of variability in child data by pinpointing different sources for different types of variability. We conclude with a discussion of the model and problems of research.

1. UNIFORMITY AND VARIABILITY IN CHILD LANGUAGE

Two major observations about the acquisition of sounds have driven previous accounts of the acquisition of segments. We term these *global uniformity* and *local variability.* By global uniformity we mean that if one looks at the larger picture, one sees that in early acquisition children acquire roughly the same set of basic sounds in roughly the same order and that this holds both within a language and across languages. By local variability, we mean that children may show some disturbances in the actual ordering of the sounds, though generally the early sounds are still taken from among the same basic set of sounds.

Approaches to acquisition that emphasize global uniformity are best exemplified in the universalist model set forth in Jakobson (1941/1968). Approaches that focus instead on local variability are represented by the cognitive-interactionist model developed in the work associated with Ferguson and colleagues (see Ferguson & Farwell, 1975; Macken & Ferguson, 1983; Vihman, Ferguson, & Elbert, 1986). In this section we outline the basic assumptions of each of these approaches and identify some of the problems they present.

1.1. The Jakobson Model

Jakobson (1941/1968), in some of the earliest theoretical work on child language acquisition, proposed a model of segment acquisition based on the ordered acquisition of phonological contrasts. Regardless of the language being learned, sounds should be acquired in the same order, with those sounds that are commonly found in the languages of the world being acquired early and those that are less frequent cross-linguistically being acquired later. The sound inventory of a language is constructed based on a universal hierarchy of oppositions, with the child coming to the task of acquisition without any contrasts and successively acquiring a set of contrasts according to the universal hierarchy of oppositions. As oppositions are acquired, sounds are added. Jakobson's theory has both a determinist and a universalist aspect. It is deterministic in that the order of acquisition is invariant and universal in that the ordering is based on a universal feature hierarchy. This theory was adopted in much early work on child phonology.

As discussed by Menn (1980), Jakobson's model was based on a general phonological theory rather than actual child data. As detailed studies of the acquisition of sounds by individual children were carried out, doubt was cast on the validity of the universalist position. One of the primary objections to the Jakobsonian perspective has been that it provides no account for the variability present in child phonology (see Macken, 1980; Macken & Ferguson, 1983). Ferguson and Farwell (1975) stated: "Jakobson's concern with generalizations about order of acquisition leaves no room for considering the nature of individual differences in phonological development. Yet any careful comparison of different children learning the same language shows differences in the individuals' paths of development" (p. 435). This statement was made in spite of the fact that the children studied by Ferguson and Farwell followed very similar paths consistent with "many of Jakobson's predictions" (p. 435). The cognitivists' claim is that any universalist theory is incapable of handling both variability across children learning the same or different languages and variability within a particular child's developmental pattern (Macken & Ferguson, 1983).

Some researchers have attempted to save the deterministic aspect of Jakobson's theory although sacrificing the universal order of acquisition. Ingram (1988); Goad and Ingram (1987); and Pye, Ingram, and List (1987) all recognized the problems of variability for a theory such as Jakobson's. Goad and Ingram accounted for the cross-linguistic variability by rejecting the claim that there is a universal order of acquisition. That is, they rejected the universal feature hierarchy; instead, they claimed that the order of acquisition is determined by the inventory of a given language. Although we respect their attempt to rescue at least the deterministic aspect of Jakobson's theory, we feel that their approach is also open to criticism. It is not clear what the precise mechanisms are that determine the order of acquisition within any language. Goad and Ingram appealed to the functional load of a phonemic opposition, with those phonemes with a high functional load being acquired first. Several problems arise in a model of this nature. One concerns the level at which we are to consider functional load. Is it the functional load of a contrast, say the voiced/voiceless contrast, or is it the functional load of individual segments, say a voiceless alveolar stop? It is, thus, not clear exactly what is being acquired, segments or oppositions. Furthermore, the child would appear to require some foreknowledge of the total inventory of the language in order to determine the functional load of an opposition. Even if functional load could be accurately defined, this model still fails to offer an account of the overall similarity of acquisition cross-linguistically, apart from the observation that the functional load of certain oppositions is similar across languages. Nor does it offer an account of the differences in order of acquisition that may occur within a single language. We argue that both aspects of the Jakobsonian theory can be maintained once the problem of variability is properly sorted out.

1.2. The Cognitive Model

Macken and Ferguson (1983) (following work by Ferguson & Farwell, 1975; Kiparsky & Menn, 1977; and others) proposed a cognitive model of the acquisition of phonology. Under the cognitive model, the child is seen as an active hypothesis tester, and the ordering of acquisition of sounds is viewed as probabilistic rather than deterministic in nature. The model postulates three cognitive processes that the child uses while acquiring phonology: selection, creation, and hypothesis testing. All of these strategies show the child's active involvement in acquisition; and because of the cognitive, nonlinguistic nature of these processes it becomes understandable that each child may indeed take a different route in acquiring the phonology of a language. Probabilistic universals of acquisition are recognized, but it is claimed that it is entirely possible for the most difficult sound of a language to be among the first sounds acquired (Menn, 1983). This model predicts substantial individual differences between children, a prediction that does not appear to be borne out by the data on child language. Stoel-Gammon and Cooper (1984) presented data to support the cognitive approach, but a reanalysis by Goad and Ingram (1987) showed that the variation is, to a large extent, overreported because of the bias in favor of variation provided by the method of analysis. The model is also vulnerable in its treatment of universal tendencies. Macken and Ferguson recognized this problem and suggested that language-specific innate mechanisms might be required to account for the similarities in developmental sequencing within and across languages. A more damaging criticism of the model, as Macken and Ferguson realized, is that the model is compatible with any set of data. Beyond variation both within the same language and cross-linguistically, the model makes no empirical predictions. Thus, by emphasizing variability, the model sacrifices generality.

It is clear what must be accounted for: In the acquisition process, overall similarities are found in the sequence of acquisition cross-linguistically, but individual variation is found both within and between languages.

In the next section, we examine inventory shapes in order to show the limited ways in which inventories can differ. This leads to our proposal regarding segment structure.

2. INVENTORIES

Cross-linguistic comparisons of inventories reveal that small inventories are similar and that as inventories expand, differences emerge. A common observation (e.g., Lindblom, 1988; Maddieson, 1984) is that inventories consist of two types of segments, basic and complex. Basic consonants are generally restricted to three places of articulation (labial, coronal, and velar), a nasal/oral distinction, and a stop/fricative distinction. The stops usually show three places of articulation, the nasals two, and the fricatives one or two places of articulation. A single liquid is generally included in the basic inventory as well. Complex segments involve the addition of laryngeal features, secondary articulations, subdivisions of place of articulation, and the like.

Yagaria, Roro, and Finnish are three unrelated languages with small inventories and thus only basic segments. All show three-way place distinctions in stops, two-way place distinctions in nasals, and up to two coronal liquids. Fricatives are also restricted in terms of place of articulation. Roro in fact has no specified place of articulation for fricatives, having only an /h/ in the fricative inventory.[1] (We omit laryngeal contrasts, glides, and length in presenting these inventories.)

(1) Yagaria   Roro   Finnish
     (Indo-Pacific)   (Austro-Thai)   (Ural-Altaic)
     p   t   k   ʔ   p   t   k   ʔ   p   t   k
     (v) s   h   h   s   h
     m   n   m   n   m   n
         l   r   l
                                             r

---

[1]All inventories in this section are taken from Maddieson (1984). These inventories show a certain amount of abstraction over those presented in Maddieson, as we have not included marginal segments or those found only in borrowings. We have assigned glottal stop and /h/ as laryngeal stop and fricative, respectively, in Yagaria and Roro, following the charts in Maddieson. We consider laryngeals to be segments lacking a Place node; see, for instance, Steriade (1987) for discussion. In Finnish the /h/ might well be the fricative counterpart of /k/.

Lindblom argued that it is only after the basic consonants are present in an inventory that any elaborations are added. Diyari and Nootka, shown in (2), have more complex consonant inventories and illustrate some of the different ways in which place of articulation can be expanded. Diyari elaborates on place of articulation by adding coronal distinctions, as is evident in both the stops and the sonorants. Nootka, on the other hand, adds postvelar distinctions, as can be seen in the stops. (We ignore manner and laryngeal distinctions in these languages.)

(2) a. Coronal elaboration
  Diyari (Australian)

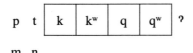

p	t̪	t	ʈ	c	k
m	n̪	n	ŋ	ñ	ŋ
	l̪	l	ɭ	ʎ	

 b. Dorsal elaboration
  Nootka (Amerindian)

p	t	k	kʷ	q	qʷ	ʔ

 m n

Work on the acquisition of phonology has revealed that cross-linguistically, children in the beginning stages of acquisition show relatively small inventories that are similar across languages, reflecting the situation found in inventories among languages of the world (see de Boysson-Bardies & Vihman, 1991). Locke (1983) made an explicit comparison and proposed to divide the sounds of the world's languages into two types: repertoire sounds and nonrepertoire sounds. Repertoire sounds, equivalent to what we have termed the basic sounds, occur in most of the languages of the world and in the babbling of infants; they are also among the first sounds acquired by children. Nonrepertoire sounds are seen as more complex and rarer among the world's languages. They may not occur in babbling and are acquired later by children.

Our theory accounts for the observations about inventory elaboration and child acquisition. To see how this is so we turn to an outline of our theory of segmental representation and then show how it provides a path for elaboration, or a learning path.

3. THE STRUCTURE OF PHONOLOGICAL
REPRESENTATIONS

The model of phonology that we assume is outlined in this section. As stated earlier, we take a minimalist approach to the acquisition of segmental representation. The initial phonological representations of the child are relatively impoverished, with little or no structure. This structure is elaborated under pressure from the phonology: Positive evidence involving the acquisition of a contrast between two segments forces the addition of structure to the representation. As contrasts are added to the phonology, more complex segments are acquired.

We address in this section the pieces of our theory that are critical to the model of acquisition, namely, segment structure and underspecification.

3.1. Segment Structure

We begin with a basic outline of the theory of segment structure that we have developed in recent work (Avery, in preparation; Avery & Rice, 1989; Rice, 1993; Rice & Avery, 1990, 1991b). We assume, following the work of Clements (1985), McCarthy (1988), Sagey (1986), and others, that segments have internal structure and that features are grouped together under higher level organizing nodes. Dependency relationships are represented structurally, with a dependent feature represented as a daughter of a superordinate organizing node.[2]

We assume that there are four major constituents in a segment, dominated by the organizing nodes, Laryngeal, Air Flow, Sonorant Voice (SV), and Place. Each organizing node has a subtree involving two types of relations, dependency and markedness. At any point of expansion there is a marked and an unmarked option. These options are represented in the subtrees in (3), with the feature appearing in parentheses being the unmarked option for the immediately dominating node. Also important is the dependency defined through the structure involved in the expansion of a given node. Thus, if the Place node is expanded to Dorsal, this entails the presence of Peripheral, which entails the presence of Place. (See Avery & Rice, 1989, for phonological arguments in favor of the specific organization given.) SV, Air Flow, and Laryngeal display the same type of dependency relationships.[3]

---

[2]The particular structure that we adopt is based on work by Avery and Rice (1989) and Rice and Avery (1991b). Details of the structure that are not relevant to this discussion are ignored, but see the preceding references for more details.

[3]The dependencies under SV, Air Flow, and Laryngeal are less well established than those under Place. The structure of the SV node is argued for in Rice and Avery (1991b). For discussion of the Laryngeal node, see Lombardi (1991), Avery (in preparation).

As is clear from the subtrees given in (3), the Place node organizes place features, the Laryngeal node organizes laryngeal features, and the Air Flow node organizes stricture features that are relevant to air flow in the oral cavity. A less familiar node is the SV node, argued for in Rice and Avery (1990, 1991b), Piggott (1992), and Rice (1993b), with SV standing for *sonorant voicing* or *spontaneous voicing*. This node organizes those features normally associated with sonorant segments such as nasals, laterals, and r-sounds.[4] Obstruents lack the SV node.

(3)

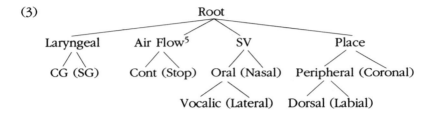

3.2. Markedness and Underspecification

We assume, following many other phonologists (e.g., Archangeli, 1984; Kiparsky, 1982; Steriade, 1987) that redundant information is absent from underlying representation. This is represented in (3) by the parentheses around one of the dependents at each bifurcation. Coronals are generally considered to be unmarked for place of articulation (see, for example, papers in Paradis & Prunet, 1991), and this is shown in (3) by the parentheses around the feature Coronal. The implication of this is that a prototypical coronal consonant is represented by a bare Place node. Similarly, at the SV node, the feature Nasal is unmarked, and thus the prototypical nasal consists of just an SV node (and relevant place of articulation). The unmarked features are default features added for the purposes of phonetic implementation and, in general, do not play a role in the phonology.

Some sample prototypical representations of several consonants are given in (4) and (5). Only Place and SV structure are identified, as only these are relevant to this discussion.

---

[4]The following abbreviations are used: Cont = continuant, CG = constricted glottis, SG = spread glottis. We should also note that in other work we have argued against the fanlike structure of the segment presented in (3) (see Rice & Avery, 1991b). In that work we argued that Air Flow dominates SV, which in turn dominates Place. As this particular organization is not important to the present discussion, we present the simpler model in (3).

[5]Our understanding of the Air Flow node is not sophisticated enough for us to comment on it more fully other than to say that is establishes the stop/continuant contrast.

(4) Prototypical representation of stops at three places of articulation

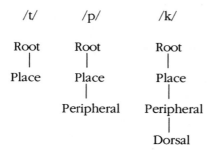

/t/   /p/   /k/

Root   Root   Root
 | | |
Place   Place   Place
                | |
          Peripheral   Peripheral
                              |
                           Dorsal

(5) Prototypical representation of the sonorants /n/ and /l/

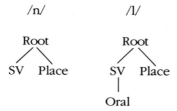

/n/   /l/

Root   Root
 ╱ ╲   ╱ ╲
SV   Place   SV   Place
                  |
                 Oral

The stops and sonorants differ in that the sonorants include the SV node. Place of articulation is underspecified: /t/, /n/, and /l/ do not have a Coronal node but receive this by a default rule; likewise, /p/ receives Labial by a default rule, being represented as just a Peripheral node.[6]

Arguments for organization under the SV and Place nodes can be found in Avery and Rice (1989) and Rice and Avery (1990, 1991b). The arguments are based primarily on assimilation processes: A segment with less structure under SV or Place can assimilate to one with more such structure, whereas one with more structure does not assimilate to one with less structure. Thus, coronals may assimilate to segments at all places of articulation, whereas labials and dorsals do not assimilate to coronals; see section 3.3.[7]

---

[6]Saying that the features in parentheses are universally inserted is actually an oversimplification. Two choices are available at an organizing node: Either the default feature is filled in or that feature fails to fill in and the node itself is interpreted. For example, if the feature Coronal is not filled in at the Place node, a consonant that is generally thought to be a velar arises; see Rice (1993a). When Nasal is not filled in at SV, a voiced sound results; see Rice and Avery (1990). Although beyond the scope of this chapter, this failure of default features to fill in may account for some of the problems of interpreting child data.

[7]Elsewhere, we have argued that constraints on segmental complexity also play a role in the elaboration of segments; but this would take us beyond the scope of this chapter (see Rice & Avery, 1991b; 1993).

The segment structure that we propose thus encodes constituency (organizing nodes), and markedness (absence of unmarked features in the phonology). Furthermore, the expansion of any constituent may be to a nonterminal node that itself acts as an organizing node, having dependents with a marked and an unmarked option.

3.3. Contrast

So far we have suggested that unmarked features are absent in underlying representation, being added only for the purpose of phonetic implementation. This represents an oversimplification of the facts, however. We briefly examine feature specification in this section, focusing in particular on the notion of contrast.

We take as an example the specification of the feature Coronal; see Avery and Rice (1989) for details. In a language in which there is only a single coronal place of articulation, the Coronal node is absent, and the coronal consonant is represented as a bare Place node, as in the diagrams in (4) and (5). In such languages, coronals display special types of patterning, frequently assimilating to segments at other places of articulation such as labial and dorsal. However, labials and dorsals do not assimilate to coronals. This is illustrated with the Korean data in (6) and English data in (7).

(6) Underspecification of Coronal in Korean
    pat+ko   →   pakko   'to receive'
    kot+palo →   koppalo   'straight'
    pap+to   →   papto (*patto)   'rice also'

(7) Underspecification of Coronal in English
    bad boy   →   ba[bb]oy
    bad game →   ba[gg]ame
    big day   →   bi[gd]ay (*bi[dd]ay)
    rib day   →   ri[bd]ay (*ri[dd]ay)

In languages with more than one distinctive place of articulation within the coronals (for instance, with both alveolars and retroflexes), coronals do not assimilate across articulators. In this case a plain /t/ might assimilate to a retroflex or a palatal but fails to assimilate to a labial or a velar. Such patterning is found in a number of languages, including Sanskrit (Avery & Rice, 1989), Telugu (Gilbert, 1992), and many Australian languages (Hamilton, 1993). Thus, the patterning of a typical coronal varies, depending on whether there is a sole coronal place of articulation or contrasting coronal places of articulation.

This behavior shows that in languages without distinctions under the Coronal node, the feature Coronal is absent underlyingly, whereas in languages with distinctive places of articulation within the coronal range, the Coronal node must be present underlyingly for all contrasting coronals. The notion of contrast is thus important to the theory in that it is the addition of contrasts that drives the addition of structure.

3.4. Interpretation of Representations

An important aspect of our theory concerns the phonetic interpretation of representations. Consider a very early stage in the acquisition of phonology, a stage at which the child has a distinction only between consonants and vowels. According to Jakobson, at this stage the child is likely to have [p] and [a], these being maximally distinct. Under our theory the status of these two sounds as sounds is unspecified apart from a consonant-vowel split. The child at this stage has only a single consonant and a single vowel, and beyond this there is no further specification. That the consonant is realized as [p] and the vowel is realized as [a] is not relevant to the phonology. In our estimation the child has an unmarked consonant, and the realization of this consonant as [p] is not the result of the specification of that consonant as a labial sound. From a phonological point of view the sound could be just as easily realized as a [t] or even a [k]. That this sound is often, though not always, realized as a [p] could be due to articulatory constraints on the child (i.e., the child has little control over the tongue musculature), or to other factors of a nonphonological nature. What is crucial to our theory is the prediction that the first distinction with respect to place of articulation will be between a coronal and a peripheral, a distinction that should be between /t/ and /p/. It seems that this prediction is in general borne out. (See, for example, Ferguson & Farwell, 1975, who stated that the three children they studied had "labial and alveolar stops as their first sounds" [p. 435].)

Thus, when acquiring a sound system, the child begins from an impoverished structure with a wide range of possible realizations for any particular segment. This is a reflection of the ample phonetic space that may be allotted to that segment because there are few contrasts. As the system is built up, the phonetic space decreases and the variability decreases.

3.5. Summary

In this section, we have discussed several aspects of our theory: universal segment structure, markedness, contrast, and interpretation. In acquisition, the segment structure is elaborated through the addition of marked structure. A given phonological representation is interpreted with respect to the oppositions that are present in an inventory, leading to possible variable realization of the same opposition.

4. ELABORATION OF STRUCTURE: THE LEARNING PATH

Important to our theory is the notion of elaboration. When structures such as those in (4) are considered, it is apparent that the difference between places of articulation lies in the amount of specified structure present: Coronals have only a Place node, labials have one node in addition to the Place node, and dorsals have yet an additional node. Our proposal is that inventories must be built up in this step-by-step fashion, with the acquisition of new contrasts being nothing more than the addition of structure to segments. Segment structure is elaborated in a monotonic fashion, with the starting point set at completely unmarked structure. Our central hypotheses are stated in (8).

(8) a. *Minimality:* Initially the child has minimal structure.
    b. *Monotonicity:* Inventories are built up in a monotonic fashion.

Minimality forces the assumption that the child's initial phonological representations will be impoverished. Additional structure is forced onto a segment only as contrasts are introduced into an inventory. For example, if an inventory has only a single distinctive place of articulation, it may not even be necessary that the Place node be present in the phonological representation. The introduction of a place contrast involves a distinction below Place, and the Place node is obligatorily present on the unmarked segment, whereas the segment with which it contrasts has a Peripheral node. A further distinction causes the addition of a Dorsal node. This is the only pathway available in the acquisition of the three basic places of articulation; that is, addition of structure proceeds a single step at a time, or monotonically. Thus, it must be the case that the first place contrast is between coronal and noncoronal. The next contrast differentiates the noncoronal places of articulation. The normal implementation of this is a coronal/labial/velar distinction. The development can be seen in (9).

(9) No Place distinctions | Two-way Place distinction | Three-way Place distinction

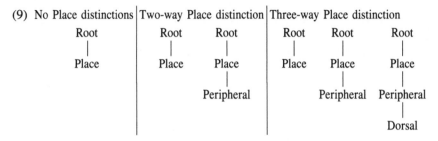

Structure is built up only as required by increasing contrasts in the inventory. Furthermore, the elaboration must follow a predetermined path within any particular organizing node. Place must be present to select Peripheral, Peripheral to select Dorsal, and so on. If a language has a Dorsal, it must also have a Peripheral.

So far we have considered elaboration only within a single organizing node. Although within a given node only a single pathway is possible, when the entire structure of a segment is considered, it becomes obvious that not all inventories need expand in the same way, as different organizing nodes may be expanded in different languages. For instance, some languages might add further places of articulation, others more sonorants. What we claim is that the possibilities are limited and that the basic segments appear first. The inventories of Diyari and Nootka in (2) show two different expansions of Place: In one case coronal contrasts develop through the addition of structure under the Coronal node, and in the other case postvelar contrasts are introduced. In addition these inventories differ in the degree to which SV is expanded. The number of sonorants can be increased by adding further places of articulation; they can also be increased by adding further manners of articulation within the sonorant class.

This model allows inventories to expand in different ways, as it is possible to extend places of articulation and manners of articulation independently. However, it is important to notice that the number of possibilities is limited by the structure itself. Within each constituent, a well-defined initial path must be satisfied before further elaboration is allowed.[8]

Given this model of elaboration, we now turn to the acquisition problem: How do we account for both the similarities and the variation found in the acquisition process? In this section, we examine two types of variability: noncontrastive variability, that is, variability arising from absence of structure, and structural variability, variability depending on the order in which the different nodes are elaborated.

4.1. Noncontrastive Variability: Different Realizations of the Same Segment

In the model that we have proposed, we have argued that structure is minimal and is added only under the pressure of contrasts. Thus, if the child has only a consonant/vowel contrast, the actual phonetic realization of the consonant or the vowel is irrelevant. Whether the consonant is produced

---

[8]There are dependencies between branches, as discussed in Rice and Avery (1991c). These dependencies account, for instance, for the absence of labial laterals in languages of the world. We dub the required constraint the *Structural Complexity Constraint*, arguing that this constraint disallows a segment from having an excess of structure overall. This topic is beyond the scope of the present chapter.

TABLE 2.1
Tessa's Realizations of the Word *Boat* over a 5-Month Period

Target	Session	Phonetic Transcription	Number of Productions	Age
boat	1	$[p^o\text{ɔ/o}]_{3x}$, $[p^o\text{ɔ}ʔ]$	4	1;4;28
	2	$[p^o\text{ɔ}]_{4x}$, $[p^o\text{ʌ}ʔ]$	5	
	3	$[p^o\text{ɔ}]_{3x}$, $[p^o\text{o/ɔ}ʔ]_{3x}$	6	
	4	$[p^o\text{ɔ}p^hk^h]$, $[p^o\text{o}t^h]$, $[p^o\text{ʌ}p'p^h\text{ʊk}]$, $[p^o\text{ʌ}k^h]_{2x}$, $[p^o\text{ɔ}k^h]_{2x}$, $[p^o\text{ɔ}k^hk^h]_{2x}$, $[p^o\text{a}p^hk^h]$, $[p^o\text{ʌ}k^hk^h]$	11	1;5;30
	5	$[p^o\text{ɔ}p^h]_{2x}$	2	1;6;15
	6	$[p^o\text{o}p^h]$, $[p^o\text{o}ʔ]$	2	
	7, 8	—	—	
	9	$[p^o\text{ʌ}p^h]_{3x}$	3	
	10	—	—	
	11–16	$[p^o\text{o}t^h]$, $[p^o\text{o}t']$	2–3 times/ session	• 1;9;2

Note. Adapted from "Cognitive Aspects of Phonological Development: Model, Evidence, and Issues," by M. Macken and C. Ferguson in *Children's Language*, Volume 5 (p. 266), by K. E. Nelson (Ed.), 1983, Hillsdale, NJ: Lawrence Erlbaum Associates. Adapted by permission.

as [p t k m n ŋ] or even other consonants is of no significance whatsoever; the only contrast is that between C and V.

As an example of noncontrastive variability, consider the data in Table 2.1, taken from Macken and Ferguson (1983). Here we are interested in the realization of the final consonant of the word *boat*.[9] Macken and Ferguson's subject Tessa appears to have a place distinction in word-initial position as evidenced by the consistent realization of the initial labial, though this could conceivably be a production strategy and we would need to see other words in Tessa's vocabulary to be certain that there is a contrast. As yet, however, she does not have any place distinction in final position.[10] As there are no place distinctions, we might expect to find variability in the realization of the final consonants, and this is exactly what happens. In the earliest stages Tessa is developing the necessary structure for the realization of a final consonant. When the position is there, it is initially realized as a glottal stop. At the next stage (Session 4), it appears that she has a final consonant that is realized as labial, coronal, or dorsal, with dorsal being the most common realization, perhaps under the influence of the preceding vowel. At a later

---

[9]C^0 represents an unaspirated stop; C^h, an aspirated stop; and C', an unreleased stop.

[10]We distinguish word-initial and word-final position. Languages frequently show far more restricted inventories in word- or syllable-final position (see, for instance, Goldsmith, 1990, for discussion) than they do in word- or syllable-initial position. This suggests that in speaking of inventories, it is actually necessary to distinguish inventories in different structural positions within a word.

stage, the final consonant is realized more consistently as [p]. At this stage, there is probably a rule spreading the Peripheral node of the initial consonant or of the round vowel (see Levelt, in press) onto the final consonant. Finally, the consonant is realized consistently as [t], indicating that a place distinction has been acquired in final position.

In (10), also from Macken and Ferguson (1983), we see the variable realization of the word *elephante* as found in the speech of Si, a 21-month-old child acquiring Spanish.

> (10) *elephante* (Spanish), Si 1;9;12
>   [pfantɪndɪ], [hwantuti], [panti], [bantɪndi]

The data show the variable realization of the initial fricative /f/ of the stressed syllable. As can be seen, it is realized as a labial affricate, labial glide, or labial stop, indicating that the child is able to make a place distinction but that the manner distinction has not yet been acquired. Again, this is an example of noncontrastive variability.

Ferguson and Farwell (1975) also presented a good deal of noncontrastive variation. For example, one child showed variable realization of laryngeal features within stops, as in (11a) and (11b). This same child also lacked a stop/continuant distinction, with variation between labial stops and continuants as in (11c).

> (11) Variable realization of sounds (from Ferguson & Farwell, p. 426)
>   a. b ~ pʰ ~ p
>   b. d ~ tʰ
>   c. b ~ β ~ bw ~ ɸ

We claim that a large part of the variability found within a child is the result of lack of specification or contrast. As discussed earlier, before the acquisition of particular contrasts, there may be several possible phonetic realizations of the target. These can be thought of as free variants of a particular phoneme, resulting from the fact that little structure is specified and thus the phonetic range allowed in the representation is very broad.

4.2. Structural Variability: Possible Learning Paths

Our theory defines various possible ways in which a learner can build up an inventory of segments, just as it defines various ways in which inventory shapes can differ. In this section we consider some of the paths a learner might take, through an examination of the SV and Place nodes.

Consider a learner who acquires a consonant contrast at a given stage within place of articulation, giving an opposition between the coronal place of articulation and other places of articulation. The distinction between sonorants and obstruents is not yet relevant. The representations would be as in (12).

(12) Stage 1 representations, addition of Peripheral

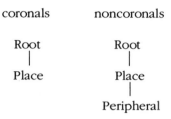

The consonants may be realized as oral or nasal because the oral/nasal contrast is not yet relevant for the child. In this case the child would have something like /p~b~m/ versus /t~d~n/, with perhaps other variants as well.

Alternatively, at the same stage, the child might create an obstruent/sonorant contrast, with place of articulation being noncontrastive. Representations would be as in (13).

(13) Stage 1 representations, addition of SV

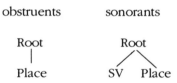

For this child, the obstruent/sonorant contrast is important, but the place of articulation contrast is not. Thus, the obstruent and sonorant may each be of a range of places of articulation, as Place is not yet distinctive; and we might expect to find /t~d~p~b/ versus /n~m/.[11]

At Stage 2, further complexities develop. The child who elaborated at place of articulation could take this a step further, adding Dorsal to the representation as in (14).

---

[11] It is possible that at this stage the voiced sounds are part of the sonorant set and not part of the obstruent set. Rice and Avery (1990) argued that there are many languages in which the voiced stops are sonorants.

(14) Stage 2 representations, addition of Dorsal

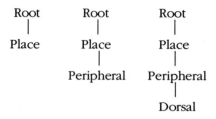

Now we may expect the child to have a set of contrasts such as /p~b~m/ versus /t~d~n/ versus /k~g~ŋ/.

Alternatively, the child could add SV structure, creating an obstruent/sonorant contrast. The representations in (15) would be added to those in (12).[12]

(15) Stage 2 representations, addition of SV

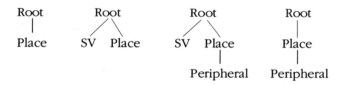

Now we may expect the child to have a set of contrasts such as /t~d/ versus /n/ versus /m/ versus /p~b/.

Consider again the child who first elaborated at Stage 1 by adding SV structure, as in (13). This child might now create a contrast at the Place node, yielding the additional representations in (16).

(16) Stage 2 representations, addition of Peripheral

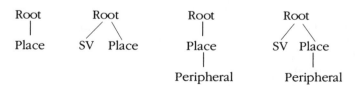

Alternatively, that child who first elaborated SV at Stage 1 could add SV structure, as in (17), rather than Place structure as in (16).

---

[12]The Structural Complexity Constraint mentioned in footnote 8 predicts that the structure with both SV and Peripheral might be less common, as it has both SV and elaborated Place structure.

(17) Stage 2 representations, addition of Oral

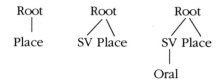

This elaboration would create a contrast between nasals, with just an SV node, and other sonorants, with the Oral node in addition, thus distinguishing between /p~t~k/ versus /m~n/ versus /l/. This seems to be a less common elaboration at an early stage, although the early presence of laterals in Quiché (see Pye, Ingram, & List, 1987) may be accounted for with this path.

An example of children following different paths can be found in the work of Goad and Ingram (1987), who reanalyzed data from three children, originally reported in Stoel-Gammon and Cooper (1984). Two of the children acquired a nasal/oral contrast before a stop/continuant contrast and the third acquired the stop/continuant contrast first. Within our model, the first two children added SV first, whereas the third child added Air Flow first.

What we have termed structural variability results from the choices available within the segment structure. Limitations to this type of variability are a consequence of the limited structure available to the learner.

4.3. Individual Variability

So far we have discussed two types of variability: noncontrastive variability and structural variability. Another type of variability is identified in the acquisition literature, individual variability (see Ferguson & Farwell, 1975; and, in particular, Vihman, Ferguson, & Elbert, 1986). Two types of individual variability pose no particular problems for our model: favorite sounds and frequency effects. It has been noted that individual children may have sounds that are particularly favored at a given stage. It might be expected that the child would develop such sounds as long as there is no phonological relevance to the choice of sounds. For instance, Ferguson and Farwell reported a child who had as favorite sounds sibilant fricatives and affricates. This, we suggest, is simply a particular choice the child makes for the realization of a bare Place node; there is phonologically nothing important about this choice (although it may be important in other ways). Others have reported on the importance of frequency effects. For example, de Boysson-Bardies and Vihman (1991) reported that systematic differences exist between the babbling and first words of infants from different language backgrounds that can be related to the phonetic structure of the ambient language. Although frequency of a sound in an ambient language may well have an effect, it does not appear to override the general constraints placed by our model.

5. CONCLUSION

In this chapter we have argued for a deterministic model of language acquisition based on the presence of phonological universals. Our model allows for two types of variation, one arising from lack of significant phonological oppositions and the second being a consequence of the small number of different structural paths made available to the child. If an account of variability is presented within a deterministic model, then the key argument against the deterministic model is vitiated, leading one to wonder about the validity of adopting a probabilistic cognitive approach. The model that we propose is able to (a) capture the overall uniformity across child language, a fact not well accounted for by either the cognitive model or the language-specific deterministic model of Goad and Ingram; and (b) account for the existence of some variability both within and between languages.

We can offer a universal model that accounts for variability largely because of the vast changes that have taken place in phonological theory in the past several years. The view of phonology represented in Chomsky and Halle (1968) and subsequent work, and from which much of the work on acquisition derives, is rule-based, viewing speakers as performing a series of operations that take them from an underlying representation to a phonetic representation. Language acquisition within this model is framed in terms of phonological rules that essentially change the adult input into the child output. Children are in a sense viewed as miniature adults, but adults who make mistakes or modifications due to output constraints that can be written as rules. Within our model, children do not have the adult grammar but, instead, their own grammar. The structure-elaborating constituency model that we propose allows for a vastly different view of the acquisition of phonology from that assumed in much of the acquisition literature and will, we hope, allow for new insights into the acquisition process.

ACKNOWLEDGMENTS

An earlier version of this chapter was presented at the Boston University Conference on Language Acquisition in October 1991. Many thanks to the participants at the conference for helpful suggestions. We would also like to thank Elan Dresher, Bill Idsardi, Betsy Ritter, Ron Smyth, and Tom Wilson for helpful comments and discussion.

CHAPTER THREE

Segments and Syllables in Early Language Acquisition

E. Jane Fee
Dalhousie University

In the past 10 years there has been a noticeable trend toward incorporating the findings of linguistic theory into models of language acquisition. Unfortunately, as tends to be the case in all aspects of linguistics, this trend has been much less noticeable in phonology than in syntax. Although nonlinear and metrical models now represent the mainstream of phonological research, only rare studies make any attempt to integrate these new visions of phonology into studies of phonological acquisition (e.g., Bernhardt, 1992b; Demuth, in press; Fee, 1991; Ingram, 1989c; Iverson & Wheeler, 1987; Menn, 1978).

The focus on explanations for linguistic phenomena, rather than simple descriptions, marks a second important research direction of the past decade. One consequence of this line of research has been a growing interest in the theory of Universal Grammar (UG), which links cross-linguistic and developmental phenomena. The theory of UG allows us to explain how children eventually achieve the grammar of their language, and why children from distinct language backgrounds show similar patterns of linguistic development.

In this chapter I develop a framework for determining how children represent their earliest productive lexical items, based on a UG-driven theory of phonological acquisition that incorporates current models of nonlinear phonology. I argue that UG provides a set of rules for building melodic and prosodic structure that dictates the shape of children's early words. Because of the restrictions imposed by prosodic representations, children's word forms differ in certain principled ways from adult targets. The focus of this work is on the representation of children's earliest phonological forms, those that are constrained by UG, and on the explanations for differences between children's representations and those of adults.

The organization of this chapter is as follows. In section 1 some descriptive characterizations of early phonological development are discussed. In section 2 a general picture of nonlinear phonology is presented for those not familiar with current developments in the field, with a particular emphasis on the theory of prosodic constituency. In section 3 I discuss how the primitives of nonlinear phonology can be integrated into a theory of phonological acquisition, with an attempt to distinguish the language-universal from the language-particular aspects of such a theory. In section 4 I summarize this model and discuss some of its implications for our understanding of children's early underlying representations, and for a general theory of phonological development.

1. SOME CHARACTERISTICS OF EARLY PHONOLOGICAL DEVELOPMENT

Although there is very little agreement in the acquisition literature regarding the theoretical mechanisms that drive children's early phonological development, it is relatively uncontroversial that children's word forms during the second year of life have a specific set of characteristics. Three particular characteristics are addressed here: (a) the canonical shape of children's early words, (b) the set of phonological processes that have been used to characterize discrepancies between a child's forms and adult targets, and (c) the relationship between early segmental acquisition and syllable structure.

1.1. Canonical Shapes

Jakobson (1941/1968) stated that during the initial stages of phonological development, the words used by children from all linguistic backgrounds are predominantly CV monosyllables and reduplicated CVCV bisyllables. Subsequent research on the acquisition of English supported this claim but demonstrated that consonant-final forms are available at a relatively early age for at least some children (Brannigan, 1976; Ingram, 1976; Winitz & Irwin, 1958). As in all aspects of language acquisition, there appears to be a great deal of variation in the syllable shapes used by individual children.

In looking at the development of children's early canonical forms, Ingram (1978) presented data from his daughter, Jennika, from 1;3 to 2;0. Jennika's most common syllable types during this period are given in (1).[1]

(1) Jennika's Syllable Types (revised from Ingram, 1978)

	Monosyllables		Multisyllables
Age	**CV**	**CVC**	**CVCV**
1;3	.89	.11	.87
1;6	.14	.66	.47
2;0	.13	.79	.36

At 1;3 Jennika's most common syllable types are CV and CVCV (we are not told if the CVCV forms contain identical consonants and/or vowels), with CVC forms representing only 11% of all monosyllabic forms. By the age of 2;0 the proportion of CV monosyllables decreases to only .13, whereas the proportion of CVCs increases to .79. CVCV forms decrease to .36 by this same age. These data demonstrate that early in phonological development, CV and CVCV forms represent the majority of early word shapes, but that by the age of 2;0, forms containing final consonants are more common.

1.2. Phonological Processes

Stampe (1969, 1972) proposed that children's early phonological systems are constrained by a set of natural processes that represent innate mental constraints on the child's productive abilities. Stampe did not attempt to determine the complete set of processes but, rather, discussed several processes, such as Word-Final Devoicing and Palatalization, in detail. Ingram (1976) suggested that processes can be divided into three types: Syllable Structure Simplification processes, Assimilation processes, and Substitution processes. Some examples of these are given in (2).[2]

(2) Phonological Processes

Syllable Structure Processes
a. *Final Consonant Deletion:* Final consonants are deleted.
   cat → [kæ]

---

[1]The proportions of CV and CVC syllable types are the proportions of monosyllables these syllable types represent, whereas the proportion of CVCV forms are the proportions of multisyllables that this syllable type represents.

[2]The English data used in this chapter are my own data from Christopher, from approximately 1;8 to 2;0.

b. *Unstressed Syllable Deletion:* An unstressed syllable is deleted.
   Andrea → [æjæ]
c. *Cluster Reduction:* A consonant cluster becomes a singleton.
   clothes → [koz]
   blanket → [bakə]

Assimilation Processes (Reduplication)

d. *Total Reduplication:* A consonant and vowel of a target syllable appear twice in the child's word, producing a $C_1V_1C_1V_1$ form.
   Patrick → [bæbæ]
e. *Partial Reduplication:* Either a consonant or a vowel of a target syllable appears twice in the child's word, resulting in a $C_1V_1C_1V_2$ or $C_1V_1C_2V_1$ form.
   Peter → [bibə]
   Andrea → [æjæ]

Substitution Processes

f. *Stopping:* A fricative is replaced by a homorganic stop.
   this → [dI]
   another → [nʌdə]
g. *Fronting:* Palatals and velars are replaced by alveolars.
   cheese → [tiz]
h. *Gliding:* A liquid is replaced by a glide.
   light → [jai]
i. *Voicing:* A voiceless consonant becomes voiced.
   Patrick → [bæbæ]

Each of these processes describes differences that exist between the target word form and the child's rendition of that target. There is little agreement in the literature as to the exact set of processes that characterize early development. Grunwell (1982), for example, assumed that normal phonological development can be described using a particular finite set of processes, but that children with phonological disorders may make use of processes outside of this set or may make use of normal processes in variable or persistent ways. Grunwell's data do show that the most common processes occurring in normal development are those shown in (2). Shriberg and Kwiatkowski (1986) listed 43 processes that have been discussed in the acquisition literature, although they claimed that this list is only suggestive and not exhaustive.

1.3. Segmental Acquisition and Syllable Structure

Many researchers have noted that segmental acquisition is dependent on syllable or word position, with the majority of consonants acquired first in word-initial position. Hodson and Paden (1983) showed that children between 1;6 and 1;9 omitted final obstruents of the adult targets (represented in their analyses as postvocalic obstruent omissions) 45% of the time. Prevocalic consonant omissions, on the other hand, were relatively infrequent, occurring only 14% of the time at this same age. Ingram (1981) examined the frequency with which particular consonants are matched (i.e., replication of the target consonant) in word-initial and word-final positions.[3] In a study of 15 normal children between the ages of 1;5 and 2;2, it was found that consonants were matched more often in initial position than in final position. These figures are shown in (3).

(3) Proportion of Matches (revised from Ingram, 1981)

Word Position	**Proportion of Matches**
Initial	52.8
Final	21.4

In looking at the proportion of matches of specific sounds, Ingram's data demonstrated that all consonants, with the exception of [p], [k], [s], and [r], were matched more frequently in initial than in final position. Stoel-Gammon (1985) also found that consonants were correctly produced more often in initial position than in final position, with the exception of [r].

2. CURRENT PHONOLOGICAL THEORY

Although these descriptive characterizations of children's early word productions are relatively well accepted, there has been little attempt to explain why phonological development proceeds as it does. In this section and those that follow I demonstrate that these characteristics of early phonological organization can be explained, given a UG-based theory of phonological development based on nonlinear models of phonology. Each of the phenomena characterized in section 1 is the result of the constraints that are imposed on children's earliest phonological representations by UG. These same UG-based constraints can be shown to operate in adult phonological systems and, in fact, represent the unmarked universal aspects of phonological systems.

---

[3]Ingram (1981) also presented data concerning the proportion of matches in ambisyllabic position. According to current theories of the syllable, discussed in section 2.1, all consonants belong to distinct syllables at the phonological level. Consequently, I deal exclusively with word-initial and word-final positions in this chapter. In the early acquisition data, word-initial and word-final positions should, in most cases, be equivalent to syllable-initial and syllable-final position.

2.1. Levels of Representation

Since the publication of Goldsmith (1979) the emphasis of phonological research has been on the investigation of representations, with a consequent reduction in the power of phonological rules. Research since 1979 has shown that phonological features are hierarchically organized and may in fact exist independently of segments; hence the term *nonlinear phonology*. Nonlinear phonology provides two distinct levels of structure: the melodic level, where featural information is represented; and the prosodic level, where aspects of syllabification, stress, and word structure are represented. These levels are schematically illustrated in the representation of the word *deep* in (4).

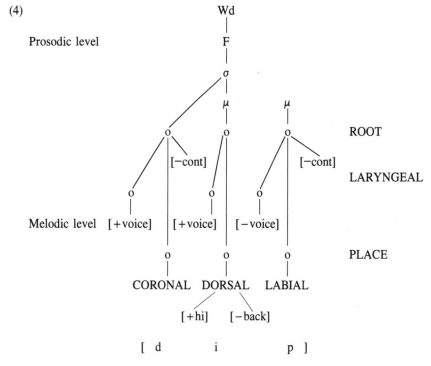

The word *deep* is made up of a single syllable. Many suggestions have been made regarding the appropriate internal organization for the syllable itself (Kahn, 1976; Levin, 1985; Steriade, 1982), although this issue is not crucial for the proposals developed here. Recent work has shown that the prosodic level of structure is highly developed, with hierarchical organization both above and below the syllable node. I assume the organization of the prosodic level used in McCarthy and Prince (1986), which employs the set of prosodic categories in (5).

(5) Prosodic Categories
Wd	prosodic word
F	foot
σ	syllable
μ	mora

The mora (μ) is the prosodic unit that reflects syllable weight, the foot (F) is important in the representation of stress systems, and the prosodic word (Wd) represents the phonological category corresponding to the word. The syllable node in *deep* branches into two morae; in English, closed syllables and syllables containing diphthongs or tense vowels are assumed to be bimoraic (Hayes, 1989).

The lower level of structure present in (4) is the melodic level, where the featural content of segments is represented. Researchers such as Clements (1985) and Sagey (1986) have argued that the melody is organized in hierarchical fashion and is made up of both nodes (e.g., ROOT, LARYNGEAL, PLACE, CORONAL, DORSAL, and LABIAL) and features ([voice], [cont], [high], and [back]). I do not argue for a particular model of feature geometry here; and in all illustrations the melodic level is abbreviated, using phonetic symbols. In (4) the melodic portions of the vowel and final consonant are linked to morae, whereas the melodic portion of the onset consonant is directly linked to the syllable node.

Another theoretical innovation in the past two decades has involved the exclusion of predictable information from lexical representations. Archangeli (1988) discussed the issue of underspecification of phonological constituents, showing that it is relatively uncontroversial that predictable prosodic structure is omitted from underlying representation, yet the same is not true for melodic structure. In English, syllable structure and stress assignment are built by rule, and therefore only in very marked cases will elements such as syllables or stress be present underlyingly. In contrast, it is assumed that in the nonconcatenative morphological systems of Semitic languages, syllable structure is represented lexically, whereas linkings between the syllabic and melodic levels are added during the course of a derivation.

The issue of the underspecification of melodic features is a more complex issue than that regarding prosodic structure, because it relates not only to which features are underlyingly present or absent, but also to which values of features exist lexically. Archangeli and Pulleyblank (1986), Steriade (1987), Avery and Rice (1988), and den Dikken and van der Hulst (1990) each presented different views of the types of nonpredictable melodic information that are permitted in underlying representations.

If we assume that in English, underlying representations do not contain predictable prosodic information, the lexical representation of *deep* will resemble (6).

(6) [d] [i] [p]

Prosodic information is missing entirely from this underlying representation. At the melodic level, only features or feature values that are not predictable are included (abbreviated here as the symbols [d], [i], and [p]). A prosodic structure for *deep* will be built, by rule, during the course of the derivation. Both universal and language-specific rules will be required to construct the surface representation, which will be similar to that shown in (4). Vowels will always be linked to morae, whereas consonants may be linked either to morae or directly to syllable nodes.

Lexical representations may differ from the representation in (4), which shows a one-to-one relationship between prosodic and melodic elements. In some theories of feature representation segments may exist that have no associated underlying features (Archangeli & Pulleyblank, 1986); and in this case, no feature hierarchy will exist underlyingly, because it has no features to support. Floating features, which are features that are underlyingly unassociated to skeletal slots, are also assumed to exist in many models (cf. Archangeli & Pulleyblank, 1986; Piggott, 1990). Floating features generally fulfill a morphological function in languages.

2.2. Rules

Nonlinear phonology and theories of feature geometry have led to a much clearer view of the structure of phonological representations. This, along with the move in syntax to limit rule types (Chomsky, 1981), has led phonologists to a constrained view of the number and types of phonological rules that may occur in any language. Following works such as Archangeli and Pulleyblank (1986) and Piggott (1990) I assume the set of possible phonological rules in (7).

(7) Phonological rules

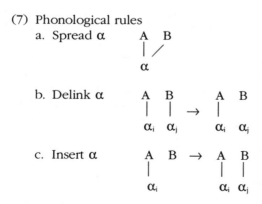

The rule of Spread α, shown in (7a), allows for the addition of an association line between a feature or node and some segment. This process permits a single node or feature to be shared by two distinct segments. In section 3.3.3, I demonstrate that this rule is important in the resolution of mismatches that occur between the child's representation and the intended target.

The rule of Delink α, shown in (7b), allows for the deletion of an association line, with the consequence that a feature will be left unassociated at some point in the derivation. If this feature is not reassociated by some subsequent rule of the phonology, it will have no phonetic realization.

The rule of Insert α, shown in (7c), provides for the addition of an association line or an element such as a feature. This rule can then save a previously delinked element, or add a new feature or node to the representation.

3. TOWARD A THEORY OF PHONOLOGICAL DEVELOPMENT

In the 1960s and 1970s it was assumed that language acquisition took place as the child created rules compatible with the linguistic data, with an evaluation metric aiding the child in the choice between competing rules or rule systems. More recently, the theory of UG has replaced the rule-writing approach, in part because it was found to be extremely difficult to understand or even characterize the evaluation metric, and in part because it was difficult to ascertain how children would ever arrive at the appropriate adult grammar. In the theory of UG the set of possible hypotheses that are necessary for acquisition are assumed to be innate. Although this type of theory requires more innate machinery than the rule-writing approach, it permits a more restricted view of the types of hypotheses that children can make about language.

There are two important consequences of the theory of UG. First, it provides us with a principled model of language acquisition, in that we must assume that children begin acquisition with the set of principles and categories provided by UG. Second, it greatly increases the importance of acquisition data for linguistic theory in general, because stages of acquisition must represent possible human grammars. This produces a very different picture of acquisition than was prevalent in the earlier period of research, as summed up by Menn (1978): "Child language is a form of linguistic communication, but it is not a form of adult language" (p. 157).

In developing a model of phonological acquisition I assume the basic premises of a theory of UG. The child is equipped with a set of innate principles and categories that shape the direction of phonological acquisition. The acquisition process consists of the child acquiring language-specific aspects of grammar, and those aspects of grammar that are peripheral to UG.[4]

In Ingram (1976, 1989a), early phonological acquisition was divided into four stages, involving: (a) prelinguistic development, (b) the acquisition of the first 50 words, (c) the phonology of single morphemes, and (d) later developments. The period during which the first 50 words are acquired lasts from about 1;0 to 1;6 and spans the time when children are producing mainly single-word utterances. Vocabulary development during this period is relatively slow, and the child's words tend to be more idiosyncratic than during later stages. Beginning at about 1;6 most children demonstrate a rapid increase in the size of their vocabularies and begin to combine words into utterances.

Following Ingram, I assume that phonological organization begins not with the acquisition of the first 50 words but at around 1;6, with the phonology of single morphemes. I assume that during the acquisition of the first 50 words, children may represent their words as learned wholes, but that by about 1;6 the child's vocabulary has become too large to manage without some organizational system. This predicts that there may be qualitative differences in the representations found during these two periods.

3.1. Components of the Theory

In developing a UG-based model of phonological acquisition, it is essential to clarify which aspects of development are determined by UG, and which must be learned through exposure to the input language. We expect that in the initial period of phonological organization children's representations will be characterized by just those aspects of the phonological system that are supplied by UG, and that as they learn that certain modifications are required to fit the language being learned, their phonological systems will change to reflect language-particular aspects of phonology. In the discussion that follows, I attempt to outline both the aspects of phonological acquisition that are directed by UG and those aspects that must be learned.

3.1.1. Prosodic Structure. A good deal of phonological research has shown that the universal syllable shape is CV (Jakobson, 1941/1968; Jakobson & Halle, 1956; Maddieson, 1984). This fact is built into the theory of prosodic morphology discussed in section 2.3 by assuming the primitive status of the minimal or core syllable, a syllable that is maximally filled by a single consonant and vowel. I therefore assume that UG provides the child with a rule for building the core syllable (σ_c), which is also maximally a

---

[4]Chomsky (1981), Fodor (1989), and Piggott (1990) each presented some proposals regarding the peripheral areas of linguistic theory.

monomoraic syllable (σ_μ). At the earliest stages of phonological organization children will be capable of building only monomoraic syllables, consisting of simple vowels preceded by single onset consonants. To account for child syllables that do not contain onset consonants, I further assume that only the moraic projection is obligatory. Language-specific rules that allow the child to represent syllables containing coda consonants, complex onsets, and complex vowels will be later acquisitions.

It is argued in Fee (1992) that UG also provides the child with a rule for building the minimal word (Wd$_{min}$; see also Demuth, in press). McCarthy and Prince (1986) suggested that the Wd$_{min}$ = F = [$\mu\mu$]. If children are initially able to represent only monomoraic syllables, then the Wd$_{min}$ can be filled only by two monomoraic syllables. The assumption that the Wd$_{min}$ plays a major role in early phonological development will help to explain why so many of children's early word forms are bisyllabic. The units *word* and *syllable* will be distinct entities from the earliest period of phonological development, with the rule for building the Wd$_{min}$ acting to make children's words bisyllabic, and that for building the σ_μ acting to make the component syllables as simple as possible.[5]

Children acquiring languages that permit bimoraic syllables must learn that syllables can contain two morae before the Wd$_{min}$ can be filled by a monosyllabic bimoraic form. This again predicts that words containing long vowels, diphthongs, or coda consonants will not appear until a later stage of development. Similarly, words containing three or more syllables will be later acquisitions for children from all linguistic backgrounds.

3.1.2. Melodic Structure.   Research such as that of Ingram (1981, 1986) has shown that between 1;0 and 2;0, children acquiring English have smaller phonological inventories than adults. This is also true of children acquiring languages such as K'iche (Pye, Ingram, & List, 1987) and Hungarian and Spanish (Fee, 1991). Translated into a featural account, these facts suggest that children have control of fewer features than are required for the adult phonological system of their language.

Some possibilities for featural acquisition were outlined in Iverson and Wheeler (1987), Rice and Avery (1991a; this volume, chap. 2), Brown and Matthews (1992), and Fee (1992). Iverson and Wheeler argued that many of the errors made by very young children can be accounted for by assuming that particular features have been mistakenly associated at the suprasegmental or prosodic level, rather than at the melodic level. In a UG-based model of acquisition, an incorrect hypothesis of this kind is impossible for a child

---

[5]I ignore the prosodic category F in this chapter because I am not looking at stress systems. For an insightful treatment of the development of stress systems using current phonological theory, see Fikkert (1992) and Demuth (in press).

to make. In this chapter it is assumed that development proceeds according to the constraints of UG, as in the models discussed in Rice and Avery, Brown and Matthews, and Fee. In these models it is assumed that features are acquired gradually, but that UG provides the structure to which features, once acquired, are associated.

3.1.3. Rules. One final aspect of phonology that will form part of children's innate knowledge is the set of phonological operations given in (7). These rules provide the mechanisms that can account for the manipulation of phonological elements in all languages. Children will then be restricted to the insertion, deletion, or spreading of elements of their phonological representations in order to provide well-formed representations.

3.1.4 Summary. Summarizing the preceding discussions, the following picture of the phonological component of UG emerges:

(8) 1. *Levels of Structure*
    a. Rules for building prosodic structure:
       $Wd_{min} = \sigma_\mu\ \sigma_\mu$
       $\sigma_{min} = \sigma_\mu$
    b. Melody: Unmarked aspects of hierarchical structure
   2. *Rules*
    a. Spread
    b. Delink
    c. Insert

These are the mechanisms that will initially constrain children's phonological representations and should therefore characterize children's earliest words.

3.2. Building Prosodic Structure

As an example of how the mechanisms in (8) work, I first discuss a child's form [bebi] for the target *baby*, that is, a case where the child's form matches the target. I assume the child's underlying representation consists of the information in (9):

(9) [b] [e] [b] [i]
    Unmarked aspects of hierarchical structure

UG provides the child with certain unmarked aspects of the feature hierarchy (e.g., the structure and certain unmarked features/nodes or feature values).

The child's representation may also contain some learned information, permitting the child to represent the appropriate melodic content of the target.

The rules that build the Wd_{min} and the σ_μ are provided by UG, and these prosodic units will be erected over the melody during the course of the derivation, as shown in (10).

(10)

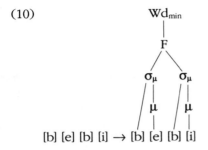

$$\text{[b] [e] [b] [i]} \rightarrow \text{[b] [e] [b] [i]}$$

If we assume that the prosody is constructed from the top down, the Wd_{min} will have to be filled by two monomoraic syllables. The two morae are linked to the two vowels of the melody, and the consonants can link to syllable nodes. The child's surface form is then identical to that of the target.

3.3. Mismatches Between the Child's Form and the Target

In (10) the number of feature combinations is equal to the number of slots provided for in the prosodic level, and the child's production is the same as the target. One of the predictions made by the theory of phonological organization developed here is that there may be mismatches between the target form and the child's representation of that same form, when the number of feature sets and prosodic slots are not the same. Two possible types of mismatches are possible, and each is discussed here, along with possible resolutions of the mismatches.

3.3.1. Child's Form Is Less Complex Than Target. The first type of mismatch between the child's representation and the intended target will arise when there is more prosodic information present in the target than the child can represent. A mismatch may occur when the child attempts a trisyllabic target such as *banana*, as shown in (11).[6]

---

[6]In fact this example is also a case of spreading of the initial nasal consonant and vowel, but in order to simplify I treat the two consonants as having distinct feature sets. Spreading is dealt with in section 3.3.2.

(11) Target: banana [bənænæ]

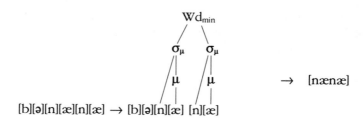

$$[b][ə][n][æ][n][æ] \rightarrow [b][ə][n][æ] \; [n][æ]$$

In this case, I assume the child knows where stress falls in the adult target. The leftmost mora of the prosodic structure is constructed over the leftmost stressed syllable, with the result that the initial syllable of the target is not linked to the prosody. The child's form will consequently be realized as bisyllabic [nænæ], rather than as a trisyllabic form. The unassociated melodic constituents will not surface phonetically, because they have no dominating prosodic structure. The type of target distortion shown in (11) has traditionally been described as Unstressed Syllable Deletion (see (2b)), a process that occurs frequently with polysyllabic targets (see Archibald, this volume, chap. 5).

A similar type of mismatch will occur when the target contains a consonant cluster, as in the child form [bakə] for *blanket.*

(12) Target: blanket [blaŋkət]

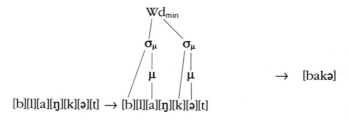

$$[b][l][a][ŋ][k][ə][t] \rightarrow [b][l][a][ŋ][k][ə][t]$$

In this example, the restrictions of the prosodic structure constrain the child's form to pick up only a single consonant from the complex onset of the target. Likewise, neither of the coda consonants of the target will surface in the child's form, because they cannot be associated to prosodic constituents. The change in the onset cluster is described as Cluster Reduction, as in (2e),[7] whereas the omission of the coda consonants is described as Final Consonant Deletion in (2a).

---

[7]Sonorancy, or some similar requirement, may well be an issue in cluster reductions in acquisition, because [s]-plus-stop clusters are most often realized as the stop itself (Ingram, 1976). In both cases it is the least sonorous member that is preserved.

3.3.2. Child's Segmental Material Differs From Target. In the preceding examples we have assumed that children can correctly represent all the melodic constituents of target forms. As discussed in section 3.1.2, the acquisition literature in fact demonstrates that children have limited knowledge of the features of their language, particularly at the earliest stages of phonological acquisition. A second type of mismatch is then predicted to occur when the child's melodic representation is distinct from or less complex than that of the target. It may be that the child cannot provide melodic information for all prosodic positions, or it may be that the child simply has melodic information that is different from that of the target.

In a child's production [nʌdə] for the trisyllabic target *another*, the child's melodic representation for the intervocalic fricative of the target appears to be different from that in the target. If [ð] is not in the child's phonological inventory at the time the target is attempted, then it will not be possible to supply a melodic representation for this sound.[8] Given that one of the most common substitutions for /ð/ is [d], I assume that this substitution pattern, and others like it, are due to immaturities at the segmental level of structure. Such immaturities can be built into the theory of UG using markedness theory and feature geometry or a theory of underspecification.[9] The child's representation of *another* is as shown in (13).

(13) Target: [ənʌðər]

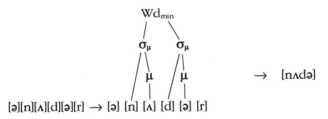

$$\rightarrow \quad [\text{nʌdə}]$$

[ə][n][ʌ][d][ə][r] → [ə] [n] [ʌ] [d] [ə] [r]

In this particular form, the child's underlying representation contains melodic information distinct from that of the target. Several phonological processes can be used to describe this form: Unstressed Syllable Deletion (the omission of the initial vowel of the target), Stopping (the use of unmarked [d] for /ð/), and Final Consonant Deletion (the omission of the final [r]).

A mismatch may also occur when the child's form does not contain all the melodic information of the target. In an investigation of children's early consonant assimilations, Vihman (1978) suggested that children produce assimilated forms (a) when a sound is not in the child's inventory (e.g.,

---

[8]Most studies of segmental acquisition agree that [ð] is one of the later consonants acquired by children (e.g., Templin, 1957).

[9]See Fee (1991) for a justification of the use of redundancy rules to provide substitutes in this fashion.

[bibə] for *Peter*, if voiceless stops are not yet in the child's inventory), or (b) to simplify a word form so that the child can focus on some other aspect of the word (e.g., [bæbæ] for *Patrick*, where the complexity of the second syllable consonant cluster is removed). Fee (1991) demonstrated that although both these factors contribute to the occurrence of assimilated forms, stress may also play a role in forms containing assimilated vowels. In Spanish, which has a complex stress system, it is the unstressed syllable that assimilates to the stressed syllable in children' early words (e.g., [papa] for *zapato*, where stress is on the penultimate syllable in the adult target). I then assume that any one of these possibilities may explain why children cannot supply the complete set of melodic constituents for a target form.

If we assume that all prosodic slots that exist in the child's form must surface in some fashion, then we can explain why assimilated forms occur. Given a bisyllabic minimal word form that has melodic content for only a single syllable, the rule of Spread α from (7) will permit the child to provide surface melodic specifications for the unspecified syllable. This process is demonstrated for the target *Patrick*, shown in (14).

(14) Target: Patrick [pætrɪk]
     Child's underlying melody: [b] [æ]

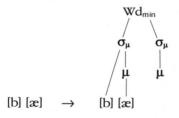

Here I assume that the child can initially represent only the first consonant and vowel of the target, and that UG has provided the substitute [b] for /p/ of the target. The structure for the Wd$_{min}$ is built, but only the initial syllable of the word is filled by melodic information. If the child makes use of the rule of Spread α, the features of [b] and [æ] can be used to fill the final syllable of the prosodic form, as shown in (15).

(15) Resolution: Spread [b] and [æ]

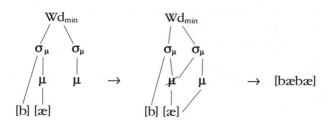

In descriptive terms the child's form [bæbæ] for *Patrick* would involve the processes of Voicing (2i) and Total Reduplication (2d). The fact that totally reduplicated bisyllabic forms have been reported to occur for monosyllabic target words (Fee & Ingram, 1982; Vihman, 1978) indicates that there must be some prosodic constituent that is driving the child toward the representation of a bisyllabic form. If this were not the case, then we might expect children simply to truncate words when they do not have sufficient melodic information. Monosyllabic forms may be used by the child at this stage of development, but because these do not adhere to the restrictions provided by UG, they must be represented as lexical wholes and are therefore not truly part of the child's phonological system.

A bisyllabic child form such as [bibə] (2e) would represent Spreading of the initial consonant only, with distinct featural representations for the two vowels. This type of form is often called Partial Reduplication. Partially reduplicated forms that have identical vowels but distinct melodic representations for the consonants also exist in the acquisition literature. The form [æjæ] in (2e) is representative of this type of process.

Spreading processes must adhere to the constraints that operate on all phonological representations. One of these is the Crossing Constraint (Goldsmith, 1976), which says that association lines do not cross. For simplicity's sake I have not indicated the features that specify [b] and [æ] in (15), but we must assume that these specifications are such that association lines do not cross. [æ] cannot be specified with features that spread from [b], or crossing would take place. Child forms where spreading does occur should then provide one possible source of evidence as to the features that are underlyingly specified in children's phonological representations (see Stemberger & Stoel-Gammon, 1991).

The rule typology in (7) provides for three possible rules: Spread α, Delink α, and Insert α. The data examined here provide evidence only for Spread α—the rule that will be used to provide surface feature specifications for underlyingly unspecified segments. We would predict, however, that evidence may be found for the rules of delinking and insertion in children's early lexical representations.

4. SUMMARY

In this chapter I have attempted to integrate the melodic and prosodic components of current nonlinear phonological theory into a theory of phonological acquisition. This conception of acquisition leads us to a clear picture of the UG-constrained representations that will be used by children at the earliest stages of phonological development and provides an explanation for the characterizations of early phonological development that were noted in section 1.

The theory of phonological organization presented here also makes test-able predictions regarding the nature of children's early representations. Given that the Wd$_{min}$ is assumed to be one of the prosodic units provided by UG, and that this category must be filled by two monomoraic syllables, we predict that children's word forms should be minimally bisyllabic. We would expect that the canonical form of children's words should change when phonological organization begins. Forms that are simply lexically learned may be monosyllabic, because they will not have to adhere to the phonological constraints of UG. Words that are constrained by the phonological system should, in contrast, be bisyllabic. We would also predict that at some later point, children acquiring languages that permit bimoraic syllables (like English) will learn that syllables may be either monomoraic or bimoraic. At this point bimoraic forms containing long vowels or coda consonants will become possible.

Although there have been attempts to determine whether the child's initial unit of phonological organization is the feature, segment, syllable, or word (cf. Ferguson and Farwell, 1975; Macken, 1979; Moskowitz, 1970), the model developed here tells us that features, syllables, and words are all organiza-tional units for the child at this early age. This model predicts that the unit *segment* exists only as a derivative notion and has no primitive status.

The theory of early word formation developed in this chapter allows us to explain why children's early word forms have such restricted syllable shapes and why certain phonological processes or substitution patterns seem to be characteristic of children's early productions. Our theory predicts that the set of phonological processes are simply descriptive devices detailing differences between child and target forms. Explanations for the occurrence of these processes can come only from an examination of children's phonological representations.

This theory of early word formation also helps to explain why early phonological acquisition appears to be so dependent on syllable structure. Children may be capable of providing featural information for a particular sound or class of sounds, but in certain positions (i.e., syllable-finally, or in clusters) these sounds cannot be mapped to prosodic positions and will therefore have no phonetic realization.

An interesting implication of the work presented here is its contribution to the debate on the nature of children's underlying representations. Certain authors have suggested that children's representations are not the same as adults', because their perception of adult forms is incorrect or incomplete (e.g., Braine, 1976; Macken, 1979; Vihman, 1982). Others have argued that children's underlying representations are identical (or at least very similar) to adults', given that their perceptual abilities are in advance of production skills (e.g., Ingram, 1976; Menn, 1978; Smith, 1973). The model of word formation presented here suggests that children's representations may in many cases be different from those of adults because their phonological systems do not yet contain the language-specific mechanisms that are required for complete representations.

ACKNOWLEDGMENTS

An earlier version of this chapter was presented at the Boston University Conference on Language Development, October 1991. This work was supported in part by doctoral fellowships from the Social Sciences and Humanities Research Council of Canada, grant number 452-89-2413, and the H. R. MacMillan Family.

CHAPTER FOUR

The Acquisition of Negative Constraints, the OCP, and Underspecified Representations

David Ingram
University of British Columbia

Issues of learnability have been far more prevalent in research in syntactic theory and syntactic acquisition than they have in the comparable areas of phonology. This chapter is a preliminary inquiry into three general learnability issues: (a) the nature of the input (or evidence), (b) parameters, and (c) principles of acquisition. These general issues are addressed by focusing on a specific aspect of each.

The general issue of evidence concerns the use of positive versus negative evidence in language acquisition. Here, I address the more specific issue of the learnability of negative constraints in phonological theory. Such constraints are common in the literature on theoretical phonology, yet they seemingly would need to be acquired through indirect negative evidence. The second topic involves the effort to examine principles of grammar in terms of their parameters and how they are set. I discuss an attempt to do this with a widely held principle in phonological theory, the Obligatory Contour Principle. I examine arguments that the principle is parametrized in a way that accounts for the stages that children follow in the acquisition of English plural allomorphy. Last, I explore some issues concerning the child's acquisition of underspecified phonological representations. In the acquisition literature, underspecification has been assumed since the initial work of Jakobson (1941/1968). For independent reasons, underspecification has been revived in phonological theory by Archangeli and Pulleyblank (1986). I suggest specific acquisition principles that enable the child to acquire underspecified representations.

1. THE ACQUISITION OF NEGATIVE CONSTRAINTS

Although there is not a consensus, there is certainly a prevalent view in syntactic research and learnability that the child uses only positive evidence (e.g., Baker 1979). We can ask whether the same is true for phonological acquisition.

1.1. Negative Constraints and Indirect Negative Evidence

At first glance, the learner appears to be in a different situation in phonological acquisition than in syntactic acquisition. This difference can be traced to that between the products of the syntactic and phonological rule systems. Phonological rules apply to a fixed set of lexical entries and can thus be characterized as interpretive. Syntactic rules, on the other hand, lead to the production of an open set of possible sentences and can be characterized as generative. This difference suggests that indirect negative evidence may be available in the acquisition of the phonological system in a way that is not possible during the acquisition of the syntactic system.

Negative constraints are a case in phonology where it appears that indirect negative evidence may be available to the learner. English has a restriction on word- or syllable-initial clusters of the form in (1):

> (1) Initial stop-plus-sonorant clusters cannot agree in place of articulation:
> pl   *tl   kl
> *pw   tw   kw

Such restrictions are usually stated in phonology as negative constraints. Further, this set of facts seems easier to state as a negative constraint. We could reformulate it positively: English stop-plus-sonorant clusters must have a difference in place of articulation. Acquisition, however, would then involve quite a bit of specific learning for all the individual clusters that do occur. The simpler learning scenario would be:

> (2) 1. Acquire the set of possible clusters through positive evidence.
>   2. Identify the gaps through indirect negative evidence.
>   3. Formulate a negative constraint for the exceptions.

The greater simplicity of negative constraints for at least some patterns in phonology can be used as an argument for the use of indirect negative evidence in phonological acquisition.

A second argument that indirect negative evidence may be used in phonological acquisition concerns the lack of overgeneralizations in phonology. If children were acquiring the pattern in (1) through positive evidence, we might expect an overgeneralization such as the one in (3):

(3) Overgeneralization of (1): Assume that all obstruent-plus-sonorant clusters are possible.

Children are not normally presented with contexts that require them to create words, however, and therefore evidence of such overgeneralizations is not likely. We do get some child errors, however, that merit discussion. Children will violate English constraints and say things like *pway* for *play*. We can account for these forms as the consequences of the interaction of underspecification and universal redundancies, rather than incorrect language-specific constraints (Ingram, 1991, 1992). The underlying form for such a production is still /ple/, with a simplification of the /l/ to [w]. On perceptual tasks, children will discriminate the two (see review of this literature in Ingram, 1989a). Also, these forms will be corrected as the result of positive evidence. Such errors, therefore, are the result not of a misanalysis of English but, instead, of an inability to map an underlying distinction onto a phonetic surface structure.

1.2. Negative Constraints as Positive Constraints

An initial proposal is that children may have access to indirect negative evidence in phonology in a way that does not exist in syntax. There are, however, reasons to reject this proposal. The first argument against it is what can be called the *symmetry argument*. This is based on the claim that the child should be programmed to use the same kind of evidence in any domain of acquisition, be it syntax or phonology. It would be a peculiar state of affairs if the child were using one form of evidence in syntax and another in phonology.

A second argument is one often given against indirect negative evidence in syntax: the computation argument. The child taking negative evidence into consideration has to keep track of every aspect of the input in terms of frequency of occurrence. We can see this when we look at the constraints on English syllable-initial clusters. Besides the constraint in (1), we can also identify a constraint for the clusters in (4).

(4) *ps *pf *kp *mb *cs

This is unlike any constraint ever proposed for English. Yet, if children establish negative constraints on the basic of indirect negative evidence, then they should have a potentially infinite set of constraints that constitute knowledge of what never occurs in the phonological system. Although UG will eliminate some clusters, it will allow the ones in (4), which can be found in a range of languages. The set of negative constraints will cover everything that is allowed by UG but does not exist in the child's native language.

An alternative to proposing negative constraints is to suggest that they are nothing more than mirror images of positive statements. Such a suggestion, in fact, can be found in Itô (1986), as paraphased in (5).

(5) Itô's proposal: Negative constraints are formally equivalent to positive constraints.

If this proposal is true, we can then argue that all negative constraints suggested in the literature are actually positive constraints, and that they are acquired from positive evidence. Itô gave an example of this regarding the constraint on codas in Japanese. Japanese allows only nasals to appear in the syllable coda. Itô pointed out that this condition can be stated as a negative constraint, as in (6a).

(6) *Japanese Coda Condition:*
   a.   *C]   b. IF: C]
        |
    [−nasal]   THEN: [+nasal]

She suggested, however, that, such negative constraints are equivalent to *if-then* statements about the phonology. Such an *if-then* condition is given in (6b) for the same constraint.

1.3. The Need for Negative Constraints

Although this solution seems to get around the problem of negative evidence, there are three arguments against It's proposal in (5). I would like to show now that it appears that we need negative constraints, and that negative constraints are not always formally equivalent to positive *if-then* statements.

The first problem concerns the specification of phonological features in underlying representations. There is currently quite a debate about the nature of such specifications. There are three common views in the literature, favoring contrastive specification (Steriade, 1987), radical specification (Archangeli, 1988), or unary features (den Dikken & van der Hulst, 1990). The constraint in (6) requires more explicit examination of how such an equivalence can hold, under each of these approaches. That is, the proposal that there is a formal equivalence involving two values of a feature will require some formal machinery to get us between the two values. I doubt that anyone has contemplated how this would be done in the context of these proposals.

A second problem is that there are cases where the negative constraint is simpler to state than the positive form. An example of this is a constraint in Luyia, a Bantu language, discussed in Dalgish (1975). Luyia has a constraint on morae, that two morae cannot appear at the beginning of a word. This constraint can be stated negatively as in (7a):

(7) a. *#VV (Luyia constraint on word-initial morae)
    b. Allow #V, #CV, #CVV

As is typical in constraints like this one, the positive constraint is much more complex to state. (7b) gives the word-initial onsets and vowels that are allowed in Luyia. The frequent appearance of negative constraints in the phonological literature is due to their simplicity, as well as to their apparent psychological reality, as mentioned earlier.

A third problem in doing away with negative constraints is that they appear in some instances to serve as the trigger to a phonological repair. For example, in Luyia, the *#VV constraint is violated when a vocalic prefix is added to a verb root with a vocalic onset, as in (8).

(8) a. /u-um-a-ng-a/ → wuumaanga 'you dry'
    b. /a-umbax-a-ng-a/ → yoombaxaanga 'he builds'
    c. /u-li-lak-a/ → olilaka 'you will cover'
    d. /a-xol-a/ → axola 'he did'

This violation results in two repairs. In (8a), the /u/ becomes a glide and triggers compensatory lengthening, whereas in (8b), there is vowel coalescence and glide insertion.

How are we to trigger repairs of this sort? One common practice is to perceive negative constraints as a kind of filter. That is, all output of phonological rules is filtered through a set of well-formedness conditions. These conditions tell the system what is not allowed. This is captured very naturally by negative constraints. Such restrictions can also be captured by *if-then* conditions, but the effect is much less direct. I am not aware of any proposals that well-formedness conditions should be stated as *if-then* conditions. The strength of this argument, therefore, depends on the degree to which negative constraints provide a simpler account of such effects than *if-then* conditions.

This leads to the hypothesis that there are at least two kinds of negative constraints. One kind cites the structural environments of phonological rules and has no formal status in the theory. This would include the kind of constraint discussed earlier, which can be stated either positively or negatively. The second kind has formal status as a negative constraint. Evidence for these is that they operate to trigger repairs of the kind just mentioned.

If there are negative constraints, then we are still left with the question of how they can be acquired. A tentative answer is the one that is usually suggested in the syntax literature. This is to restrict the child's learning space through restrictions on UG and find positive evidence that would lead the child to the correct grammar.

The following is a tentative proposal regarding the acquisition of negative constraints from positive evidence. Phonological patterns are initially based on what occurs in the input vocabulary and are formulated as *if-then* conditions. Some of these, however, will be restructured into their negative form when certain conditions arise in the phonology. Further research must investigate the nature of such conditions. It is possible that this restructuring occurs when the *if-then* condition reaches a certain level of complexity that greatly exceeds that of the negative alternative. Alternatively, the restructuring may occur when a repair of some kind would be more directly triggered by a negative constraint then by a complex *if-then* condition.

2. PHONOLOGICAL ACQUISITION
AND THE OBLIGATORY CONTOUR PRINCIPLE

It is common in the syntactic literature to see principles analyzed as parametrized and, in acquisition research, to see proposals regarding the setting of such parameters (e.g., Hyams, 1986, on the pro-drop parameter). Research within phonological theory has only recently turned to the study of possible principles and parameters. One of the most extensive efforts of this kind was that of Dresher and Kaye (1990), in which several interrelated parameters were proposed for stress systems. Another attempt to explore possible parameters in phonology and acquisition was Goad (1989). This study concerned the Obligatory Contour Principle, or OCP. Unlike Dresher and Kaye, Goad not only addressed the logical issue of the acquisition of the OCP but also examined the OCP in light of acquisition data.

2.1. The Obligatory Contour Principle

First proposed in Leben (1978), the OCP was defined in McCarthy (1986) as follows:

(9) *Obligatory Contour Principle:* At the melodic level, adjacent identical elements are prohibited.

McCarthy's proposal was that the OCP is universal, that is, that it is never violated in languages.

Research on the OCP has not reached a consensus on how and when it operates (e.g., Yip, 1988). One perspective is that it operates to block the application of a rule (Borowsky, 1987; McCarthy 1986); another is that it can function to trigger a rule (Archangeli & Pulleyblank, 1986). The difference between these perspectives can be seen in two alternative analyses of the English plural allomorphs. Under the first approach, the plural is underlyingly /əz/, and there is a rule of schwa deletion that is blocked when an OCP violation would result, as in *buzzes* (/bʌz/ + /əz/). Under the second approach, the underlying form is /z/, and the occurrence of two identical segments would violate the OCP, triggering schwa insertion.

If the OCP is absolute and thus operates in one of these two ways, then this would suggest that it is never parametrized. A third possibility, however, is that it operates sometimes as a blocker and other times as a trigger (Yip, 1988). If so, the language learner would need to know how it was operating. This could be accomplished with a parametrized OCP, where one operation is associated with the unmarked or initial setting, and the other, associated with the marked setting, is determined by positive evidence. Another way that the OCP may involve parametrization is in its capacity as a trigger for repairs. Suppose, for example, that the plural morpheme in English is an underlying /z/. The OCP could allow (or trigger) any one of the following repairs: (a) creation of a geminate structure, (b) deletion of one of the identical segments, or (c) insertion of an epenthetic vowel.

A third aspect of the OCP that could involve parameters is the level in feature geometry at which the OCP operates. In the predominant number of cases discussed by McCarthy, its effects are seen when the segments involved are identical. In a few cases, however, the segments only need to be similar. One such example is our English plural case where the schwa separates the plural sibilant from all sibilants, regardless of their place of articulation.

2.2. The Acquisition of English Plural Allomorphy

Goad (1989) examined the operation of the OCP in language acquisition by studying the acquisition of the English plural allomorphs. The distribution of the English allomorphs is given in (10).

(10) [z] after sonorants and voiced noncoronal nonstrident obstruents
  [s] after voiceless noncoronal nonstrident obstruents
  [əz] after sibilants (s, z, š, ž, č, ǰ)

There is an extensive descriptive literature on their acquisition, inspired by Berko's (1958) original study. Goad first presented the well-known finding that the first allomorphs to appear are the nonsyllabic [s] and [z]. She took this as evidence that the first underlying form for the child is /z/. Also, invoking the continuity condition of acquisition (Pinker, 1984), she assumed that this is the adult underlying form as well.

Goad then turned to children's plurals for those words that require [əz] in English. She found that there were two error patterns reported in the literature. The most widespread pattern is for the plural form to be deleted for these sibilant-final words, even though it is used elsewhere (e.g., Baker & Derwing, 1982). A second pattern is that of gemination. Goad reported that at least two studies showed instances where children add a plural form to the sibilants but do not insert a schwa. This produces geminates for same-place sibilants (e.g., *roses* [rozz]), and sibilant clusters in the other cases (e.g., churches [črčs]). These two patterns of errors are summarized in (11):

(11) *Acquisition errors in English stem-final sibilant words*
Pattern 1: deletion of the plural affix
Pattern 2: addition of plural affix to all sibilants without schwa insertion

The second pattern looks like a possible violation of the OCP in that it shows identical segments occurring together, as in (12a). Goad proposed that these are not violations because the child has combined the two sounds into a single geminate consonant, as in (12b):

(12) a. X X X + X → X X X X
     | | | | | | | |
     r o z   z   r o z z

    b. X X X + X → X X X X
     | | | | \ /
     r o z   z   r o z

Goad predicted that Pattern 2 would constitute the first stage of acquisition of plurals for English word-final sibilants. Later, the child would hear words such as *roses* /rozəz/ that indicate that English does not have geminate plurals. Such evidence would lead the child to reject the geminate analysis. Subsequent repairs would also be available in a particular order. First, the child would repair potential OCP violations by deletion, which would yield Pattern 1. Finally, the child would see from positive evidence that English uses epenthesis as a repair in these forms.

Although Goad did not formulate her account as a set of parameters, it can be presented as such. (13) give a set of parameters that would lead the child to the stages she predicted. I have also adjusted the epenthesis parameter to include a default setting for identical segments only, and a marked one when it also applies to similar segments, as in the English plural. (The error pattern 1a is discussed shortly.)

(13) | *Parameter* | *Setting* | *Error if Default Setting* |
|---|---|---|
| 1. Gemination | Yes(default)/No | Pattern 2 |
| 2. Deletion | (If Parameter 1 is No) | |
| | Yes(default)/No | Pattern 1 |
| 3. Epenthesis | (If Parameter 2 is No) | |
| | Identical(default)/ | Pattern 1a |
| | Similar | |

Goad's analysis constituted one of the first attempts to develop parameters of phonological acquisition that accounted for data from acquisition. She argued that the error patterns she observed are the result of phonological parameters, rather than some vaguely defined set of performance limitations. Her analysis also had the virtue of not resorting to restructuring on the part of the child. She proposed that the child's and the adult's underlying representations of the plural are both /z/.

Let us now turn to some potential difficulties with this account of the acquisition of English plurals. One aspect that is not totally clear is how the nonidentical sibilants are handled. In the proposed first stage of plural acquisition when geminates are used, the child should treat nonidentical sibilants as sequences of two melodies with a shared strident feature, as in representation (14) for *churches*. (I assume that the strident feature is attached to the coronal node and also collapsed by the OCP.)

(14) /črč + z/

```
X X X + X
| | |   |
č r č   z
   \ /
[+strident]
```

This analysis, however, predicts that children should not delete the plural in such words when Pattern 2 appears due to the No setting for Gemination (Parameter 1). The default setting of the Deletion parameter only involves identical segments.

A possible solution is to suggest a further pattern of errors in addition to the two documented in (11). This pattern is summarized in (15):

(15) Pattern 1a (hypothetical): deletion of plural affix when identical adjacent sibilants occur but use of /z/ when sibilants are nonidentical.

This would indicate that the child has rejected the default Geminate setting for English but has not yet observed that similar adjacent sibilants pattern like identical sibilants.

There are, in fact, data in the literature that suggest that Pattern 1a is a stage in the acquisition of the plural morpheme. Baker and Derwing (1982) presented an analysis of data from 94 children, which they divided according to five clusters of behavior. (16) gives the percentages of their Group IV subjects ($n = 25$) who deleted the plural, used [əz], or used [s].

(16) Response Pattern for Group IV (adapted from Baker & Derwing, 1982)

Phonemes	Deletion	Use of [əz]	Use of [s]
/s/	68%	28%	0%
/z/	92%	8%	0%
Average	80%	18%	0%
/ǰ/	72%	20%	8%
/š/	48%	28%	20%
/č/	44%	44%	12%
/ž/	52%	36%	4%
Average	54%	32%	11%

Note that deletion occurred for 80% of the stems ending in /s/ and /z/, but for only 54% of those ending in palatal sibilants. Likewise, the gemination pattern of adding the plural without a schwa did not occur for /s/ and /z/ but did occur for the stem-final palatals, in 11% of the responses.

The data in Baker and Derwing also indicated that deletion does in fact precede gemination in acquisition, the opposite of Goad's predictions. This can be seen by observing the distribution of the three kinds of responses in (16) across the five clusters found by Baker and Derwing for stems ending with /š/. Although Baker and Derwing were very cautious not to construct developmental stages based on their clusters, the clusters did appear to be associated with an increase in age, as indicated in (17). (Note that C represents the group showing close to correct performance.)

(17) Response Pattern for Five Groups in Baker and Derwing (1982) for the Stems Ending with /š/ (Voiceless Palatal Fricative)

Group	Size	Mean Age	Deletion	Use of [əz]	Use of [s]
I	14	4.08	92%	0%	0%
II	7	4.14	100%	0%	0%
III	49	4.22	63%	29%	4%
IV	25	4.92	48%	28%	20%
C	18	5.78	0%	94%	6%

Notice that gemination actually increases as the children get older and is even being used in a few instances by the oldest group.

Such data from children's acquisition patterns suggest that the parameters proposed by Goad need revision to fit the developmental facts. First, deletion is the first way children treat potential OCP violations, followed later by some evidence of gemination. Second, epenthesis appears to precede gemination, based on the figures in (17) for Group III. Third, the fact that gemination is not widespread indicates either that our data are not accurate, or that gemination may be the consequence of factors other than the influence of the OCP.

3. ACQUISITION AND UNDERSPECIFICATION THEORY

An important component to the study of learnability is the role of acquisition data. The discussion of negative constraints primarily concerned the logical problem of language acquisition, and data were used not to challenge the nature of the OCP but to determine its parametrization. In this section, it is argued that acquisition data can be used to assess the learnability of a linguistic analysis. This is done through an examination of the analysis of Wikchamni vowels in Archangeli (1985).

3.1. Wikchamni Vowels and Underspecification

Archangeli presented an analysis of Wikchamni vowels, following a theory of radical underspecification (RU). A central goal of RU is to eliminate redundancy from underlying representations. A complex set of arguments are presented in defense of this theory that are both theory-internal and theory-external. Theory-internal arguments invoke the simplicity of the resulting rules as well as the simplicity of the theoretical machinery proposed. One theory-external argument is that RU simplifies the psychological space that is needed for the storage of lexical items.

Proponents of RU propose that most phonological features are redundant and can be specified by a set of universal redundancy rules or markedness conditions. Some redundancies are absolutes; for instance, a vowel that is [+high] will be redundantly [−low]. Others are determined by markedness; for instance, liquids and nasals are redundantly [+voice]. Underlying representations are specified only for the marked features, whereas the redundant features are specified by redundancy rules.

According to Archangeli, Wikchamni has the following five-vowel system: /i/, /y/, /u/, /a/, /o/. (I use /y/ to refer to a high front rounded vowel.) (18) gives Archangeli's specification for these vowels, along with the redundancy rules, which fill in redundant features.

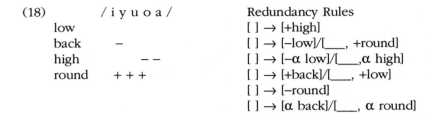

(18)   /i y u o a/   Redundancy Rules
        low   [ ] → [+high]
        back   −   [ ] → [−low]/[___, +round]
        high   − −   [ ] → [−α low]/[___,α high]
        round   + + +   [ ] → [+back]/[___, +low]
                                            [ ] → [−round]
                                            [ ] → [α back]/[___, α round]

I assume for the sake of our discussion that the Archangeli analysis is consistent with the facts of Wikchamni and the theory of RU. I would like to examine how the child might reach the system of specification in (18). Exploring this point requires a brief discussion of the acquisition of underspecification in general and the constraints on that acquisition.

3.2. The Acquisition of Underspecification

The idea that children begin acquisition with underspecified representations has been around for some time. The first and foremost proposal was in Jakobson (1941/1968) and also Jakobson and Halle (1956). Jakobson offered an account of phonological acquisition, working within the general format of Prague phonological theory. He claimed that phonological features are added to the child's first phoneme units by the Principle of Maximal Contrast. This principle states that children first select distinctive features on the basis of their maximal generality and acquire features one at a time. The sequence of acquisition presumes a hierarchical ordering of features in terms of their generality.

Jakobson's efforts fell somewhat short of a complete application of Prague theory to phonological acquisition. For one thing, he never elaborated how the child's acquisition interfaced with language-specific differences between privative and equipollent oppositions. He therefore never discussed the acquisition of neutralizations and the establishment of archiphonemes. Further, he was never very detailed on the order in which features become specified. As argued in Ingram (1988), the theory suffers more from lack of elaboration than from being discredited by available acquisition data. A more recent theory of phonological acquisition is natural phonology, a theory developed by Stampe (1969, 1972). Acquisition is seen as the gradual elimination of a series of hierarchically ordered constraints on the articulatory system. The child begins acquisition with the most severe set of constraints and overcomes these in the course of phonological acquisition.

It is possible to combine Stampe's approach with that of Jakobson and consider them in terms of current RU theory. The child will specify only those features that are marked, within some theory of markedness to be determined. Redundant features are added via redundancy rules that will have the properties of Stampean natural processes. In Ingram (1991, 1992), I attempted to develop a model along these lines. In doing so, I added two restrictions on the way in which children acquire phonological features. First, I argued that children initially represent their words phonetically, as proposed in (19):

(19) *Acoustic Representation Hypothesis:* Children first represent their early vocabulary in the form of fully specified phonetic feature matrices.

The fully specified phonetic matrix provides the child with the information he or she needs for subsequent phonological analysis.

The next step is an important process that has not been directly faced by most researchers working in language acquisition. I suggested that the child then analyzes words phonologically and establish phonological representations. This occurs in the following way:

(20) *Distinctive Feature Hypothesis:* Children phonologically analyze and represent their first words in terms of distinctive features selected from the set of available phonetic features in the fully specified phonetic representation.

These two simple hypotheses greatly constrain the nature of the phonological representations that children may form. Given the accuracy of children's early perception, they eliminate representations that may differ from the adults' on the basis of misperceptions. They also impose a naturalness condition on the child's representations. A child cannot have an underlying /u/ with the feature [−round], because the feature [−round] would not be part of the phonetic form of the vowel [u].

3.3. The Acquisition of Wickchamni Vowels

Acquisition data do not exist on the acquisition of the five-vowel system of Wikchamni. For purposes of discussion, the following stages of acquisition are proposed (based on established patterns):

(21) Stage   i y u o a (Adult vowels)
        1   i i i i a
        2   i i u u a
        3   i i u o a
        4   i y u o a

The question that now arises is what the child's representation would be for these vowels through the four proposed stages. I demonstrate that the acquisition theory I have outlined restricts what these representations may look like.

At Stage I, the child has a distinction between the low and nonlow vowels. Because there is a single vocalic opposition, we need to select a single feature to capture it. Further, we specify only the feature that is marked, following a general tenet of RU. There are only two choices—specify /a/ or specify /i,y,u,o/. If we decide to mark the /i,y,u,o/ set, the Distinctive Feature Hypothesis limits our choice. We cannot choose [+high] because /o/ is [−high]. We cannot choose [+round] because /i/ is [−round]. The only choice is to mark them as [−low]. These options are summarized in (22):

(22) Stage 1 Specification:
   a. If /i,y,u,o/ then specify [−low].
   b. If /a/ then specify either [+low], [−high], or [−round].

The next step is deciding how to choose between the various options. Archangeli's analysis in (18) provides a way in which we can choose between them. We must first assume that the redundancy rules reflect the naturalness of vocalic systems. Further, they need to be seen as guidelines to the child concerning what may be specified, even though Archangeli did not present them as such. A first approximation of these guidelines is as follows:

(23) Ordered Rules for Specification:
   1. Specify features that maximize redundancy.
   2. Specify the marked features of context-free redundancy rules.
   3. Specify the marked features of context-sensitive redundancy rules.

The first rule maximizes redundancy by specifying the feature that is needed for the fewest phonemes. In our example, it means selecting to mark /a/ over /i,y,u,o/. By selecting /a/, we redundantly fill in features for four phonemes instead of one.

The decision to specify /a/ still involves a choice between [+low], [−high], and [−round]. The second rule contains two parts. First, we look for context-free rules that refer to the features in question. There is no such rule for [low], but there are for [round] and [high]. The selection of [−round] would violate Rule 2, because [−round] is unmarked, based on the rule [ ] → [−round] in (18). We do have a context-free rule for [high], however, which fills in [+high] as the unmarked feature. This leads us to specify /a/ as [−high], as is shown in (24). The redundancy rules in (18) will fill in the rest of the features, yielding the vowels [i] and [a].

(24) Stage 1 / i y u o a /
        [high]   −

At Stage 2, the front/back distinction emerges for the nonlow vowels. There is a choice here between [back] and [round]. If we select [round] as the relevant feature, we would have to specify [+round] for /o,u/. We cannot specify [−round] for /i,y/, because /y/ is round and this would violate the Distinctive Feature Hypothesis. We have more options with [back]. We can specify /i,y/ as [−back], or /u,o/ as [+back]. These choices are as follows:

(25) Stage 2 Specification:
   a. If /i,y/, then specify [−back].
   b. If /u,o/, then specify [+back] or [+round].

The first rule of the Rules for Specification (23) does not help us, because there are two phonemes in both sets. Rule 2 leads us to select [+round] for /u,o/, based on the context-free rule of [ ] → [−round]. This is shown in (26).

(26) Stage 2 / i y u o a /
   [high]   −
   [round]   + +

Stage 3 indicates the need for [high] to distinguish /u/ from /o/. The redundancy rules states that [+high] is unmarked, so /o/ will be specified as [−high], as in (27).

(27) Stage 3 / i y u o a /
   [high]   − −
   [round]   + +

Last, the child at Stage 4 distinguishes /i/ from /y/. These two vowels differ minimally in the feature [round]. Again, our redundancy rules instruct us that [−round] is the unmarked case, requiring [+round] to be specified. Marking /y/ as [+round] will distinguish it from /i/, but then both /y/ and /u/ at this point will be similarly specified as [+round]. At this point, the redundancy rules we are working with break down. There is no rule that will instruct us to separate these two vowels. The two rules that deal with [back] are context-sensitive, based on the features [low] and [round]. This does not help us here, because both vowels have the same value for these features. We therefore must adjust the last redundancy rule in (18), which ties backness to roundness. Such a change is given in (28).

(28) a. [ ] → [+back]/[___, +round]
    b. [ ] → [−back]/[___, −round, −low]

Following Rule 3 of the Rules for Specification, we can then specify /y/ as [–back], the marked feature for rounded vowels. This yields the adult system in (29).

(29) Stage 4 / i y u o a /
  [back]   –
  [high]   – –
  [round]   + + +

Our acquisition theory has been adapted as a theory for the acquisition of underspecification. I have used the redundancy rules given in Archangeli with one adaptation as a theory of markedness, adding three Rules for Specification. This theory, applied to a hypothesized set of acquisition data, has produced an underspecified system that matches the system in (18). Note that my explanation has been highly restricted by the principles proposed.

4. SUMMARY

I have presented a preliminary investigation into the issue of learnability within phonological theory. I started with the assumption that we should expect the basic issues to be the same in the acquisition of both syntax and phonology. First, we examined the extent to which we would want to restrict the child's acquisition to the influence of positive evidence. At first glance, it appeared that indirect negative evidence would be more viable in phonology, due to the existence of negative constraints. After an examination of such constraints, however, I concluded that we still should attempt to account for them in terms of positive evidence.

Next, I looked into research on the learnability of a principle of phonology, the OCP. It appears that this principle can be explored in terms of a set of principles in much the same way as in the area of syntax. Acquisition data suggest that children advance through stages in the ways in which they avoid OCP violations.

Last, I discussed the nature of phonological representations and presented a set of developmental principles that limit the ways in which a child might acquire the adult phonology. It was shown that one hypothesized set of developmental stages of vowel acquisition for Wikchamni yielded an adult system like that proposed by radical underspecification. I concluded that we need to begin to supplement the speculations on the learnability of phonological constraints with data from language acquisition, in much the same way that this has been proceeding in the last few years for syntactic acquisition.

ACKNOWLEDGMENTS

An earlier draft of this chapter was given at the Workshop on Learnability, Leiden, Holland, January 19, 1989. The working title of the earlier draft was "Issues in Learnability and Phonological Theory." I would like to thank Jane Fee, Sadanand Singh, Joe Stemberger, and Harry van der Hulst, who took time to read the earlier draft and discussed it with me. I would like to extend a special thanks to Iggy Roca, who provided extensive and extremely insightful comments.

CHAPTER FIVE

The Acquisition of Stress

John Archibald
University of Calgary

In this chapter, I first discuss some of the issues in the acquisition of word stress in a first language and then deal with some of the issues of acquiring the metrical system of a second language. Questions such as what the initial state of the child's system looks like (i.e., what the default settings are), whether there is a bias for any particular stress pattern, and whether children learn stress systematically or word by word are addressed. I also consider how stress affects other aspects of the linguistic system in terms of (a) bootstrapping, and (b) the influence on segmental truncation. In second language acquisition, I discuss the influence of the first language (L1) stress system on the acquisition of the second language (L2). The two sections have quite different styles because the tasks involved are very different. The child has to set up a system for extracting stress and representing metrical systems. The adult second language learner has already done this and has to discover how the L2 system differs from the L1 system.

1. L1 STRESS LITERATURE

In much of the first language acquisition research literature, the acquisition of stress has received what could, at best, be described as cursory attention. By far the majority of work on the acquisition of phonology (Ferguson, 1977; Ferguson & Farwell, 1975; Ingram, 1974; Macken, 1986; Menn, 1977, 1983; Smith, 1973; etc.) has focused on the acquisition of segmental phonology. Much less work has been done on the acquisition of suprasegmental phonology. Crystal (1986) wrote on the acquisition of prosody (variation in pitch, loudness, speed, and rhythm), as did Waterson (1971). However, the acquisition of stress has been addressed by only a few (cf. Allen & Hawkins, 1980; Dresher & Kaye, 1990; Fikkert, 1992; Hammond, 1990;[1] Hochberg, 1988a, 1988b; Klein 1984).

I begin by discussing certain aspects of children's ability to perceive stress, and the implications of this ability.

2. PERCEPTION OF STRESS AND PROSODIC BOOTSTRAPPING

Let us begin by asking what the consequences are of acquiring a stress system. Obviously, a stress system is part of the adult language and therefore needs to be acquired, but what good is it? One proposal is that stress is a significant contributor to bootstrapping the learner into acquiring grammatical categories (the prosodic bootstrapping hypothesis; Gleitman, Gleitman, Landau, & Wanner, 1988). As Kaye (1988) pointed out, one of the things that phonology is useful for is to indicate where edges are; for instance, edges of words, edges of phrases. Echols and Newport (1992) argued that stress may be particularly useful in helping language learners "to extract and represent approximately word-sized units from the stream of adult speech" (p. 189). They proposed that very young language learners have perceptual biases that allow them to extract certain elements from the adult speech stream. In particular, they suggested that stressed syllables may be particularly salient for the children. They went so far as to suggest that English-speaking children lack functional categories and inflectional morphology in the early stages of acquisition because these elements are unstressed.

Echols and Newport conducted a study to test the claim that if stressed syllables were perceptually salient to children then they would tend to omit unstressed syllables more than stressed syllables. They also proposed that final syllables are perceptually salient to children, following Slobin (1985). Thus, they predicted that unstressed, nonfinal syllables are more likely to be omitted than stressed or final syllables. As they pointed out, it is unexplained why final position should be privileged. It is conceivable that the

---

[1]Hammond (1990) addressed the acquisition of L1 stress from a different perspective than did the other papers cited. He was concerned with the implications that the construct of learnability will have for the theory of metrical phonology. As a result, he did not consider developmental data but, rather, more general proofs. He argued that all occurring metrical systems are learnable on the basis of seven syllables or less. Where such input is unavailable to the learner, default values are relied on to set parameters. Intuitively, I must admit that this seems like a large window that requires somewhat exotic primary data for acquisition to occur. In this chapter I focus on developmental accounts of acquisition of stress.

conservation of final syllables, or the trochaic bias, could be the result of a more general edge effect, because English feet are constructed from the right edge, and the word tree is strong on the right. Perhaps in languages like Hungarian where metrical feet are constructed from the left edge, and the word tree is strong on the left, initial syllables would be privileged. This is suggested in an unattributed footnote in Echols and Newport. Later, I also argue that the retention of final syllables falls out from other general principles such as prosodic circumscription and parsing strategies.

Echols and Newport looked at three children in the one-word stage. The children were recorded at home and the sessions were later transcribed. Stress assignment in the children's utterances was not included, as the researchers failed to achieve interrater reliability on the coding. Thus, they did not have data on the children's stress placement, just on the effect of adult stress placement in a di- or multisyllabic word on the form of the child's word.

Syllables in the adult target were coded as either *stressed* or *unstressed*; no distinction between primary and subsidiary stress was encoded. This is unlikely to be a problem, in that both primary and subsidiary stress retain full vowel quality in English. However, the fact that the perceptual saliency of vowel quality interacts with English stress should be noted. In my L2 research (see Archibald, 1992), I argued that L2 learners use the presence of a full vowel as a cue to the presence of stress. L1 learners may, as well.

2.1. Results

Echols and Newport's data support the claim that stressed and final syllables tend to be included in production more than unstressed[2] or nonfinal syllables.[3] This is cumulative in that syllables that are both unstressed and nonfinal are most susceptible to deletion (or omission).

A general comment that must be made is that Echols and Newport did not provide us with any of the data; we do not know which words the children were attempting to say. Without knowledge of the phonological structure of the word, and the grammatical category, valuable generalizations cannot be made.

They argued that the child's perceptual abilities mature over time. In the early stages the child attends to stressed and final syllables, but as children mature they are able to attend to, and construct representations for, less salient syllables. So, following Echols and Newport, I assume that children can perceive stress. What we need to address now is the kind of mental representation they set up related to stress.

---

[2]$p < .02$
[3]$p < .005$

3. MODELS OF STRESS

Exactly how to represent stress is a linguistic problem that has attracted a considerable amount of attention. Should it be represented with trees (Hayes, 1980), or grids (Prince, 1983)? If we use grids, how should we represent constituent structure? Should we bracket constituents (Halle & Vergnaud, 1987) or mark only a single edge of a constituent (Idsardi, 1992)? One thing that is clear is that the metrical structure is somehow connected to or projected from the syllable structure. Goldsmith (1990) argued that the metrical structure is "an autonomous structure . . . whose terminal (or bottom row) elements are autosegmentally linked to syllable positions via the principles of autosegmental licensing" (p. 193).

I assume that adult models of stress assignment can be described via some sort of parametric framework, but I remain neutral as to the exact structures that such parameters erect. So, for my purposes, I assume a kind of equivalency between representations like the following:

(1)   F
      / \
      s w
      σ σ   x   x
      | | (x x)   (x x
      edit   edit   edit

I believe that nothing crucial to my arguments hinges on these distinctions. For the most part, I use tree diagrams because I refer to the unit *foot* frequently, and this is easy to read off a tree.

3.1. Moraic Phonology

Hayes (1989) elaborated on a model of syllabic phonology that incorporates a level of structure below the syllable: the mora. McCawley (1977) following Hayes, defined a mora as "something of which a heavy syllable consists of two and a light syllable consists of one" (Hayes, 1987, p. 278). This definition captures the fact that many languages treat heavy syllables differently from light syllables with respect to stress assignment, for instance. Hayes illustrated with the following structures:

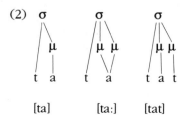

(2) σ   σ   σ

Languages vary as to which syllable types count as heavy or light. For example, in Latin CVC is considered heavy, whereas in Lardil CVC is treated as a light syllable. This, too, will have to be learned by the child. We return later to the importance of morae.

3.2. Metrical Parameters

One of the best known explicit proposals along parametric lines is Dresher and Kaye (1990). They proposed the following parameters:

(3) P1: The word tree is strong on the [Left/Right].
P2: Feet are [Binary/Unbounded].
P3: Feet are built from the [Left/Right].
P4: Feet are strong on the [Left/Right].
P5: Feet are quantity-sensitive (QS) [Yes/No].
P6: Feet are QS to the [Rime/Nucleus].
P8A: There is an extrametrical syllable [No/Yes].
P8: The extrametrical syllable occurs on the [Left/Right].

And the default settings were as follows:

(4) P1: The word tree is strong on the [Left].
P2: Feet are [Unbounded].
P3: Feet are built from the [Left].
P4: Feet are strong on the [Left].
P5: Feet are quantity-sensitive (QS) [No].
P6: Feet are QS to the [Rime].
P8A: There is an extrametrical syllable [No].

In other words, as a default, unbounded, left-strong, quantity-insensitive feet are constructed from the left with no extrametricality. As we see later, some of these defaults (but not all) receive empirical support from child language data. It has been proposed that children have an initial trochaic bias in their metrical systems (Allen & Hawkins, 1980). We address this in detail soon, but for now note that the trochaic bias hypothesis is supported if the default metrical constituents are strong on the left. That feet are assumed to be quantity-insensitive (QI) is consistent with the assumption that the minimal word is a syllabic trochee[4] (an assumption we soon address explicitly). In Idsardi's terms (see Appendix B), we could note that by assuming a quantity-insensitive system, the learners are able to project elements (x) onto the metrical grid but are unable to project parentheses onto the grid. The ability

---

[4]If it were a moraic trochee, the system would be quantity-sensitive.

to project parentheses would presumably appear on the basis of positive evidence. The data reported on the acquisition of Spanish stress (and other data) indicate that the child's initial assumption is that there is no extrametricality in the grammar.[5]

4. EXTRAMETRICALITY IN L1 ACQUISITION

This raises the question of how learners would determine whether the language they were learning had extrametricality or not. That is to say, how would they determine what the proper setting of the extrametricality parameter is? I discussed this in more detail in Archibald (1993a), but I make some brief comments here.

We can begin by noting that the Subset Principle[6] (Wexler & Manzini, 1987) cannot apply here, as the Subset Condition[7] they proposed is not met. This is because the two possible parameter settings of the extrametricality parameter do not yield languages that are in a subset relation to each other. If English had no extrametricality ([−extrametrical]) we would always find penultimate stress (assuming left-headed feet). If it had obligatory extrametricality ([+extrametrical]) we would always find antepenultimate stress. The situation is a little more complex, as we have extrametricality in English that is sensitive to the grammatical category (i.e., it works differently on nouns and verbs, for instance). Thus, the Subset Principle makes no clear predictions.

We can find a certain amount of evidence in the first language acquisition literature to support the claim that the initial setting is [−extrametrical]. Hochberg (1988b) cited some evidence from studies by Montés Giraldo (1971, 1976). Montés Giraldo gave examples of adult forms and their realization by child learners, shown in (5):

(5) | *Adult Form* | *Child Form* |
|---|---|
| cáscara | kakála |
| estómago | tomágo |
| lámpara | pampála |
| fósforo | popúlo |
| hipopótamo | popotámo |

---

[5]Indeed, according to Idsardi (1992), there is no such thing as extrametricality in the adult grammar. His model of computing prosody has phenomena previously attributed to extrametricality fall out from the interactions of other metric basics, such as an edge-marking convention.

[6]The learning function maps the input data to that value of a parameter that generates a language: (a) compatible with the input data, and (b) smallest among the languages compatible with the input data.

[7]For every parameter p and every two values i, j of p, the languages generated under the two values of the parameter are such that one is a subset of the other, that is, L $(p\,(i)) \supseteq$ L $(p\,(j))$ or L $(p\,(j)) \supseteq$ L $(p\,(i))$.

The children are shifting what in adult Spanish are antepenultimate stresses to the penult. This follows from the assumption that they do not have any extrametrical segments.[8] Extrametricality is needed to produce the adult antepenultimate stress. For example:

(6) cáscara

The child's representation would be (ignoring possible segmental differences):

(7) cascára

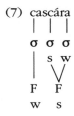

Once again, the data seem to support the claim that the initial setting of the extrametricality parameter is [−extrametrical].

5. ACQUISITION OF SPANISH STRESS

Hochberg (1988b) was interested in whether children are acquiring rules for stress assignment or are acquiring lexical stress. She considered only the stress pattern on nonverb forms in Spanish. Two points related to Spanish noun stress (Harris, 1983) are of interest here:

> Stress must fall on one of the last three syllables of the word. Although *atápama* and *atapáma* are well-formed hypothetical words, *átapama is not.

> Antepenultimate stress is impossible if the penult is a closed syllable. Hypothetical *atapámba* and *atapambá* are well formed but *atápamba is not (nor is *átapamba).

---

[8]Extrametricality is indicated with a slash overstrike.

Although stress may appear on any of the last three syllables, not all probabilities are equally likely. The following two generalizations are noted:

1. Penultimate stress is unmarked in vowel-final words:
     Unmarked: *pistóla, perdída, sabána*
     Marked: *epístola, pérdida, sábana, Panamá*
2. Final stress is unmarked in consonant-final words:
     Unmarked: *civíl, mercéd, altár*
     Marked: *móvil, césped, ámbar*

According to Harris (1983), then, Spanish stress is assigned by building left-dominant quantity-sensitive feet from right to left, and the word tree is strong on the right.

Hochberg utilized two tasks in order to investigate whether children had knowledge of these stress rules. In the first, spontaneous data were elicited from fifty Spanish-speaking children. The second task involved imitating novel Spanish words that differed in stress placement. Her prediction was that if children had acquired stress rules, then: (a) they should find regular (unmarked) forms easier to pronounce, and (b) they would tend to produce irregular forms with regular stress patterns (but would not produce regular forms with irregular stress patterns).

The subjects lived in California, but Hochberg argued that they were very much like a monolingual Spanish population. Of the 50 children studied, 12 were 3-year-olds (between 3 and 4); 23 were 4-year-olds (between 4 and 5), and 15 were 5-year-olds (between 5 and 6). All 50 children were Spanish dominant.

Subjects had to produce both imitated and spontaneous speech. In the spontaneous elicitation task the children had to name items out of a picture book. In the imitation task they had to repeat words spoken by the researcher.

5.1. Results

Hochberg argued that children do display rule knowledge in both their spontaneous production and their imitation. Furthermore, she argued that the rule-learning process is complete by age 3. Consider first the imitation results.

The more irregular the word, the more errors the children made. Children made the fewest errors on words with regular stress; more errors on words with irregular stress, and the most errors on words with prohibited stress. The differences were statistically significant ($p < .001$). It also emerged that the subjects were more likely to regularize irregular forms than they were to irregularize regular forms. For example, they would tend to produce *movíl* for *móvil*. These results robustly support the rule-learning hypothesis. What of the spontaneous task?

Hochberg argued that the spontaneous production task results also supported the rule-learning view, though less strongly. The children did tend to make more errors on irregular forms, but their error types did not tend to regularization. They were not more likely to regularize irregular forms than to irregularize regular forms. This argues that by age 3 they have mastered certain irregular forms and do not regularize them in spontaneous speech. Hochberg's study contradicted Klein's (1984) claims about the acquisition of English stress. Klein argued that children learned stress patterns word by word. However, she was looking for the existence of a general stress rule of English. Without a more sophisticated model of stress placement, the study is problematic.

5.2. Developmental Stages

Hochberg did find that the children's pronunciation improved with age. The 4- and 5-year-olds made significantly fewer errors than the 3-year-olds. In addition, the 5-year-olds' errors were less likely to be overregularization errors than the younger children's.

It appears then that children as young as 3 have acquired the rules of Spanish stress. At this age they are still making many errors in segmental phonology (e.g., substituting [l] for [r]), and in morphology (e.g., *sabo* for *sé*). Children appear to acquire this aspect of the suprasegmental domain very early.

Hochberg (1988a) focused on whether children have initial biases in the stress placement. This is a question we return to throughout the chapter. She argued for a neutral start, citing Leopold (1947): "The child begins presumably with level stress or with indifference to the distribution of stress, both in babbling and at the outset of speaking. Then the stress habits of the community assert themselves quickly and decisively" (p. 24). Allen and Hawkins (1980), on the other hand, argued that children are biased toward a trochaic foot. Allen and Hawkins suggested that children are more likely to delete an initial unstressed syllable in front of a stressed syllable, resulting in the stress pattern ′ ˅ (a trochee), than they are to delete an unstressed syllable after a stressed syllable, resulting in the stress pattern ˅ ′ (an iamb). This would predict that, given a target word like *banana* [bənǽnə] where the stress pattern is ˅ ′ ˅, the child would be more likely to delete the first syllable than the third. Therefore we would expect some version like [nǽnə] more often than something like [bənǽ] for the target form. Ingram (1986) documented this preference for deletion of unstressed initial syllables.

Again, the children Hochberg studied were natives of California but monolingual Spanish speakers. The children were about 1;6 at the start of the project and were recorded weekly for 10 months in both spontaneous and elicited imitation tasks. She identified all of the polysyllabic words in each session. Sadly, she did not include either polysyllabic pronunciations of adult monosyllables, or monosyllabic pronunciations of adult polysyllabic words, so some potentially useful sources of information on phonological processes are missing. The selected polysyllabic words were transcribed.

5.3. Results

Hochberg argued for the neutral start hypothesis and not for the trochaic bias, in that her subjects were not more accurate on producing words with initial stress than on producing words with final stress. However, the differences were not statistically significant (for spontaneous production, p = .9683; for imitated production, p = .1328, on paired, two-tailed t tests). I would suggest, though, that without looking at the monosyllabic versions of adult polysyllabic words, we do not have enough information to reject the trochaic bias hypothesis.

She also argued that if the neutral start hypothesis were correct, then we would expect no preference for trochaic stress patterns at the beginning. That is to say, words like *cása* should initially be produced with correct stress at chance level but will become more accurate over time. She argued that this was what her data supported, presenting developmental data on these *cása*-type words. Statistically, there does seem to be a significant difference (p = .013) between the two spontaneous results, but no significant difference between Time 1 and Time 2 on the imitated results (p = .133). That is to say, the subjects did appear to improve in their spontaneous production, but not in their imitated production. In addition, it is hard to interpret these results on the accuracy of words of the s-w (strong-weak) pattern (trochees) without comparison data on the accuracy of words of the w-s pattern (iambs). We would like to see if these word classes are behaving significantly differently.

6. ACQUISITION OF DUTCH STRESS

Fikkert (1992) investigated the acquisition of Dutch stress. She was also concerned with stress-related phenomena such as truncation and argued that disyllabic words with initial stress behave differently than disyllabic words with final stress with respect to truncation.

She set out two basic questions in the study of L1 stress:

1. Do children learn stress on a lexical basis or by rule? (Hochberg, 1987, 1988a; Klein, 1984)?
2. Do children have a bias toward a particular foot type when learning stress? (Allen & Hawkins, 1980; Hochberg, 1988b)?

Let us look at the second question first. Fikkert commented that Hochberg's (neutral start) and Allen and Hawkin's (trochaic bias) results are

TABLE 5.1
Accuracy Levels for Trochaic Words

Subject	Time 1 Accuracy (%)		Time 2 Accuracy (%)	
	Spontaneous	Imitated	Spontaneous	Imitated
1	40	56	70	76
2	44	56	75	94
3	37	56	79	65
4	80	80	95	80[a]

[a]Hochberg does not actually give these figures for Subject 4. I am reading them off a graph in the text; therefore they are approximate.

not completely incompatible. Both studies found that words with penultimate stress were more common than words with final stress in the speech of the children they studied. The data from Samantha (see Appendix A) and Sophie, discussed later, also support this claim. Fikkert argued that when we look at other phonological phenomena such as deletion preferences we find strong arguments for the trochaic bias.

Now let us turn to the first question. How are children learning stress? Are they learning word by word (lexically) or are they learning rules? Fikkert pointed out that if children are learning stress lexically, we would expect them not to have systematic deviations from the adult model. If, however, they are acquiring rules, then we would expect systematic deviations from the adult system. She argued that her data clearly showed a systematic performance. Let us look at her data.

Fikkert, as I said, was looking at the acquisition of Dutch stress. She looked closely at what she called *truncation* phenomena. Truncation results in a reduction of the number of syllables in a word and is what has commonly been called *deletion*. However, she argued that it is not a deletion precess but a process that involves the mapping of a melody to a specific template via prosodic circumscription (Idsardi, 1992; McCarthy & Prince, 1990).

She assumed that child grammars are constrained by universal general principles of phonology and described child phonological systems with reference to such devices as mora, syllable, foot, and prosodic word, as illustrated hierarchically in (8):

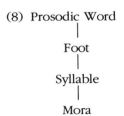

(8) Prosodic Word
    |
    Foot
    |
    Syllable
    |
    Mora

Fikkert argued that if we were really talking about a deletion process, we would not find the asymmetry that initial unstressed syllables are more likely to be deleted than final unstressed syllables. In other words, if we were to write deletion rules to account for both environments, we would produce the following two rules:

(9) a. $\breve{\delta} \rightarrow \emptyset / \underline{} \acute{\delta}$
    b. $\breve{\delta} \rightarrow \emptyset / \acute{\delta} \underline{}$

Why would we find one rule and not the other? Her data argue that, in fact, initial unstressed syllables are deleted more often than final unstressed syllables. She noted the differences in behavior indicated in Table 5.2. I ran a paired, two-tailed t test on these numbers; and the differences are statistically significant ($p = .0001$).

She also noted that whether a disyllabic word had initial or final stress in its adult form also had some effect on the number of stress errors children made on that form. She showed that children make more errors on final stressed words than on initial stressed words. Her data are shown in Table 5.3. Again a paired, two-tailed t-test revealed that the differences were significant ($p = .0071$). Adult forms with final stress are (a) more prone to truncation, and (b) more prone to stress errors for children. This, she argued, was evidence that iambic words are treated differently than trochaic words by children.

6.1. Developmental Stages

Fikkert outlined the following developmental stages in the production of disyllabic words with final stress. In Stage 1 they are produced as monosyllables with the final, stressed syllable being the one that is produced. For

TABLE 5.2
Unstressed Syllable Deletion

Subject	Final Deletion (%)	Initial Deletion (%)
1	5	92
2	5	48
3✓	4	94
4	5	57
5	1	29
6	1	41
7	7	62
8	9	100
9	2	11
10	0	76
11	4	23
12	0	14
Average	3.2	53.9

TABLE 5.3
Stress Errors

Subject	Initial Stress Errors	Final Stress Errors
1	3	0
2	5	29
3	3	75
4	2	42
5	7	12
6	6	51
7	10	26
8	6	0
9	3	33
10	17	18
11	5	11
12	12	60
Average	6.6	29.8

instance, adult *ballon* [balɔ́n] is produced by the child as [lɔn]. In Stage 2, both syllables are produced but the child places stress on the first syllable. For instance, *ballonnen* [balɔ́nən] is pronounced by the child as [búɔnə]. In Stage 3 the child produces the word with level stress, and in Stage 4 the word is pronounced with the adult stress pattern.

She observed, from these data, that (a) the stressed syllable of the adult form is not deleted in the child form at any stage, and (b) the stressed syllable in the adult form need not be stress bearing in the child form.

Fikkert then explained the developmental sequence.

6.1.1. Stage 1. Fikkert argued that the child is operating on the foot structure of the word, not on the syllable level. It is a foot that is being truncated, not a syllable. In Dutch, disyllabic words with initial stress form one foot; and as we have seen, these forms are rarely truncated. Trisyllabic forms with medial stress have their initial foot truncated. For instance, *vakantie* 'holiday' [vakɑ́ntsi] is produced as [kɑ́ntsi]. The adult structure would be:

(10)
```
        W
       / \
      w   s
      F   F
      |  / \
      w  s  w
     vakɑ́ntsi
```

What remains for the child is the stressed foot of the adult form: [kɑ́ntsi]. So at Stage 1, we see the child producing the segmental material found in the stressed foot of the adult form. This segmental material is then mapped onto a trochaic template (a left-headed foot), which is argued to be the minimal word (W_{min}). Fikkert suggested that this is a universal template, or at least a default value, because it is the only quantity-insensitive foot in the foot typology of Hayes (1991) or McCarthy and Prince (1990).

She argued that the process that the child is engaged in is similar to McCarthy and Prince's prosodic circumscription. Via this process, a base is divided into two parts, the *kernel* and the *residue*. For Fikkert, the child retains the kernel and truncates the residue as it cannot be mapped onto the trochaic template. Consider the adult target *ballon* [balɔ́n]. The adult form would be represented as:

(11)

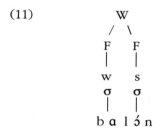

The child would take the stressed foot of the adult form [lɔ́n] and project it onto a trochaic template supplied by UG:

(12)

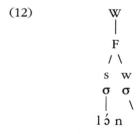

This would account for such productions as [lɔ́n] but would also account for the fact that an extra syllable is often added to such forms (e.g., [bɔ́mə]), where the added syllable is unstressed. The trochaic template allows this structure. Note that this would also predict that we should find adult mono-syllables realized with an extra syllable after the stressed syllable, and we do. For instance, adult *trein* [trɛ́in] is realized in child speech as [tɛ́inə].

6.1.2. Stage 2. At Stage 2 the child is producing two syllables. Fikkert argued that the child continues to produce the final stressed syllable from the adult form and now adds the leftmost syllable. She noted that the child now appears to be referring not to the adult foot or the adult word but to elements that are not prosodic units in the adult form. For instance, adult *krokodil* [kròkodíl] is realized as a disyllable but with the first and third syllables chosen, becoming [krókdil].[9] The child's production at this stage still consists of one foot. It looks to me as if the child is extracting the stressed initial syllable and adjoining it to the existing foot. That this stressed syllable would be perceptually salient to the child was borne out by Echols and Newport (1992). The child may be looking, then, not for the leftmost syllable but, rather, for the stressed syllable. At Stage 1, the child can scan only for a single stressed syllable. At Stage 2, the child is able to scan for another stressed syllable.

6.1.3. Stage 3. Fikkert argued that at Stage 3 the child allows more than one foot in his or her productions. This change may well be driven by the perception of more than one stressed syllable in Stage 2. These two feet are assigned level stress by the child. Fikkert explains this by saying that the child is unaware of the main stress rule or thinks that the adult word is made up of two words.

I later provide a reanalysis of these two stages.

6.1.4. Stage 4. At the final stage Fikkert stated that the representation is adultlike.

Fikkert's explanations are most satisfying for Stage 1 behavior. After that things seem to get somewhat vague. She explained nicely why, at Stage 1, disyllabic words with initial stress are rarely truncated and why there are fewer stress errors on these forms—they match the UG template. The child continues to build his or her own systematic phonological representation of stress.

6.2. Minimal Word

The construct of minimal word appears to be a useful one here and, as a result, the question of what form the minimal word takes needs to be addressed explicitly. McCarthy and Prince proposed that the minimal word (Word$_{min}$) is a bimoraic foot. Fee (this volume, chap. 3) argued that Word$_{min}$ = 2 monomoraic syllables ($\sigma\ \sigma$), where each syllable is maximally a single mora:

(13) $\sigma\ \sigma$
$\quad\ \ |\ \ |$
$\quad\ \ \mu\ \mu$

---

[9]Fikkert did not give the stress assignment on this form. I am assuming the main stress is still assigned by the trochaic foot.

Fikkert (1992) argued that the Word$_{min}$ is a syllabic trochee. I support Fikkert's analysis (as opposed to McCarthy and Prince's) in that, if the minimal word was a bimoraic foot, we would predict that children would be able to represent both CVCV and CVC syllables at the initial stage of grammar, as both structures are bimoraic:

(14)

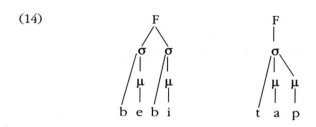

In fact, as is well documented, children acquire CV syllables before they acquire CVC syllables. This, too, would argue against an analysis that suggested that the prosodic template supplied by UG was underspecified (with respect to syllables or morae) and that the trochaic template could be filled by either two morae or two syllables, whichever was encountered first on the scan. Therefore, I would maintain that the Word$_{min}$ is a syllabic trochee:

(15)   F
             / \
            s   w
            σ   σ

Following Fee (this volume, chap. 3), I assume that the minimal syllable is monomoraic. Hence the structure of Word$_{min}$ would be:

(16)   F
             / \
            s   w
            σ   σ
            | |
            μ   μ

7. ACQUISITION OF ENGLISH STRESS

Fletcher (1985) presented some data from a longitudinal case study that is relevant here. Admittedly the focus of the study was not the acquisition of phonology, but transcripts are provided that indicate stress placement (on an orthographic script). The subject, Sophie, was recorded at ages 2;4, 3;0, 3;5, and 3;11. By far the most obvious aspect of Sophie's stress placement is her accuracy, from the first session. In the first session Sophie produced 22 words for which the adult target was either di- or multisyllabic. Of those 22 words, Sophie had correct stress placement on either all 22 or 21 of the 22, depending on the scoring. The item in question was *plásticìne*, which Sophie produced as [si:n]. If we do not make a distinction between primary and subsidiary stress, then we can say that Sophie produced a stressed syllable. If we make the primary/subsidiary distinction, then Sophie got this one wrong. Two forms are of interest at this stage, as they illustrate the phenomenon of truncation. These forms are:

(17) *Target*   *Child Form*
    plásticìne   [si:n]
    anóther   nóther

In both cases, initial syllables are truncated in the child form. I see two factors involved here. The first is that what Sophie produced was the final foot of the form. Because the final syllable of *plasticine* has a long vowel, it is not extrametrical and is assigned a stress due to the quantity-sensitive nature of English stress. This would generate the structure:

(18)

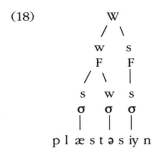

Sophie truncated the first foot. The second factor in Sophie's production has to do with rhythm. Note that in the form in (18), the main stress appears to fall on the final syllable. If this were Sophie's representation, then she would be producing the syllable with main stress. But note too that the adult form has primary stress not on the final syllable but on the initial syllable. It is usually proposed that the manner by which words like *plasticine* get the stress back to the antepenult is via stress retraction. It appears that Sophie had not yet acquired the rhythm rules of English, but she had acquired the stress rules.

Truncating the first foot would also explain her production of *nother* for *another*. The structure would be:

(19)

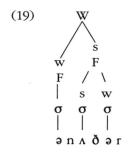

Once again, Sophie produced the final foot of the adult target.

In the second sample, at age 3;0, Sophie produced 27 words for which the adult target was either di- or multisyllabic. Of these 27 words, she got the stress right in all 27. Again, there are two things worth commenting on at this stage. One is that she continued to produce the truncated form of *nother* for *another*, but she did not produce a truncated form for the adult target *medicine*. If she were producing a foot, we would not expect the final syllable to be produced, unless there is a universal bias for trochees ′ ˅ and dactyls ′ ˅ ˅ as opposed to iambs ˅ ′ and anapests ˅ ˅ ′. Later in the chapter I propose a parsing solution to this problem.

One change that occurred in Sophie's system at this point was that she could get stress as far back as the antepenult, as a result of interaction with morphology. So in forms like *tídying*, she assigned the stress on the base form *tídy* and then added the suffix -*ing*, which does not affect stress placement. This, in fact, was the only form of the 27 where the stress (in both child and adult form) was not on the penult.

In the third sample, at age 3;5, Sophie was still producing mainly penultimate stress. She produced 33 words that were either di- or multisyllabic. Of these 33 she produced 28 with penultimate stress, 3 with final stress, 1 with antepenultimate stress, and 1 with preantepenultimate stress. She still showed evidence of truncation in forms like *gótten* for *forgótten*, *córder* for *recórder*, and *ténding* for *preténding*. In these cases she was still producing the final foot of the adult target. However, there were also cases where she did not truncate. One case was another token of the word *recórder*, which she produced as *recórder*. So, even for a single lexical item, variation had begun to appear. And we find forms like *Elízabeth* and *béautifully*, which were not truncated.

In the fourth sample, at age 3;11, Sophie produced 35 words where the targets were either di- or multisyllabic. She had correct stress placement on

TABLE 5.4
Sophie's Stress Placement in Multisyllabic Words

		Stress Placement Correct			
Sample: Age	Number of Targets	Penult	Final	Antepenult	Preantepenult
Sample 1: 2;4	22	19	3		
Sample 2: 3;0	27	26	1		
Sample 3: 3;5	33	28	3	1	1
Sample 4: 3;11	35	21	4	8	2

all of them, and was starting to utilize a much greater range of syllable positions for stress (as shown in Table 5.4). We also note that at this stage she produced the form *anóther* with no truncation, but a new form *guána* appeared as a truncated form of *iguána*. As has been widely documented (Menn & Matthei, 1990), newly acquired lexical items are often subject to different phonological processes than items that have been stored longer.

I summarize the four samples in Table 5.4. Throughout the study, Sophie showed that she had very accurate stress placement, and that metrical structure played a role in the truncated forms she produced. This picture of the acquisition of English stress appears to be very similar to Fikkert's picture of the acquisition of Dutch stress.

8. A PARSING SYNTHESIS

It looks as if the studies discussed in this chapter are each emphasizing something slightly different. Echols and Newport (1992) emphasized perception of the adult form. In their view, the nonstandard child form is attributable to perceptual factors, a misperception of the input. Fikkert (1992) emphasized UG. The adult input is mapped onto a universal trochaic template. Sometimes not all of the adult input can be represented by the child's system, so the form will be truncated. The child's nonstandard form results from the mapping process and truncation. Idsardi (1992), although not emphasizing the acquisitional implications of his work, set out a model for constructing metrical grids. Crucial to the model is the notion of projection of either elements or parentheses. In this view, nonstandard forms (representations) would be constructed via universal parameters. Therefore, if the child was constructing nonstandard representations, they too would be the result of projection.

I think that there are elements of truth in all the proposals. I imagine the whole process looks something like (20):

(20)

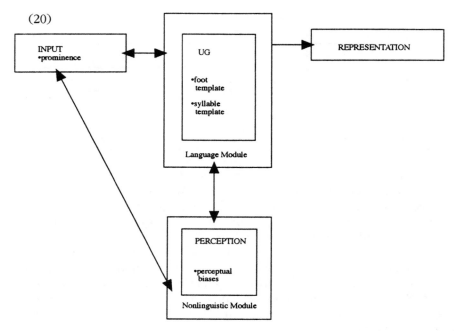

Nonlinguistic cognitive abilities, such as perception, act on the input, extracting certain parts of that input. This could be combined with a modification to Idsardi's parameters to read something like: Project stressed syllables. Children can project stressed syllables because they have certain nonlinguistic abilities. This input is then mapped onto given UG structures such as metrical templates. This will constitute the child's representation.

What this leads me to propose is some sort of parsing strategy for the child. Drawing on the perceptual abilities identified in Echols and Newport (1992), the following possibilities might appear reasonable.

8.1. Perceptual Bias for Stressed Syllable

One possibility is that the child extracts the stressed syllable from the input and then maps that syllable onto a universal template. Although capturing certain facts, this explanation is problematic in that it cannot explain why syllables following the stressed syllable are not usually truncated as are syllables preceding the stressed syllable.

8.2. Perceptual Bias for Stressed Foot

Following Fikkert (1992), we might assume that the child has a perceptual bias for the stressed foot in the input. Thus, the child would extract the stressed foot from the input and map that onto a universal prosodic template.

The problem with this model is that it assumes the representation it is trying to build. That is to say, the child would be scanning for and extracting a foot and then mapping it onto a universal foot.

8.3. A Combined Proposal

I think there is a way to combine the best of both of these views in order to understand how children are perceiving the input and assigning prosodic structure to it. I propose that the parsing process goes something like this:

1. Perceive and store entire input string. I assume the input string at this stage to be an adult word. The word is stored as a string of phonetic elements. For instance, the adult word *another* would be stored initially as (21):

(21) ə n ʌ ð ə r

I feel that this is a necessary stage in the parse in order to account for certain production/perception asymmetries that are observed in child language (Menn & Matthei, 1990). If children can perceive things they cannot produce, we would like there to be some sort of representation that explains the perception ability.

2. Identify the stressed syllable. Following Echols and Newport (1992), I assume that the child has a predisposition to be able to perceive stressed syllables. The child will scan from right to left until a stressed syllable is encountered. At this stage, then, the child will be operating on a form something like (22):

(22) ə n ʌ́ ð ə r

3. Project the stressed syllable head onto the next level of structure. This would result in the structure (23):

(23)   σ
          |
      ə n ʌ́ ð ə r

4. Syllabify the stressed syllable. This has to happen now so that we have some way of explaining why the [n] does not subsequently disappear. The [n] needs to be assigned to the same constituent as [ʌ]. The resulting structure would be (24):

(24)

5. Circumscribe the string. Following Idsardi (1992), I assume that a process of phonological circumscription is operative at this stage. "The circumscription operation parses a form into two pieces: the base and the residue" (p. 43). Idsardi adopted this notion and applied it to stress systems, in the following way:

(25) Divide a form into two domains at the main stress. (p. 43)

Idsardi argued that it is necessary to have certain metrical operations operate only on the residue (some deletion processes), whereas other processes apply to the base (e.g., conflation). As a result of circumscription, the structure will look something like this:

(26)

6. Truncate the residue. This results in the structure (27):

(27)

    σ
   /|
  n ʌ ð ə r

7. Syllabify the base. This generates the representation (28):

(28)

    σ   σ
   /| /| \
  n ʌ ð ə r

8. Project the base onto the universal prosodic template of a trochaic foot:

(29)   F
         / \
        s   w
        σ   σ
       /| /| \
      n ʌ ð ə r

If there are syllables still remaining that have not been mapped onto the trochaic template, these syllables would be deleted by Stray Erasure (Steriade, 1982) as a result of a violation of prosodic licensing (Itô, 1986). Prosodic licensing stipulates that phonological material must be incorporated into the next higher level of prosodic structure or be deleted.

This parsing strategy allows us to account for the fact that syllables after the main stress tend not to be truncated as often as syllables before the main stress. The different status of these positions relative to the stressed syllable could be due to the direction of scanning. If we assume that the scan takes place from right to left, then all material that has been scanned is less likely to be truncated. Once the stressed syllable is encountered, the scan stops. Any unscanned material will be a candidate for truncation as a result of circumscription.

The developmental stages defined by Fikkert can now be explained more satisfactorily. In Stage 1, the child is extracting the stressed syllable and mapping it onto the universal template. In Stage 2, the child maps the base onto the universal template and is now able to produce trochees. The characteristics of Stage 3, however, still remain unexplained. Why is the child producing level stress on the two syllables? The explanation I would propose relates to the expanded parsing capabilities. In Stage 1, the child is able to scan for a single stress. In Stage 2, the child is able to scan for another stress and generate forms like [krókdil]. In Stage 3, the child's representations appear to be governed by a principle that assumes one stressed syllable per foot. Therefore, when the parsing scan extracts two stresses, as in [kròkdíl], the child, at this stage, assumes that there must be two feet. Each stressed syllable would be projected to a foot. Now this would suggest that at Stage 3 we would find structures like (30):

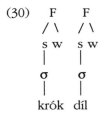

(30)

This would predict that there are segmental slots that could be filled at this stage. Fikkert's data in (31) indicate that the predicted forms are attested:

(31)	Dutch	English Gloss	Adult Form	Child Form
	kameel	camel	/kamél/	[kíkɔmɔ́i]
	konijn	rabbit	/konɛ́in/	[tɔ́tɔtɛ́in]
	kameel	camel[10]	/kamél/	[kánəmèu]
	ballonnen	balloons	/balɔ́nən/	[báulowlɔ́mə]

---

[10]The two examples of *camel* are taken from different children.

The existence of these four-syllable ditrochaic words seems to justify this analysis.

9. STRESS IN L2

I now discuss how adult language learners acquire the metrics of a second language. L2 stress has received very little attention in the literature (James, 1988; Mairs, 1989; Pater, 1991; Youssef & Mazurkewich, 1993). In a number of papers, I have considered how second language learners acquire stress. My broad conclusions suggest that (a) adult interlanguages do not violate metrical universals, and (b) adults are capable of resetting their parameters to the L2 setting. The subjects I observed were quite good at putting English stress on the right syllable.[11] Thus, their interlanguages reflect UG principles, correct L2 parameter settings (from resetting), and incorrect L1 parameter settings (from transfer).

In Archibald (1992) I looked at the acquisition of English stress by Polish speakers. In Archibald (1993a) I looked at Spanish speakers, and in Archibald (1993b) I looked at Hungarian speakers. In fact, the Spanish study was a pilot study for Archibald (1991). Under the basic research design used in these studies, the subjects performed both production and perception tasks related to stress assignment. First they had to read a list of words, and then they read sentences out loud. Stress placement was transcribed for the key words. Then the subjects listened to the same words they produced as they were read out loud on a tape recorder by a native English speaker. The subjects had to mark the syllable on which they perceived stress to occur. In both the production and the perception tasks, transfer of the L1 parameter setting into the L2 grammar was evident.

Table 5.5 illustrates how languages may differ in their parameter settings. When the parameter settings are different in the first and the second language, we have the potential for transfer. Often, the L1 parameter settings transfer into the L2.

9.1. Spanish → English

As can be seen in Table 5.5, Spanish and English stress are virtually identical. One of the places where we can see L1, influence, though, is in the transfer of diacritic extrametricality markings. This can help us to explain certain L2 errors. Consider the word *cannibal* in Spanish, *caníbal.* The underlying representation must be (32):

---

[11]Responses were about 70% correct for the production task, and about 85% correct for the perception task. The tasks are described in the following text.

TABLE 5.5
Parameter Settings in Four Languages

Parameter	Spanish	Polish	Hungarian	English
P1 (word tree)	right	right	left	right
P2 (foot type)	binary	binary	binary	binary
P3 (built from)	left	left	left	left
P4 (strong on)	right	right	left	right
P5 (QI/QS)	QS	QI	QS	QS
P6 (sensitive to)	rime	NA	nucleus	rime
P8A (extrametrical)	yes	no	no	yes
P8 (extrametrical on)	right	NA	NA	right

(32) [kaníbaɫ]

In (32), the final consonant is extrametrical. Otherwise we would get the unmarked stress pattern [kanibál]. When asked to produce this word in English, [kaníbal] was elicited in informal research sessions. The lexical marking of extrametricality seems to have been transferred into English. Now this word, of course, is a cognate, and it could be claimed that this is just a simple case of transfer. However, I do not think it is trivial for us to be as explicit as we can be as to what exactly is transferring. This gives us some information as to what elements of the lexical representation do transfer. If there is extrametricality marked in the learner's lexicon, then this will transfer.

9.2. Polish → English

Polish stress is fixed for the most part and is assigned to the penultimate syllable. Polish differs from English in how it treats extrametricality and quantity sensitivity. Both of these differences affect the interlanguage grammars of Polish subjects learning English. Because Polish lacks extrametricality, the Poles frequently produced penultimate stress in English words that have antepenultimate stress because of extrametricality. For example, the word *cabinet* has stress on the antepenult in English because the final syllable is extrametrical. The Polish subjects, lacking the extrametricality marking, placed the stress on the penult. One exceptional subclass that emerged for the Polish subjects included words ending in *-a*. Polish has a suffix *-a* that is marked as extrametrical. In English words that ended in *-a*, Polish subjects often assigned antepenultimate, rather than penultimate, stress. For example, they would produce *cínema*, not *cinéma*.

In addition, the Polish subjects showed no evidence of referring to the internal structure of the syllable when assigning stress. They were building quantity-insensitive feet. For example, the closed penult of a word like *agénda* was no more likely to attract stress than the tense vowel in the penult of a word like *aróma*.

9.3. Hungarian → English

Hungarian is also a language of primarily fixed stress. Main stress occurs on the initial syllable of a word. This is the result of the word tree being strong on the left in Hungarian (in English it is strong on the right). Hungarian, like English, is quantity-sensitive; but, unlike English, it is sensitive to the structure of the nucleus. Thus, in Hungarian a branching nucleus will attract stress, as opposed to English branching rimes attracting stress.

These two differences, in fact, account for the majority of the Hungarian subjects' errors. They tended to transfer their L1 parameter settings and assign initial stress to English words. In addition, syllables with long vowels (as opposed to syllables closed by consonants) tended to attract stress for the Hungarian subjects, as they would in the L1. Initial stress could be seen in productions like *ágenda* rather than *agénda*. The role of the difference in the domain of quantity sensitivity was evident in the fact that the branching nucleus in the penult of a word like *aróma* was more likely to attract (correct) stress than the branching rime of a word like *agénda*, which was often produced as *ágenda*.

10. CONCLUSIONS

There are still relatively few empirical studies that investigate the acquisition of stress in either L1 or L2. In this chapter I summarized some exisiting work and proposed certain mechanisms to account for the observed facts in first and second language acquisition. In L1, I argued that such factors as non-linguistic perception, UG templates for syllable and foot structure, prosodic circumscription, and parsing strategies could explain a range of phenomena such as stress placement and truncation. In L2, UG principles, parameter resetting, and the mechanism of transfer of L1 parameter settings were proposed to explain the stucture of an interlanguage.

Empirical investigations of phonological representations and processes serve to shed light on many of the central questions faced by acquisition researchers today. What does the final state grammar look like? What does the initial state look like? What do the intermediate states look like? Are they governed by UG? What processes affect representations? How does the input affect the representation of linguistic knowledge? I have addressed all of these questions in this chapter, thus demonstrating the import and utility of investigating the interaction of phonological acquisition and phonological theory.

APPENDIX A

TABLE A.1
Samantha's Data (2;6)

English		Spanish	
Target	*Form*	*Target*	*Form*
puppies	pápis	rana	yána
purple	pípəl	bruja	byúxa
yellow	yéyow	mansanas	mansánas
Babar	bábá:	chicita	kikíkə
crocodile	kakodáyo	cara	káya
Cinderella	sɪnəwéyə	vasso	báso
crying	fwayɪ́ŋ	casa	yáka
Snow White	sów wáyt	nueva	yéma
apples	ǽpows	naris	neníy
outside	áwsayd	niños	níños
Alicia	alíysyə		
Maria	miyníə		
Joshie	ǰášiy		
Gary	gáriy		
Oda	ódə		
Maya	máyə		
horsie	hɔ́siy		

Target	Form
apple	ǽpu
baby	bíbí
bunny	bʌ́ní
	bʌní
buttons	bʌ́téns
	bʌ́tɪns
	bʌténs
chimney	čími
corner	kʌ́nʌ
doggie	gɔ́gi
donkey	gɔ́ki
frisbee	fízi
flowers	fáwz
hammer	hǽmʌ́
	hǽmʌ
horsie	ʌ́ti
mirror	míə
monkey	mɔ́ki
paper	pépʌ
	pépʌ́
penny	péni
pliers	páəz
pocket	pákít
	pakít
puzzle	pəzú
	pə́zú
scissor	sízʌ
soldier	sódʌ
suitcase	ʌkés
	hʌ́kés
	ʌtkés
table	tebú
	tébo
triangle	daiʔǽ
	daiŋgú
turtle	tə́tú
	tʌ́tu
water	ʌ́ti
	wʌdə́
zipper	zɪpʌ́
	dípɔ́
broken	bókín
	bókin
heavy	ɛ́ví
	ɛ́vi
turning	tʒ́nɪŋ
	tʌ́lɪnɪŋ
away	əwé

APPENDIX B
Idsardi's Parameters

Line 0 element projection:
Project a line 0 element for each element that can bear stress.

Line 0 parenthesis projection:
Project the $\left\{ \begin{array}{l} \text{left} \\ \text{right} \end{array} \right\}$ boundary of certain syllables onto line 0.

Edge-Marking Parameter:
Place a $\left\{ \begin{array}{l} \text{left} \\ \text{right} \end{array} \right\}$ boundary to the $\left\{ \begin{array}{l} \text{left} \\ \text{right} \end{array} \right\}$ of the $\left\{ \begin{array}{l} \text{left} \\ \text{right} \end{array} \right\}$ -most element.

Headedness Parameter:
Project the $\left\{ \begin{array}{l} \text{left} \\ \text{right} \end{array} \right\}$ -most element of each constituent (onto the next higher line on the grid).

Iterative Constituent Construction Parameter:
Insert a parenthesis every two elements starting from the $\left\{ \begin{array}{l} \text{left} \\ \text{right} \end{array} \right\}$ -most element.

CHAPTER SIX

The Acquisition of Tonal Systems

Katherine Demuth
Brown University

1. THE ACQUISITION OF TONE: AN OVERVIEW

Autosegmental approaches to phonology developed, in part, from attempts to capture the systematic yet apparently complex grammatical tone systems found in many African languages (Goldsmith, 1976; Leben, 1973; Williams, 1976). Since that time, the development of phonological theory has contributed greatly to the understanding of other nonlinear problems that had previously eluded traditional segmental analysis (cf. Goldsmith, 1990). The field of acquisition, however, has been slow to adopt and integrate new perspectives from theoretical phonology. Much work on the acquisition of phonology has utilized a segmental approach based primarily on insights from structural linguistics (Jakobson, 1941/1968) or Chomsky and Halle (1968), henceforth SPE (Smith, 1973). Even recent volumes on the acquisition of phonology (e.g., Ferguson, Menn, & Stoel-Gammon, 1992) have focused primarily on segmental issues. This is despite the fact that some early researchers realized the importance of a prosodic approach to acquisition issues (e.g., Kiparsky & Menn, 1977; Spencer, 1986; Waterson, 1971, 1987). In this chapter I pursue an autosegmental analysis of both lexical and grammatical tone, investigating the acquisition of tonal representations, tonal sandhi rules, and the mapping between tonal and segmental tiers in Sesotho, a southern Bantu language.

1.1. The Acquisition of Lexical Tone

In any study of tone a distinction must be drawn between the lexical or
grammatical uses of pitch, which involve language-based form-meaning correspondences, and the early use of intonation for affective purposes. From
what we know of the acquisition of intonation in English, it appears that
some discourse and pragmatic aspects of the system are acquired early. In
fact, it is reported that young children perceive prosodic contours and pitch
excursions from infancy (Mehler et al., 1988). On the other hand, other
prosodic aspects of English, such as stress assignment, are apparently not
fully acquired until around 12 years (cf. Crystal, 1986).

Studies of lexical tone languages like Mandarin, Cantonese, and Thai
uniformly report that distinctions in pitch become recognizably phonemic
about the same time as, or before, segments, at around 1;11 to 2;2 years
(cf. Clumeck, 1980; Crystal, 1986). It is also suggested that even 1-year-olds
can begin to discriminate lexical items that are tonal minimal pairs (Tse,
1978). Much of the research addressing the acquisition of tone took place
before the full development of autosegmental phonology and therefore dealt
mostly with issues of lexical tone. These studies include the examination of
spontaneous speech in early Thai (Tuaycharoen, 1977), Mandarin (Chao,
1973; Clumeck, 1977; Li & Thompson, 1977), and Cantonese (Tse, 1978; cf.
Clumeck, 1980, for an overview). These studies indicate that children generally control the production of lexical tone by the age of 2, prior to the
full control of segments. Kirk (1973) also reported that naturally occurring
imitations by 2- to 3-year-old Gã-speaking children of southern Ghana more
accurately rendered tonal patterns than either rhythm or segments.[1] It would
appear, then, that children learning such languages may be able to assign
the correct underlying tonal representation to words from an early age.

1.2. The Acquisition of Tone Sandhi

In this chapter I am concerned not only with the acquisition of lexical tone,
but also with the acquisition of tonal rules, or tone sandhi. From the few
studies that address this issue, it appears that tone sandhi is more difficult
to learn than lexical tone, (Demuth, 1989, 1991, 1993; Li & Thompson, 1977).
For example, Li and Thompson (1977) noted that lexical tone in Mandarin
was acquired early but reported that tone sandhi was acquired as late as 5
years. Studies of the acquisition of tone and tone sandhi in several Bantu
languages, where tone plays a prominent grammatical as well as lexical role,
support this finding. Some of the general patterns found are outlined here.

---

[1]Gã, however, has some tone sandhi; a fuller study of the Gã tonal system and the aspects
of it that children control is needed before further conclusions can be drawn.

Chimombo and Mtenje (1989) examined the acquisition of negation constructions and tone in three Chichewa-speaking children between the ages of 1 and 2;6. They found that tonal patterns were acquired before segments and morphemes were well formed, but that the tonal rules that apply to different negative constructions were not fully in place by 2;6 years. Moto (1988) provided a brief sketch of how both lexical and postlexical tonal phenomena are acquired in Chichewa, but this work has yet to be pursued.

Demuth (1989, 1991, 1993) reported that pervasive tone sandhi may actually impede the acquisition of lexical tone. Data from a longitudinal, in-depth study of one child between the ages of 2 and 3, plus findings from a cross-sectional study of 11 children between the ages of 2;11 and 5, indicated that younger children overgeneralize the use of High (H) tone on lexical verbs; yet they generally use tone correctly in the marking of person (first and second person = Low (L) tone, third person = H tone). Findings also involved H tone spreading, acquired by 3 years, and OCP effects, which are still being acquired at 3. These findings and their theoretical import are discussed in detail in this chapter.

Evidence from the acquisition of tone in Zulu is consistent with the picture that emerges from the aforementioned studies. Suzman (1991), in a naturalistic study of nine Zulu-speaking children between the ages of 2;6 and 4, reported that nouns were generally produced with correct tone, much as in the acquisition of lexical tone reported in Asian languages. Similarly, tone was generally used correctly in the marking of person. However, only slightly more than half of the verbal constructions included appropriate tone. Overgeneralization of H tone was especially prominent among 2-year-olds, whereas 4-year-olds showed increased accuracy at 60%–80%.

The acquisition of grammatical tone systems such as those found in most Bantu languages provides especially rich ground for studying how children learn complex phonological systems. Although the findings reported here focus on the acquisition of tone, they are also relevant for theoretical questions concerning acquisition in other prosodic and phonological domains, as well as for informing the construction of acquisition theory in general.

1.3. Theoretical Issues

Linguistic theory and acquisition theory are only beginning to influence our understanding of how phonology is acquired. However, there appear to be certain recurrent patterns emerging from studies of the acquisition of tonal systems, and any theory of phonological acquisition should be able to account for these phenomena. For example, the Bantu studies mentioned earlier reported the overgeneration of H tone on verb roots. How does the child determine how many underlying tones to posit for the language being learned? And given a specific set of tonal primitives, how does the child determine which one should be employed as a default tone? Previous studies also reported the predominance of sequences of like tone in children's early productions. Perhaps children have a default setting of automatic H tone spread. Or perhaps the sequence of like surface tones is due to the strong application of the Obligatory Contour Principle (OCP), where underlying adjacent tones are fused.

Issues such as the role played by principles of Universal Grammar in guiding the acquisition of phonology have been largely unaddressed to date. What, for instance, are the principles (such as the OCP) that might guide the acquisition of tonal systems? Likewise, issues regarding parameter setting are only beginning to be discussed (e.g., Dresher & Kaye, 1990), and only with regard to specific domains (e.g., stress systems). Could the acquisition of different types of tonal systems be captured from a parametric perspective (e.g., tonal vs. pitch accent vs. stress accent systems), and could this provide insight into the acquisition of these systems? Obviously, further theoretical work, as well as empirical studies relating to these issues, is needed to address these questions more fully.

What does emerge from all the studies reported here is that the realization of at least some types of lexical tone is well formed and in place prior to the appropriate realization of segments. This means that some aspects of tonal systems are among the earliest parts of the phonological system to be acquired. Tonal systems therefore provide a unique opportunity for examining the very early organization of children's linguistic systems.

I turn now to underlying and lexical aspects of the Sesotho tonal system, and examine one child's acquisition of the system.

2. THE SESOTHO TONAL SYSTEM

There have been several early descriptive studies of the Sesotho tonal system (Köhler, 1956; Kunene, 1961, 1972; Letele, 1955; Tucker, 1929/1969; see also Doke & Mofokeng, 1957). In this chapter I restrict my discussion to autosegmental treatments of the Sesotho tone, focusing on the verbal system (cf. Clements, 1988a; Khoali, 1991; Kisseberth & Mmusi, 1989; Mmusi, 1991).

Sesotho can be described as a grammatical tone language with a restricted tonal system, that is, a system where not every syllable, morpheme, or word must be encoded for tone in the lexicon. In other words, although it is necessary to posit High tone underlyingly, it is not necessary to posit Low tone underlyingly. This means that verb roots can be specified underlyingly as having either H or Ø tone. Those syllables, or Tone Bearing Units (TBUs), that end up with no tone specification at the surface are generally filled in with a rule of Default Low Insertion. In Sesotho, approximately half of the verb roots fall into the H tone class; recent verb borrowings (loan words) are also assigned H tone. A major issue addressed in this study is how children determine the underlying tone of verbs.

Sesotho is a pro-drop language with a basic word order of (S)V(O). The verbal complex is illustrated in (1) and (2).[2]

(1) (S) SM-(T/A)-(OM)-V-(ext)-M (O)

(2) Thabo ó-tlá-mo-rék-él-a dijó
     1T. 1SM-FUT-1OM-buy-BEN-IN 8food
     'Thabo will buy him/her food.'

Although the verb *ho-réka* 'to buy' is a H-toned verb and surfaces as such in (2), there is not always a one-to-one mapping between surface realization and underlying tonal representations. For instance, if *ho-réka* 'to buy' were used with a third person subject marker, which is also H toned, the first syllable of the verb would lose its high tone: *bá-reká dijó* 'they are buying food'. Likewise, the Ø-toned verb *ho-batla* 'to want' can surface with a H tone on the first syllable of the verb if it is used with a H-toned third person subject marker: *bá-bátla dijó* 'they want food'. In other words, subject markers may influence the surface realization of tone on the following verb root. One of the acquisition problems for the child is to figure out, given these variable surface tone realizations, what the underlying lexical tone of a verb root may be.

Although Sesotho makes use of several basic grammatical tonal melodies, dependent on the tense/aspect/mood of the construction, this chapter focuses on the present and future tense forms, and on the tonal phenomena that apply at underlying and lexical levels of the phonology.

After a brief discussion of lexical tone assignment to verb roots, I discuss rule-assigned tone on subject markers. I then illustrate the rule of High Tone Doubling (HTD) and the effects of the Obligatory Contour Principle (OCP).

3. THE DATA

Demuth (1992b) provided a general profile of Sesotho-speaking children's morphological and syntactic development. The data discussed in this chapter come from a monolingual Sesotho-speaking boy (H)—one of the children

---

[2]Glosses are as follows: BEN = benefactive, CONJ = conjunction, DEM = demonstrative pronoun, FUT = future tense, ext = verbal extensions, IN = indicative, LOC = locative, M = mood, O = lexical object, OM = object marker, PASS = passive, PERF = perfective aspect, PN = independent pronoun, POSS = possessive, PREP = preposition, PRES = present tense, S = lexical subject, SM = subject marker, T/A = tense/aspect, V = verb root, ′ = high tone, + = mid tone, low tone = unmarked. Numbers indicate the noun class to which different nouns belong (e.g., *motho* 'person' and other singular human nouns = noun class 1, *batho* 'people' and other plural human nouns = noun class 2, *dijo* 'food' = noun class 8). First and second person singular/plural SMs and OMs are therefore marked as 1s/p and 2s/p respectively. A modified version of Lesotho orthography has been used.

discussed in that study. Audio recordings were made during spontaneous, naturalistic interactions between the child and his older cousin, mother, grandmother, and peers. Recordings consisted of 3 to 4 hours of interaction taped at 5-week intervals over a period of 12 months. The data consulted for this study were produced during sessions at 2;1, 2;6, and 3;0 years of age. The data were drawn from the utterances that included a full verb phrase. By this criterion, the three sessions yielded 243, 496, and 582 utterances, respectively.

Audio recordings were made with a Superscope directional microphone and a Superscope/Marantz cassette recorder. The child's utterances, which had been transcribed in broad phonemic transcription, were retranscribed for tone by a non-Sesotho speaker and verified by the author at 90% accuracy. Any questionable utterances, where tone was not clearly audible, or where the disagreement between the two transcribers could not be resolved, were not included in the study. Transcription conventions include the marking of High tone ('), falling tone (∧), mid tone (+), downstep (↓), and upstep (↑), with Low tone left unmarked. Upstep is not part of the Sesotho phonemic inventory; however, children sometimes reset the tonal register, often for emphasis (cf. examples (12) and (13)). Although the number of examples that unambiguously address a particular tonal phenomenon varies between the sessions sampled, the examples nevertheless exhibit significant developmental trends.

As noted earlier, this study examines present and future tense constructions, without object markers. The decision to focus on these particular forms was twofold: First, these constructions are abundant at children's early stages of acquisition, though they begin to decrease at around 3;0 years as children began to use an increasing diversity of tense/aspect forms and many more object markers. Second, these constructions provide ample evidence for the acquisition of underlying tonal representations and the application of tone sandhi rules in various domains, as well as the appropriate contexts for the occurrence of OCP effects and Tier Conflation problems.

I turn now to an examination of lexical tone assignment to verb roots and the acquisition of underlying tonal representations.

4. UNDERLYING LEVEL

4.1. Lexical Tone Assignment to Verb Roots[3]

Tone on Sesotho verb roots is assigned underlyingly in the lexicon (either H or Ø). If the verb is lexically marked for H tone, a H tone is then predictably associated with the first syllable of the verb root at the lexical level; if the

---

[3]Tone bearing units (TBUs) left unspecified for tone at the surface are filled in with a late postlexical rule of Default Low Insertion. Perpendicular lines (|) = initial tone associations, slant lines (/) = associations that arise through spreading. + indicates a mid tone (a lowered high tone) found at certain phrasal boundaries (cf. Khoali, 1991).

verb root is Ø toned, it will surface with a L tone on the first syllable. Examples of each are presented in (3).

(3) *H-toned verb root*   *Ø-toned verb root*
    ho-bóna   'to see'   ho-batla   'to want'

The examples in (3) are relatively transparent as to their underlying tonal specification. However, as we see in the following section, most verbs undergo tone sandhi, or tonal rules, which results in multiple surface tone patterns for a given verb root. Children learning grammatical tone languages must therefore abstract away from these surface forms in order to posit the correct underlying tone of a particular verb root. We might expect this type of lexical acquisition to be a difficult process, taking place gradually over a long period of time. In contrast, we might expect the acquisition of tone in rule-governed domains to be acquired more easily, and perhaps earlier. We turn now to a discussion of how underlying lexical tone is acquired.

The acquisition of H- and Ø-toned verb roots between 2;1 and 3;0 years exhibits some interesting developmental trends. The numbers of tokens and the percentages of verb roots surfacing with appropriate H or L tone, respectively, are presented in Table 6.1.[4]

H-toned verb roots were produced with H tone at least 75% of the time across all three ages sampled. In contrast, Ø-toned verb roots were not as consistently produced with L tone: Only 35% of Ø-toned verb roots at 2;1 years surfaced with L tone, the remainder surfacing with H tone on the first syllable. There was, however, a significant developmental trend toward appropriate marking of Ø-toned verb roots, with 47% correct by 2;6 years and 93% correct at 3;0 years.

Typical examples of early H-toned verb roots are given in (3) and (4). The critical syllables are underlined. Where the child's utterances differ segmentally or tonally from the appropriate adult equivalent; the latter is included on the following line in parentheses. Morpheme breaks are provided in the child's utterance when possible.

(3) 2;1 yrs.   te-a-<u>hána</u>
                (ke-a-<u>hána</u>+)
                1sSM-PRES-refuse
                'I refuse.'

---

[4]Although the total number of verbal utterances at 3;0 years was greater than that of the previous sessions, the number of present and future tense tokens available was much lower due to the child's increased use of other tense forms (e.g., the *tló* future), as well as the increased use of H-toned object markers and third person subject markers.

TABLE 6.1
Appropriate Marking of Lexical Tone on Verb Roots

Age	H-Toned Roots		Ø-toned roots		Number of Utterances
	N/Total	%	N/Total	%	
2;1	24/31	77	6/17	35	243
2;6	32/38	84	15/32	47	496
3;0	12/16	75	13/14	93	582

(4) 3;0 yrs.   o-ngólá lengólo?
                2sSM-write 5letter
                'Are you writing a letter?'

Typical examples of Ø-toned verb roots are given in (5) and (6), where the asterisk (*) indicates a tonally incorrect form.

(5) 2;1 yrs.   *a-kúla
                (o-a-kula)
                2sSM-PRES-sick
                'You are sick.'
(6) 3;0 yrs.   ke-kopa motohó
                1sSM-ask 3porridge
                'I'm asking for porridge.'

Some verb roots surfaced as H in one utterance but as L in the next. Thus, although there is a significant improvement by 3;0 years in the appropriate marking of tone on verb roots, there are still inconsistencies, especially with H-toned verbs. One might wonder why such inconsistencies exist, and what this means for the construction of underlying tonal representations on verb roots. It is possible that some of these later fluctuations might indicate that the verb has not yet been assigned to a particular verbal tone class. However, as seen in the following sections, certain other tonal errors are found at around 3;0 years, also involving H tones produced as L.

In sum, the majority of H-toned verb roots were produced as H at all ages sampled, and there was significant development toward the appropriate marking of Ø-toned verb roots by 3;0 years. This means that, at 2;1 years, the majority of both H- and Ø-toned verb roots were produced as H, almost as though a Default High Strategy were being used to mark verb roots at this time. Note, however, that 35% of Ø-toned verbs surfaced with L tone, indicating that verbs were already divided into two tonal groups. What, then, do the child's underlying tonal representations actually look like at 2 years? Does the child know it is not necessary to mark L tone underlyingly? We return to this issue in section 5.3, once the acquisition of tonal rules and further evidence for Underlying Representations have been presented.

In this section we have found that the accurate marking of lexical tone on Sesotho verb roots does not occur immediately, as it does in lexical tone languages like Mandarin, but appears gradually, with improved accuracy over time. Indeed, it appears that an early working strategy is to mark verb roots as H until sufficient exposure to the language provides evidence that some should be marked as L or Ø. In other words, the child appears to be using a Default High Strategy in the marking of lexical tone.

Other parts of Sesotho grammar, in particular, closed-class items such as subject markers, are assigned tone by rule. I turn now to an examination of the acquisition of tone on subject markers, and to an investigation of how lexical tone rules in general are acquired.

5. LEXICAL TONE RULES

5.1. Subject Markers

The tone of subject markers (SMs) is determined by the person and by the tense/aspect/mood of the construction. In the present affirmative, first and second person SMs take Ø tone, and third person is marked for H. This is shown in (7) (where the H tone spreads to the next syllable).

(7) *H-toned SMs*   *Ø-toned SMs*
    o-batla . . .   ke-batla . . .
     | /
    H
    ó-bátla . . .   ke-batla . . .
    'S/he wants X.'   'I want X.'

I showed earlier that a Default High Strategy was used as an initial strategy in positing underlying tone on verb roots. We might therefore predict that either (a) the acquisition of subject markers would parallel that of verb roots (i.e., subject markers would surface predominantly as H), or (b) there would be an early and consistently appropriate distinction between H- and Ø-toned subject markers. With the notable exception of H-toned subject markers at 3;0 years, the findings presented in Table 6.2 argue for the latter.

Table 6.2 shows around 80% accuracy in the appropriate marking of both H- and Ø-toned subject markers at 2;1 years. In other words, there appears to be no Default High Strategy used in the marking of SMs. Why should this be the case? The answer may lie in both the categorial difference between SMs and verb roots, and the nature of tone sandhi and tone recoverability: Subject markers represent a closed class, and the application of tone is rule governed, not lexically determined. Furthermore, the inherent tone of subject

TABLE 6.2
Appropriate Marking of Tone on Subject Markers (SMs)

	H-Toned SMs		Ø-Toned SMs		
Age	N/Total	%	N/Total	%	Number of Utterances
2;1	13/17	77	48/58	83	243
2;6	12/15	80	65/78	83	496
3;0	19/33	58	29/34	85	582

markers is generally realized on the surface. Therefore, we would expect children to acquire the correct tone on subject markers earlier and more easily than that on verb roots. Typical examples are given in (8) and (9).

(8) 2;1 yrs.   é-a kae?
                (ó-ya kae?)
                1SM-go where
                'Where is s/he going?'

(9) 2;1 yrs.   a-echá hápe
                (ke-etsa hápe)
                1sSM-do again
                'I'm doing (it) again.'

As might be expected, a large portion (43 = 74%) of the Ø-toned subject markers at 2;1 years are the first person singular subject marker *ke* 'I'. Note furthermore that tone on the subject markers in (8) and (9) is marked appropriately prior to the well-formedness of the segments in these morphemes.

Table 6.2 shows that Ø-toned subject markers surfaced as L consistently across time, with an accuracy rate of over 80%. This differs, however, from the marking of H-toned subject markers, where there is a regression in the appropriate marking of tone at 3;0 years. Compare the appropriate surfacing of L tone in (10) with the inappropriate realization of H tone on the subject markers in (11a–b).

(10) 3;0 yrs.   roná re-ngola ká-ng?
                 (roná re-ngólá ká-ng?)
                 1pPN 1pSM-write PREP-what
                 'As for us, what are we going to write with?'

(11) a. 3;0 yrs. *a-chécha
                 (é-á-checha)
                 9SM-PRES-reverse
                 'It's reversing.'

(11) b. 3;0 yrs. *e-á-fihla ká tlu-ng
                  (é-yá-fihla ká tlu-ng)
                  9SM-FUT-arrive PREP 9house-LOC
                  'It will get into the house.'

In (11a) the subject marker and tense marker have been collapsed into one syllable; even so we would expect an H tone to be preserved, but it is not. In (11b), where both subject marker and tense marker are present, a H tone surfaces on the tense marker only. We see in the following sections that tone sandhi rules involving OCP effects are in the process of being acquired at around 3;0 years, and that the regression in performance on H-toned subject markers is a result of the inappropriate mapping of those tonal melodies onto syllables, or tone bearing units (TBUs).

This section has shown that there is a critical difference in the developmental marking of tone on subject markers and verb roots. In particular, early stages of acquisition show a Default High Strategy applied to the marking of underlying lexical tone on verb roots, whereas subject markers are relatively accurately marked at 2;1 years. Why should there be a difference in the appropriate marking of tone on these two forms? I suggest that the differences are due to both recoverability and categorial phenomena. First, subject markers generally retain their tone at the surface, but the underlying tone of verb roots frequently differs from its surface form. In other words, the tone that surfaces on verb roots is often influenced by tone sandhi rules, whereas the tone that surfaces on subject markers is not. And second, subject markers do not constitute lexical items in the same sense that verb roots do. Rather, they are bound clitics and are assigned tone predictably by grammatical rule in the word formation part of the grammar. In contrast, the tone of verb roots is lexically idiosyncratic, learned verb by verb and marked in the lexicon. Once a rule is learned, it can be applied across the board. In contrast, the learning of underlyingly assigned lexical tone proceeds slowly on an item-by-item basis, hampered by problems of recoverability.

In sum, subject markers are clitics assigned tone by rule, but verb roots must be assigned tone as part of an abstract underlying lexical representation. The latter takes even longer to learn when there is a large amount of "noise," or tone sandhi. The acquisition of various tone sandhi rules provides further clues as to the form of the child's early underlying representations. We turn now to a discussion of these tonal rules and how they are acquired.

5.2. High Tone Doubling (HTD)

High Tone Doubling has two triggers: the lexical H tone of the verb root itself, as in (12a), or the H tone on a subject marker, as in (12b). H tone then spreads to the next syllable. These are illustrated in (12).

(12) *Contexts for High Tone Doubling (HTD)*
    a. On verb roots   *ke-rékéla* . . . *'I am buying . . .'*
    b. i. From SM to verb root   *ó-lé ma* . . .   *'S/he is plowing . . .'*
        ii. From SM to T/A marker *ó-á-lema*   *'S/he is plowing.'*

Only HTD from H-toned subject markers onto the verb root (e.g., (12bi)) provides evidence for underlying tonal representation on verbs. This is shown in (13).

(13) *Form*   *Underlying Representation*   *Status of HTD*
      ó-lé ma . . .   H/Ø   Applies
      ó-le ma . . .   H/L   Blocked

Nonetheless, the occurrence of HTD on verb roots, as in (12a), and from subject markers onto tense/aspect markers, as in (12bii), provides independent verification that HTD has been acquired. I discuss both types of HTD and the acquisition of each.

5.2.1. Verb Roots. The rule of High Tone Doubling, where a H tone associated with the first syllable of a H-toned verb root doubles, or spreads to the next syllable, is illustrated in (14).

(14) High Tone Doubling on verb roots
        ke-rekela . . .
         | /
         H
        ke-rékéla . . .
        'I'm buying X for Y.'

The rule of High Tone Doubling is distinct from the rule of Iterative High Tone Spread (i.e., spreading of a H tone to the end of the word)—a rule that applies in the perfective (e.g., *ke rékílé* . . . 'I bought X.'). The child must determine that these two rules apply in different contexts. We might expect that children would initially collapse these two rules into one, being unaware of the different phonological domains in which they apply.

The critical examples that provide evidence for the acquisition of HTD involve H-toned verb roots of four syllables, or H-toned verb roots of three syllables that are nonfinal in the verb phrase. Few verb roots from the child's corpus fit this criteria; the majority, especially in the earlier samples, are di- or trisyllabic phrase-final forms. Of the former that are H-toned, only one did not show apparent HTD when in nonfinal position in the verb phrase. Note, however, that those examples that did show apparent HTD also permit an Iterative Spreading analysis. Thus, those cases cannot be used as evidence that the rule of HTD has actually been acquired.

Of the verb roots that qualify, only a few, such as (15), show unambiguous HTD; others, like (16), show Iterative Spreading.

(15) 2;6 yrs. séfofánu syá-↑bídíka kwána
(sefófáne sé-a-bídíka kwána)
7airplane 7SM-PRES-turn LOC
'The airplane is turning about over there.'

(16) 2;6 yrs. *wená á-máthélá ↑má::::ne Chabadímachetse kwana
(wená o-mathela mâ:né Chabadímaketse kwána)
2sPN 2sSM-run to LOC Ch. LOC
'You're running WA:Y over there at Chabadimaketse, far away.'

However, by 3;0 years, most H-toned verb roots show appropriate application of HTD, as seen in (17) and (18).

(17) 3;0 yrs. tsa-sébétsa mo
(ke-a-sébétsa móna)
1sSM-PRES-work LOC
'I'm working here.'

(18) 3;0 yrs. te-bi b(í)néla (A)si Mamélo
(ke-bínéla Aúsi Maméllo)
1sSM-sing for sister Mamello
'I'm singing for Sister Mamello.'

Note that in (18) the child self-corrects, the verb root starting out with L tone, but surfacing with H tone (the parentheses around the vowels indicate partial devoicing).

If HTD is being applied to verb roots at 3;0 years, we might expect to find it applying with subject markers as well. We turn now to a consideration of HTD from subject markers.

5.2.2. High Tone Doubling (HTD) from Subject Markers. The H tone on the subject marker spreads to the following syllable, either onto the onto the verb root, as in (19a), or onto the tense/aspect marker when one is present, as in (19b).

(19) *High Tone Doubling (HTD) from subject markers*
a. *HTD onto verb*   b. *HTD onto T/A marker*
o-lema . . .   o-a-lema
| / | /
H   H

ó-léma . . .   ó-á-lema
'S/he's plowing X.'   'S/he's plowing.'

The acquisition of HTD from subject markers is of particular interest as it holds the key to an understanding of children's development of underlying tonal representations on verbs. Specifically, HTD from the subject marker onto the verb root, as in (19a), should take place only if the verb root is toneless (i.e., has Ø tone); if the verb root is L, spreading should not apply (i.e., the first syllable of the verb would already bear a tone and would block spreading).

The context for unambiguous application of HTD is that in which H-toned subject markers are used with Ø-toned verb roots. Although examples are few at 2;1 years, there does not appear to be early application of HTD, as shown by the lack of Doubling onto the verb root in (20).

(20) 2;1 yrs.   *á-eta móda
                 (á-étsa móna)
                 6SM-do LOC
                 'They're doing (it) here.'

It is frequently the case that the subject marker and tense/aspect marker have been collapsed into one syllable, thus obscuring the segmental context for the application of HTD. We might expect, however, that coalescence would precede the assignment of tone, and that the H tone would spread to the first syllable of the verb stem. However, as seen in (21), there is no overt evidence that HTD has applied.

(21) 2;6 yrs.   *á-nyola kho:fú yéna
                 (é-á-nyoloha khofú éna)
                 9SM-PRES-ascend 9dumptruck 9DEM
                 'It's ascending, this dumptruck.'

Indeed, there are even cases, like (22), where both the subject marker and the tense marker are realized, but the H tone has not spread to the tense marker.

(22) 2;6 yrs.   *é-a-tsamaya koloi yaka
                 (é-á-tsamaya koloi yáka)
                  9SM-PRES-leave 9car 9POSS-my
                 'It's leaving, my car.'

Other cases show possible Iterative High Tone Spread rather than Doubling, though (23) could also be a case where the Ø-toned verb root is being incorrectly treated as H.

(23) 2;6 yrs.   *á-wélá nth(ò) éná. . .
                 (é-á-wela ntho éna. . .)
                  9SM-PRES-fall 9thing 9DEM
                 'It's falling, this thing. . .'

By 3;0 years, however, HTD from subject markers seems to have been acquired, as shown by the appropriate application of Doubling to both the verb root in (24) and the tense/aspect marker in (25).

(24) 3;0 yrs.   é-tsáma ká tsê:lâ:
                (é-tsámaya ká tsela)
                9SM-leave PREP 9road
                'It's leaving by the road.'

(25) 3;0 yrs.   dikólóy tse di . . . di . . . dí-á-tsamay(a)
                (dikolói tséna dí-á-tsamaya)
                10car 10DEM 10SM-PRES-leave
                'These cars are leaving.'

Note the parallel between examples (22) and (25), where similar sentences are uttered 6 months apart, the second time with the appropriate HTD pattern. Note also that the same verb (*ho-tsamaya* 'to leave') appears in both (24) and (25), with HTD onto the first syllable of the verb root in (24) and HTD applying on the present tense marker in (25). In other words, it would appear that by the age of 3 the rule of HTD and the domains to which it applies have been acquired.

In this section we saw that the rule of High Tone Doubling (HTD) applies to both verb roots and subject markers. Although there is no evidence that the child knows of, or knows how to apply, HTD at 2;1 or 2;6 years, by 3;0 years the child appears to be able to control its use and apply it to the appropriate morphological domains. This is evidenced by examples showing the appropriate application of Doubling (as opposed to Iterative Spreading), as well as the application of HTD on both verb roots and subject markers. In the next section I discuss the implications of these findings for our understanding of the acquisition of underlying tonal representations.

5.3. From Surface to Underlying Representations

Any child facing the acquisition of a phonological system must consider the surface forms he or she hears and, from those, construct appropriate underlying representations. Given the Sesotho tonal system, the acquisition of HTD provides some evidence for how and when this occurs. Consider Table 6.3.

We know that the child posits two tonal verb classes from the earliest utterances examined, but it is not clear at this point whether the underlying representations being posited are H/L or H/Ø. The form that underlying representations take does not become clear until HTD has been acquired. By 3 years HTD originating from the verb root is systematically applied as we see in Table 6.3. This is evidence that the child is aware of HTD and

TABLE 6.3
Summary of Evidence for Underlying Representations (URs)

Phenomenon	Age	Acquisition	UR
Underlying form of verb roots	2;1 yrs.	H vs. other	H/?
	2;6 yrs.	H vs. other	H/?
	3 yrs.	H vs. other	H/?
HTD from verb root	2;1 yrs.	No	
	2;6 yrs.	No	
	3 yrs.	Yes	
HTD from SM onto verb root	2;1 yrs.	N/A	
	2;6 yrs.	N/A	
	3 yrs.	Yes	H/Ø

controls at least one domain to which it applies. It is at this same time, however, that we find HTD originating from H-toned subject markers and, most critically, spreading onto adjacent verb roots. Appropriate H/Ø underlying representations are therefore present for verb roots by the age of 3. This is not to say that individual lexical verbs are all assigned to the appropriate tonal class, but only that the appropriate primitives of underlying tonal representations have been determined.

The developmental summary provided in Table 6.3 leaves open the possibility that children might have some type of early default representation of the tonal system. Given the overgeneration of H tones in the earliest utterances examined, we hypothesize that children start with either an exhaustively underspecified system, where all verbs are predictably associated with H tone, or perhaps an exhaustive underlying H specification for all verbs. These hypothetical representations are given in Fig. 6.1, where v = verb root, as listed in the lexicon.

However, by 2;1 years, some of the child's verbs surface with L tone; by this point the child seems to have determined that there two classes of verbs, those that are assigned H tone underlyingly, and those that are not. The question remains: Are those early representations fully specified (i.e., H/L), or are they more adultlike at this point, being selectively underspecified (i.e., H/Ø)? Three possible underlying representations employed at around

FIG. 6.1. Possible underlying representations (URs) prior to 2 years.

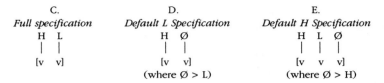

FIG. 6.2. Possible underlying representations (URs) at 2 years.

2 years can be schematized as in Fig. 6.2, where v = verb root, as listed in the lexicon.

The representation given in C would imply that some L-toned verb roots are originally classified as H and would need to be reclassified at some future point. This has the undesirable result of changing underlying representations, something that is generally seen as problematic from the perspective of learnability theory. An alternative proposal would be that given in D, where verb roots are either assigned a H tone underlyingly, or left unspecified, to be filled in later with a default L tone. This form of underlying representations still retains the undesirable attribute of forcing a reclassification of some verb roots from H to Ø at a later stage of development. A solution to this problem might be the representation given in E, where unclassified verb roots are assigned a default H tone until the child is able to assign them to the appropriate class. This would have the same effect of overgenerating H-toned verb roots (i.e., capturing the effect of the Default H Strategy), but without forcing the reassignment of verb roots to different tone classes.[5] The ultimate change in the grammar, then, comes as one change in the tonal inventory (i.e., L > Ø), rather than the reclassification of tonal representations on individual lexical items. The lesser cost involved in this type of change provides a more attractive solution for the learnability problem and at the same time captures nicely the effects of the observed Default H Strategy.

In Sesotho, OCP effects have the potential for blocking or reversing the effect of HTD, with further implications for our understanding of the acquisition of underlying representations. We turn now to an examination of OCP effects, where underlying representations again play a critical role.

6. OBLIGATORY CONTOUR PRINCIPLE EFFECTS AND TIER CONFLATION

In the phonology of many languages, identical phonological entities such as vowels, tones, or prominently stressed syllables are prohibited from occurring in adjacent positions. Languages deal with this problem in different ways, in some cases fusing two like elements to yield only one, in other

---

[5]I thank Glyne Piggott (personal communication, 1993) for this observation.

cases modifying one such that two like elements are no longer adjacent. With regard to tone, the restriction is often one that prohibits two H tones from being adjacent on the tonal tier. We follow recent work on the OCP in Sesotho and closely related Setswana (Khoali, 1991; Kisseberth & Mmusi, 1989; Mmusi, 1991) in referring to these OCP effects as Delinking, rather than Blocking rules.

6.1. Right-Branch Delinking (RBD)

The OCP manifests itself in the Sesotho tonal system in several ways, each providing a resolution to an illicit HH tonal sequence. Of concern here are two rules of High Tone Delinking: Right-Branch Delinking (RBD), and Left-Branch Delinking (LBD). In RBD, the tone from the subject marker, which has spread to the tense/aspect marker, must be delinked, thereby breaking up the HH sequence on the tonal tier to produce a HLH sequence. This is illustrated in (26).

(26) *Right-Branch Delinking (RBD)*
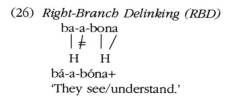
ba-a-bona
H   H
bá-a-bóna+
'They see/understand.'

Note that RBD allows HTD to apply and then undoes its effect with the use of a Delinking rule. This is, in effect, a repair strategy, a solution some phonologists would prefer to avoid by simply not letting the HTD apply in the first place (i.e., adopting a Blocking rule instead). However, Sesotho still needs a rule of Left-Branch Delinking, as is seen in the following section. Furthermore, examples like (29) indicate that the child may be applying HTD before application of the OCP. Thus, it would appear that the acquisition scenario is indeed one of *apply and repair*, rather than *block*.

6.2. Left-Branch Delinking (LBD)

LBD applies in a somewhat different domain: When a H-toned verb root is adjacent to a H-toned subject marker, it is the underlying tone on the verb root that gets delinked, again producing a HLH surface pattern. This is shown in (27).

(27) *Left-Branch Delinking (LBD)*
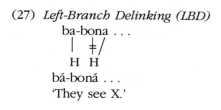
ba-bona . . .
H H
bá-boná . . .
'They see X.'

Note that a Blocking rule is of no use in this domain, where lexical tones have already been associated. We turn now to a discussion of how RBD and LBD are acquired.

6.3. Acquisition of OCP Effects and Tier Conflation Problems

Because subject markers and tense/aspect markers are frequently coalesced in early child speech, it is difficult to determine if Delinking rules have been acquired even by 3;0 years. However, from those examples where a clear segmental distinction is made, in examples like (28)–(30), there is no evidence that RBD has been acquired, even with a commonly and correctly used H-toned verb root like *ho-hána* 'to refuse' in (29) and (30).

(28) 3;0 yrs.	*ebílé kodoi yáká <u>é-á-tjéna</u>+		[HHH]
	(ébilé kolói yá-ká <u>é-a-kéna</u>+)		[HLH]
	CONJ 9car 9POSS-my 9SM-PRES-enter		
	'In fact, my car is going in.'		
(29) 3;0 yrs.	*<u>e-á-hána</u>+		[LHH]
	(<u>é-a-hána</u>+)		[HLH]
	9SM-PRES-refuse		
	'It refuses.'		
(30) 3;0 yrs.	*<u>wa-hána</u>		[LH]
	(<u>ó-a-hána</u>+)		[HLH]
	1SM-PRES-refuse		
	'He refuses.'		

No Delinking has applied in (28), with a HHH surface pattern resulting. In contrast, examples like (29), with a LHH surface pattern, indicate that some Delinking may have taken place, but that the application of the rule has applied after HTD and has involved the wrong TBU. Critically, the H on the tense marker should be delinked, not the H on the subject marker.

In (30) the subject marker and tense/aspect marker have coalesced, leaving only two TBUs to receive a three-syllable HLH melody. In similar situations many Bantu languages preserve tone, creating a contour tone (e.g., falling, rising). However, the child appears to map the HLH melody onto the available TBUs in a one-to-one mapping from right to left, thereby omitting the initial H tone. The result is that only the LH part of the tonal melody gets mapped onto syllables, the initial H tone having no place to dock. Here we see evidence that the child knows about the Delinking rule, but that, due to subsequent coalescence, the initial H tone is not realized at the surface. It would appear, then, that the child has the correct representation on a separate tonal tier, but that the incorrect surface form results from a problem of mapping tones onto the available TBUs. We call this the Tier Conflation problem.

Examples such as (29) and (30) are interesting for at least two reasons: First, recall from Table 6.2 that there was a regression in the appropriate marking of H-toned subject markers (from 80% correct at 2;6 years to 58% correct at 3;0 years). I suggest this is due to the inappropriate mapping of the HLH melody onto Tone Bearing Units. Examples such as (29) and (30) indicate that OCP effects are being learned at 3;0 years, but that the domain to which they apply has not yet been fully acquired, the L frequently falling on the subject marker, even in cases where coalescence has not taken place.

Second, as noted earlier, the choice of a Delinking rule rather than a Blocking rule to account for the resulting L tone on tense markers is, to a certain degree, a theory-internal matter. However, in examples like (29), where the tense/aspect marker surfaces with H tone, it appears that High Tone Doubling has already taken place. RBD then applies, but mapping of the HLH melody onto TBUs is not appropriately realized. The acquisition evidence therefore supports the adoption of a Delinking rule rather than a Blocking rule.

Further support for the use of a Delinking rule rather than a Blocking rule, comes from the fact that a rule of Delinking is needed to account for LBD cases. Although there is some evidence of LBD at 2;6 years, as in (31), the majority of examples are more like that shown in (32), where no Delinking takes place.

(31) 2;6 yrs.   bá-kuká mollo   [HLH]
                  2SM-pick up 3fire
                  'They're taking the flame.'

(32) 2;6 yrs.   *kolóy yá-ká é-thóthá mokúdú: [HHH]
                  (kolói yá-ká é-thothá mokúdúbe)   [HLH]
                  9car 9POSS-my 9SM-carry 3horse dung
                  'My car is carrying horse dung.'

There is, however, another set of examples that indicate the child does have some awareness of LBD around 2;6 years. We have noted that underlyingly H-toned verb roots are generally produced as H at 2;6 years. There is, however, a set of four examples where H-toned verb roots surface with L tone on at least the first syllable. These are cases where the subject marker is (ungrammatically) omitted, and the stressed pronoun nná 'me' is used. The first syllable on the verb root surfaces as L, producing a HLH pattern, as in (33).

(33) 2;6 yrs.   *ná bidíkísa   [H LH]
                  (nná ke-a-bídíkisa)   [HLLHH]
                  1sPN 1sSM-PRES-turn
                  'Me, I'm revolving (it).'

Through the omission of several syllables, two H tones become adjacent on the tonal tier, and the child has delinked the second of these. Thus, although the domain of application is not quite appropriate, such examples may be early attempts at applying LBD. What is particularly interesting about examples like (33) is that they provide evidence for the independence of tonal and segmental tiers by 2;6 years.

By 3;0 years, LBD more frequently applies in obligatory contexts like that in (35) but continues to be overgeneralized to inappropriate contexts like that in (36).

(35) 3;0 yrs.	le-↑léng dé-dulá k(áe)?		[HLH]
	(lé-léng lé-dulá káe?)		[HLH]
	5-other 5SM-live where		
	'Where does the other one live?'		
(36) 3;0 yrs.	*ébiléng o-tlá-shap-úwa Molólo		[LHLH]
	(ébiléng o-tla-sháp-úwa Molólo)		[LLHH]
	CONJ 2sSM-FUT-PASS Mololo		
	'As a matter of fact, you will be lashed, Mololo.'		

We saw earlier that mapping of the HLH melody resulting from RBD was inconsistent. Here we see that inappropriate mapping of LBD provides further evidence that the child has some notion that a HLH pattern is required, but that control of the domain to which it applies has yet to be fully mastered. In other words, Tier Conflation continues to pose a problem at 3;0 years, even when all the TBUs are present.

It should be noted that LBD appears to be a variable rule—present in some dialects and not in others (Demuth, 1991; Khoali, 1991). What is particularly interesting about this rule is that it appears to be idiolectal: Some speakers in Lesotho have the rule of Delinking and others do not. In other words, examples like (32) would be correct in some speakers' grammars. Although the child's parents and grandparents did use the rule, the child is presumably exposed to variable input, perhaps accounting, in part, for some of the observed overgeneralization. Note, however, that RBD is an obligatory rule in all speakers' grammars, and yet Tier Conflation problems are also found there. Thus, variable input cannot be the primary explanation behind the child's inconsistent application of Delinking rules.

In this section we saw that the language-particular realization of OCP effects are in the process of being acquired at 2;6 years, but that overgeneralization of Delinking rules to inappropriate segmental domains persists at 3;0 years. It would therefore appear that the child realizes a HLH melody is involved but does not yet control the domain to which it applies. This illustrates the early independence of tonal and segmental tiers but also shows that the acquisition of tonal mapping, or more generally, Tier Conflation, is not a straightforward process. Finally, we found that HTD is acquired first, with Delinking applying to the output of HTD. This points to the existence of ordered rule application in the child's grammar, rather than the use of a Blocking rule that prohibits HTD from applying in the first place.

What does this say about the status of the OCP in early child grammars? We have treated the OCP here as a rule that shows rule-governed overgeneralization patterns. The alternative would be to say that the OCP is active from the beginning of acquisition but manifests itself in the form of Fusion as opposed to Delinking. The fact that early utterances in Sesotho and other Bantu languages have an abundance of consecutive surface H tones might then be explained by invoking a Fusion setting for the early OCP. What we do know, however, is that (a) the language-particular realization of the OCP must be learned, and (b) the OCP cannot be applied until underlying representations are available for it to act upon. In a language in which there are several realizations of the OCP, and in which underlying representations are difficult to determine, we might expect the appropriate application of OCP effects to be delayed. It is then no coincidence that underlying lexical representations and OCP effects are acquired around the same time, as the former provide the context for application of the latter.

7. DISCUSSION

In this chapter I present findings from one child's acquisition of underlying tonal representations and lexical tone rules in Sesotho, a southern Bantu language with a rich inventory of tone sandhi phenomena. First, I found that an early Default High Strategy was used in the marking of verb roots. This contrasted with the early acquisition of tone on subject markers, which undergo less tonal sandhi and are grammatical items assigned tone by rule. Second, the rule of High Tone Doubling (HTD) appears to be acquired by 3;0 years, and it is also at this point that appropriate H/Ø underlying tonal representations are being used. Finally, the language-specific realizations of the Obligatory Contour Principle are beginning to be acquired between 2;6 and 3;0 years, with accurate application delayed due to Tier Conflation problems.

These findings provide insight not only into the acquisition of tonal systems, but into the acquisition of phonological systems more generally. They are of particular interest in understanding how children arrive at underlying representations, as well as how phonological rules and OCP effects are acquired. They are also useful for informing phonological theory, with respect both to the ordering of rule application and to the status of the OCP as either a rule or a principle of Universal Grammar. These issues are discussed further in the following paragraphs.

Most of the work on the acquisition of tone has examined lexical tone languages like Mandarin. It is generally found that the acquisition of lexical tone in such languages takes place along with the acquisition of the lexical item itself, tone often being correctly realized prior to the well-formedness of the corresponding segments. Thus, speakers of lexical tone languages like Mandarin generally have access to the correct underlying tonal representations of words by the age of 2. This contrasts with the Sesotho findings, where the underlying tone of verb roots appears to be acquired gradually over time, on an item-by-item basis. It would appear that the pervasiveness of tone sandhi rules in grammatical tone languages like Sesotho results in recoverability problems, making the mapping between surface and underlying representations a more difficult and prolonged undertaking. We might predict that the positing of appropriate underlying representations would be worked out in conjunction with the acquisition of tone sandhi effects, and this appears to be the case: The significant improvement in the appropriate marking of Ø-toned verb roots at 3;0 years coincides with evidence that (a) the rule of HTD has been acquired, (b) underlying representations are H/Ø, and (c) the application of OCP effects is under way. That is, once underlying representations have been determined, tone sandhi rules and OCP effects can then apply. In effect, then, the positing of appropriate underlying representations provides the trigger for the correct application of other tonological processes.

In contrast to lexical tone, rule-assigned tone, such as that assigned to subject markers, appears to be much easier to acquire, being present at the age of 2;1. This finding, in conjunction with evidence of a Default High Strategy, might provide motivation for the view that the earliest underlying tonal representations on verb roots are uniformly H and are assigned by rule (i.e., A in Fig. 6.1). Clements and Goldsmith (1984) suggested that such a scenario might account for the proposed historical drift from H/L to H/Ø types of tonal systems, both of which are found in Bantu languages today.

Finally, this study raises theoretical issues concerning the form of linguistic rules and the status of the OCP. Right Branch Delinking effectively reverses the result of High Tone Doubling, a result many phonologist would like to avoid. The alternative would be to posit a Blocking rule that prohibited the application of HTD in the first place. However, the acquisition data show that HTD must have applied prior to the application of OCP effects. This implies that "repair strategies" may play a role in children's early grammars. This study also raises the issue of the status of the OCP as either an organizing principle of Universal Grammar (e.g., McCarthy, 1986), or merely a language-specific rule that must be learned (e.g., Odden, 1986, 1988). Although it is not entirely clear what type of acquisition evidence would strongly support one or the other of these positions, this study shows that OCP effects are overgeneralized to inappropriate contexts as early as 2;6 years. Whether this overgeneralization is the result of the robust overapplication of a rule or the early organizing influence of a principle of Universal Grammar is unclear.

Although this chapter presents a case study of how one child constructs underlying tonal representations and acquires tone sandhi phenomena, it provides a glimpse of the types of strategies children may use in organizing their phonological systems. In so doing it raises many other questions that are yet to be fully addressed. It is hoped, however, that it provides the beginnings of a framework for further research in this area.

CHAPTER SEVEN

On the Natural Domain of Phonological Disorders

Daniel A. Dinnsen
Steven B. Chin
Indiana University

Although nonorganic speech disorders are naturally occurring phenomena in the first-acquired phonological systems of many young children, systems affected by these disorders have not accrued the theoretical status of other developing or fully developed phonological systems. There appear to be (at least) two reasons for this. First, because these systems are in some sense disordered, they have been assumed not to be subject to the same principles or constraints that govern other phonological systems. By definition, then, findings about phonological disorders have been prevented from contributing to phonological theory. Second, because these systems have generally been assumed to be simplified versions of the adult target system, most descriptions have characterized them as totally derivable from the target system by a set of relatively simple substitution processes (e.g., Edwards & Shriberg, 1983; Ingram, 1989b). Given substitution processes as the defining characteristics of the disorders, these systems would have no independent status and, not surprisingly, would be of little theoretical interest.

In this chapter we present a different perspective on the nature of phonological disorders and their relevance to phonological theory. Analyses of these systems independent of the target system have revealed them to be highly structured, intricate systems that vary in the substance of underlying representations and rules (e.g., Dinnsen & Chin, 1993a; Gierut, 1985; Maxwell, 1982; Weismer, Dinnsen, & Elbert, 1981). Substitution processes and their associated assumptions cannot adequately account for the facts regarding these systems. Additionally, although the form and structure of these systems differ significantly from those of the target system, they appear to be entirely consistent with the constraints governing other phonological systems (e.g., Gierut & Dinnsen, 1986; Ingram, 1989b). Finally, phonological disorders have presented unique opportunities to manipulate experimentally aspects of a first-acquired system through clinical treatment, to test and validate hypotheses about phonological structures and principles (Dinnsen, Chin, & Elbert, 1992; Dinnsen & Elbert, 1984; Gierut, 1992; Gierut, Elbert, & Dinnsen, 1987; Tyler & Figurski, 1994). In contrast, then, to the standard view, phonological disorders can serve as a rich and novel source of information pertinent to theories of acquisition and phonology generally.

Along these lines, a number of phenomena evident in the phonological systems of young children with nonorganic speech disorders are examined in this chapter. These phenomena are shown to bear crucially on theoretical issues relating to the degree and nature of specification in underlying representations. The discussion is organized around two major issues: radical underspecification versus contrastive specification and context-sensitive radical underspecification versus context-free radical underspecification. It is argued that a modified framework of radical underspecification is necessary to account for the full range of phenomena in disordered sound systems and that this is the only framework that can provide an account of acquisition that is compatible with what we know about fully developed sound systems.

For a discussion of the characteristics of phonological disorders, see Ingram (1989b) and Dinnsen (in press). The diagnosis of a phonological disorder is generally based on several factors, including, for example, intelligibility and performance on a standardized articulation test. Children with a phonological disorder typically produce a number of target sounds in error, which results in poor intelligibility. The errors often, but not always, resemble errors found in the speech of younger, normally developing children. The particular cases reported here represent unusually severe cases, especially when the children are compared with other children of the same age. That is, these children produced at least six different target sounds in error and scored below the first percentile on the Goldman–Fristoe Test of Articulation (Goldman & Fristoe, 1986). Their speech was also judged highly unintelligible.

1. RADICAL UNDERSPECIFICATION VERSUS CONTRASTIVE SPECIFICATION

Based exclusively on evidence from fully developed sound systems, two different theories about the substance of representations or their degree of specification have been proposed, namely, radical underspecification (e.g., Archangeli, 1984, 1988; Kiparsky, 1982b) and contrastive specification (e.g., Clements, 1988b; Steriade, 1987). The two theories make different (and in some cases contradictory) empirical claims, and different phenomena from different languages have been found to support one or the other framework. Despite these seemingly contradictory results, no resolution has been offered. Also, despite the obvious connection between issues of representation and issues of acquisition, little attention has been given to developing systems (and especially disorders) as a possible source for a resolution.

Both radical and contrastive (under)specification theories require that noncontrastive features be excluded from underlying representations. Allophonic and redundant properties of sounds are thus eliminated from underlying representations. The two theories differ, however, over the necessity of specifying all contrastive features. Within the framework of contrastive specification, all contrastive features must be specified. Thus, if the feature [voice] is contrastive in obstruents, both the + and − values of the feature would have to be specified for those pairs of obstruents that do in fact contrast by that feature. But within the framework of radical underspecification, generally only marked properties of contrastive features are specified. The unmarked or default value of a contrastive feature is underspecified along with all other noncontrastive features. In the case of contrastive voicing, then, only the [+voice] value would be specified. The underspecified [−voice] property would ultimately be filled in by a rule. For our purposes, it is possible to group all such rules together as *fill-in rules*. The empirical differences between the two theories have related to the different predictions about transparency effects and asymmetries associated with the different degrees of (under)specification.

Underspecification theory has, to a limited extent, been appealed to in a general form to account for various phenomena in developing systems (e.g., Bernhardt, 1992a, 1992b; Chin, 1993; Chin & Dinnsen, 1992; Gierut, Cho, & Dinnsen, 1993; Spencer, 1986, 1988); Ingram (1992) has assumed contrastive specification to account for at least some phenomena in normally developing phonologies. His arguments were based largely on the assumption of the Distinctive Feature Hypothesis. The hypothesis maintains that children can select only those features for distinctions that are available from the acoustic signal of the target system. This has the consequence that no feature could be selected that contradicts a feature of the target sound. Such a hypothesis is capable of accounting for certain characteristic and common error patterns in normally developing and, for that matter, disordered systems. To illustrate, consider the data in (1) from a speech disordered child, Subject 34 (age 5;5), who excludes velars from his phonetic inventory and substitutes alveolars for target velars.[1]

---

[1]This subject and all subjects mentioned in this work (unless otherwise noted) were involved in a long-term study investigating the phonological systems and learning patterns of young children (ages 3;4 to 6;8) with functional (nonorganic) speech disorders. For details of subjects, methods, and procedures, see Dinnsen (1992); Dinnsen, Chin, Elbert, and Powell (1990); Elbert, Powell, and Swartzlander (1991).

(1) Subject 34: Pretreatment (Age 5;5)

[tɪdz]	'kids'	[bæti]	'backy'	[bæt]	'back'
[teɪdz]	'cage'	[dʌti]	'ducky'	[dʌt]	'duck'
[tæts]	'catch'	[buti]	'bookie'	[but]	'book'
[tʌt]	'cut'	[sɑti]	'sockie'	[sɑt]	'sock'
[tom]	'comb'				
[tɑd]	'card'				

The target distinction between alveolars and velars has evidently been merged in this child's speech. Earlier accounts (e.g., Edwards & Shriberg, 1983; Ingram, 1989b) would have represented the substitutes as velars in this child's system along with a rule of fronting, which would convert all velars to alveolars. Such accounts are judged highly abstract inasmuch as a segment type, namely a velar, is being postulated in the child's underlying representations even though the segment type never appears phonetically. Within an underspecification framework, however, the phonetic absence of the distinction would be accounted for by underspecifying place of articulation. This means that target velars would be represented in the child's system without a specified place feature. The substitution of alveolars for target velars would be achieved by a fill-in rule, which would supply to those underspecified target velars the feature [coronal] as the default. The claim in this case would be that the child does not differentiate, in any way, target alveolars from velars. As regards the Distinctive Feature Hypothesis, it is important to note that the target velars would not be represented as coronals, which would be in contradiction with the facts of the target system; but neither would they be represented as velars. Instead, they would be represented simply in terms of a subset of the target features without a place specification.

Other common error patterns such as the substitution of stops for fricatives and the substitution of glides for liquids could be accounted for in a similar fashion (see Dinnsen, 1993; Dinnsen & Chin, 1991, for details). Essentially, however, a target-appropriate sound and a phonetically identical substitute sound would be underspecified for a particular target distinction, and the fill-in rules would supply the default value of the otherwise distinguishing feature. Such accounts are equally compatible with either contrastive specification or radical underspecification, because the target distinction is presumed to be noncontrastive in the child's system. The claim of these accounts, however, is not compatible with a number of other phenomena evident in disordered (and normally developing) systems. The crucial phenomena relate to children's perceptual abilities, their differential use of phonetically identical sounds, and the across-the-board nature of change.

Recall that the essential claim here is that the target-appropriate sound and the phonetically identical substitute are not differentiated by the child.

This claim may be well founded for early stages of normal development or for cases where perceptual deficits may be involved. But perceptual deficits appear to be relatively rare (Barton, 1976; Locke, 1980; Strange & Broen, 1980). It is commonly observed that even though some children do not produce certain sounds, they are aware of the target distinctions and can correctly identify those sounds. For example, then, an adult's pronunciation of *T* and *key* would be perceptually differentiated by the child. Also, it seems to be generally accepted that perceptual abilities develop in advance of production (Compton, 1975; Smith, 1973). Abilities of this sort suggest that children have at least some knowledge of the target distinctions, even if only at a perceptual level. Knowledge of these distinctions must, then, be represented somewhere in the child's grammar and cannot simply be underspecified. Some have argued for a two-lexicon model based on such evidence (e.g., Bryan & Howard, 1992; Chiat, 1983; Hoffman & Damico, 1988; Menn, 1983; Schwartz & Leonard, 1982; Spencer, 1986, 1988). We later argue, however, that a two-lexicon model is not necessary, at least as regards the phenomena considered here.

Another phenomenon that cannot be accounted for by simple underspecification relates to the differential synchronic behavior of an individual sound in a child's system. Although target distinctions can be merged phonetically in children's systems, as noted earlier, in some of these cases, the target distinctions appear to be preserved in some nonphonetic way by the child. That is, a given sound acts one way when it corresponds to one sound in the target system, and that same sound for the same child acts another way when it corresponds to another sound in the target system. This phenomenon is exemplified in the data in (2), from a speech disordered child, Subject 27 (age 4;11), who substitutes [t] for target /θ/ but also realizes target /t/ as [t]. Note, however, that [t]'s that correspond to target /t/ alternate with glottal stop word-medially, whereas [t]'s that correspond to target fricatives do not alternate.

(2) Subject 27: Pretreatment (Age 4;11)

a.	[it]	'eat'	[iʔən]	'eating'
	[bæt]	'fat'	[bæʔi]	'fatty'
	[but]	'boot'	[buʔi]	'booty'
b.	[tit]	'teeth'	[titi]	'teethy'
	[wit]	'wreath'	[wʳiti]	'wreathy'
	[maʊt]	'mouth'	[maʊdi]	'mouthy'

For this child, then, there appear to be two different kinds of [t], one that alternates with a glottal stop and one that does not alternate. Notice that this differential behavior corresponds precisely with the target distinction between /t/ and /θ/, suggesting that the child is aware that there is a target distinction. Similar cases have been reported for other speech disordered children (e.g., Anttonen, 1993; Fey, 1989; Gierut, 1985; Maxwell, 1979) and for normal development (e.g., Applegate, 1961; Smith, 1973). The fact, then, that children treat a given sound differently depending on correspondences with target sounds is evidence that they have some knowledge of those target distinctions and represent those distinctions in their grammars. Again, the distinction cannot be underspecified.

Yet another problematic phenomenon involves change in children's systems. It is reported that changes in erroneous productions of words for some children tend to occur across the board (e.g., Gierut, 1985; Macken, 1992; Smith, 1973). Such change can be observed for the speech disordered child, Subject 34 (noted in (1)), who, prior to clinical intervention, systematically substituted [t] for target /k/ in all word positions. After receiving conventional minimal pair treatment (Elbert, Powell, & Swartzlander, 1991) on word-final /l/ (presumably unrelated to the error pattern), this child produced all instances of target /k/ correctly, as exemplified in (3).

(3) Subject 34: Posttreatment (Age 6;3)

[kidz]	'kids'	[bæki]	'backy'	[bæk]	'back'
[keɪdz]	'cage'	[dʌki]	'ducky'	[dʌk]	'duck'
[kɛts]	'catch'	[bʊki]	'bookie'	[bʊk]	'book'
[kʌt]	'cut'	[sɔki]	'sockie'	[sɔk]	'sock'
[kom]	'comb'				
[kaʳd]	'card'				

All words associated with this error pattern were produced correctly when sampled after treatment. There were, moreover, no cases of overgeneralization. That is, there were no instances where target /t/ words changed to [k]. This type of evidence seems especially relevant to the claim that children are aware of target distinctions even though they may not produce those distinctions in their own speech. Otherwise, how would children know just which words need to be changed and how they need to be changed? In such cases, the facts motivate knowledge of distinctions that must be represented and cannot be underspecified.

These phenomena all require the postulation of an underlying distinction for segments that are phonetically identical in the child's speech. To account for these phenomena under the Distinctive Feature Hypothesis, it would be necessary to contrastively specify both values of an underlying distinction that are compatible with the facts of the target system, even though that distinction is not evident in the child's speech. For example, then, [t]'s that correspond to target /k/'s but are treated differently than target /t/'s by the child would have to be specified for some property that is consistent with target velars, say dorsal, and is sufficient to distinguish them from target

/t/'s. Also, as in earlier abstract accounts, a rule would then have to eliminate the underlying specification of dorsal to merge the distinction phonetically. Such an account is indistinguishable from earlier accounts and suffers all the limitations of those accounts. Even suspending the Distinctive Feature Hypothesis, an account of these phenomena within any contrastive specification framework is not possible because no single phonetically interpretable feature can be contrastively specified to distinguish phonetically identical segments. These phenomena are equally problematic for a theory of radical underspecification, at least as it has generally been conceived. That is, even though only one value of a distinction would need to be specified, it is not obvious what feature would distinguish two phonetically identical segments and still be compatible with the facts of the child's system.

In an effort to provide a unified account of these various phenomena, a modification to underspecification theory has been proposed in the form of *shadow-specification* (Dinnsen, 1993; Dinnsen & Chin, 1991, 1993b). The modification allows default values of a feature to be radically underspecified for some words but (shadow-)specified for other words, thus introducing a phonological distinction for sounds that are phonetically identical. Shadow-specification provides a means for specifying the default value of a feature as opposed to the radical underspecification of that same feature for two phonetically identical segments. Shadow-specification is thus only possible within a framework of radical underspecification and extends the conventional notion of distinctness. Under this extended notion of distinctness, two structures are distinct if they differ in the number or type of specified properties. For example, the two structures in Fig. 7.1 would be considered distinct because one is radically underspecified for the unmarked default feature of Place (shown in Fig. 7.1a), and the other is (shadow-)specified for that same feature (Fig. 7.1b).[2] Notice that the structures in Fig. 7.1 would have exactly the same phonetic interpretation after the fill-in rules have supplied to the structure in Fig. 7.1a the default value for place, namely coronal, and the phonetic implementation rules have applied. The consequence is that the structures in Fig. 7.1a and Fig. 7.1b are phonologically, but not phonetically, distinct. In this particular case, the structures in Fig. 7.1a and Fig. 7.1b constitute two different phonological representations for what would appear phonetically to be a single coronal consonant. This is precisely what is called for generally by the phenomena noted earlier. That is, a target sound and a phonetically identical substitute sound for a different

---

[2]We assume here a generic version of feature geometry that draws from various different proposals (see Paradis & Prunet, 1991, for discussion). We also assume place of articulation features in this geometry to be monovalent, with other features being binary. These assumptions and the differences across the proposals are not crucial to any of the arguments or issues presented here. Irrelevant details of structure are omitted.

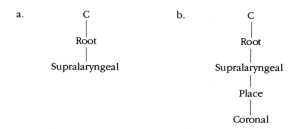

FIG. 7.1. Place distinctness in shadow-specification: (a) radically underspecified coronal, (b) shadow-specified coronal.

target are (in some cases) treated differently by children in terms of perception, phonological rules, and/or longitudinal change. This distinct specification of an unmarked feature as in Fig. 7.1b is termed shadow-specification because such structures are seen as the mere reflection of another more basic structure. That is, they crucially emerge from, resemble, and co-occur with the radically underspecified structures but also remain distinct from those structures. The combination of shadow-specification and radical underspecification allows for a two-way distinction within an unmarked category, to which children can appeal to achieve this differential behavior. Moreover, the distinction is expressed in terms of features that are entirely consistent with the child's production facts. Shadow-specifications, however, always contradict some property of the target system and thus are not compatible with the previously mentioned Distinctive Feature Hypothesis. For example, in the case of alveolars that correspond to velars, as in Fig. 7.1b, those alveolars will be shadow-specified not as dorsal, but as coronal, in contradiction to the facts of the target system. These incorrectly (shadow-) specified segments will nonetheless be distinguished from target-appropriate alveolars (Fig. 7.1a), which are by necessity radically underspecified for that same property.

A child's ability to perceive a difference in words spoken by others even though those words are not differentiated in the child's own production is, in this modified framework of underspecification theory, accounted for by representing some words as radically underspecified for a given feature, and other words as shadow-specified for that same feature. This distinction is sufficient for perceptual differentiation, even though it differs in substance from the target distinction. It is important to note in this regard that children can and do make correct perceptual judgments in terms of parameters other than those used by adult listeners (e.g., Nittrouer, 1992; Nittrouer & Studdert-Kennedy, 1987). Thus, although a child may not represent a distinction exactly as in the target system, at least a distinction is being made and the number of target distinctions is being approached. A further consequence of shadow-specification is that these perceptual differentiations are being represented in terms of properties that are consistent with the production facts. Thus, the duplication inherent in a two-lexicon model with perceptual representations and production representations is avoided.

Similarly, the differential phonological behavior of phonetically identical sounds, as illustrated in (2), can be accounted for by radically underspecifying target-appropriate /t/'s and shadow-specifying [t]'s that correspond to target /θ/'s as [−continuant]. This is illustrated in Fig. 7.2. This distinction is sufficient to identify uniquely those structures that are most vulnerable to a phonological weakening process such as intervocalic glottal stop formation, which delinks the supralaryngeal node from an already reduced structure. The additional specification in shadow-specified structures is apparently sufficient to insulate those segments from undergoing the rule. The rule preserves, and even enhances, the phonological distinction by treating phonetically identical segments differently, at least in intervocalic position.

The across-the-board nature of change with no overgeneralization, as exemplified in (3), can be accounted for by shadow-specifying erroneous substitute sounds and radically underspecifying phonetically identical target-appropriate sounds. The underlying distinction is sufficient to identify uniquely just those sounds that must undergo the change. In the case of the change from (1) to (3), target velars would be shadow-specified as coronal, as in Fig. 7.1b. A rule of sound change formulated to operate on (shadow-)specified coronals would then convert all and only those structures to specified dorsals. Target-appropriate /t/'s would not change or overgeneralize because they would be radically underspecified for the very property on which the rule of sound change is defined.

Shadow-specification crucially relies on a framework of radical underspecification. To the extent that shadow-specification is required for these various phenomena, radical underspecification is also necessary. Contrastive specification, on the other hand, is neither necessary nor sufficient to account for the full range of phenomena noted here.

But what of the apparent conflict in fully developed languages between the different underspecification frameworks? Even though shadow-specification can emerge only in a framework of radical underspecification, shadow-specification results in a certain degree of contrastive specification.

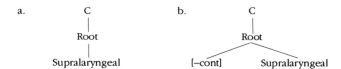

FIG. 7.2. Manner distinctness in shadow-specification: (a) radically underspecified coronal stop, (b) shadow-specified coronal stop (corresponding to target /θ/).

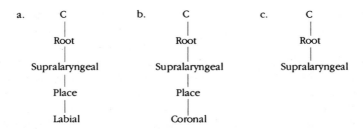

FIG. 7.3. Contrastive specification and radical underspecification by means of shadow-specification: A specified labial (a) is contrastively specified with respect to a shadow-specified coronal (b), and both are distinct from a radically underspecified coronal (c).

For example, structures that are shadow-specified as coronal (i.e., alveolars that correspond to target velars) are specified to the same degree as other structures that are specified as labial, resulting in the contrastive specification of labials and erroneous alveolar substitutes. At the same time, however, labials and target-appropriate alveolars would not be contrastively specified, because the latter would be radically underspecified for place. The display in Fig. 7.3 illustrates the effect of contrastive specification that results from a specified labial (Fig. 7.3a) and a shadow-specified coronal corresponding to a target velar (Fig. 7.3b), and the three-way distinction that obtains between these two structures and a radically underspecified coronal (Fig. 7.3c). Similarly, stops that correspond to target fricatives would be shadow-specified as [–continuant] and would be contrastively specified relative to target-appropriate fricatives specified as [+continuant]. Such a situation arises in a system where the child produces /t/'s and /s/'s target-appropriately but substitutes [t] for target /θ/. As illustrated in Fig. 7.4, target-appropriate /t/'s would be radically underspecified for continuancy, [t]'s corresponding to /θ/ would be shadow-specified as [–continuant], and target-appropriate /s/'s would be specified as [+continuant].

It thus appears that a given phonological system, especially a developing system, can tolerate the coexistence of radical underspecification and contrastive specification. The fact then that fully developed languages present mixed results in this regard is somewhat less surprising. That is, it is conceivable that in the course of development where shadow-specification (and thus both radical underspecification and contrastive specification) is warranted, a subsequent change or elaboration of the system occurs. Two different changes are suggested. One type of change in the system shifts the shadow-specification to a different and phonetically distinct specification. For instance, a shadow-specified coronal changes to a specified dorsal, as seen in the change from (1) to (3). Such a change has the effect of increasing the number of phonetic categories or distinctions, although preserving the radically underspecified character of the default category. The change also

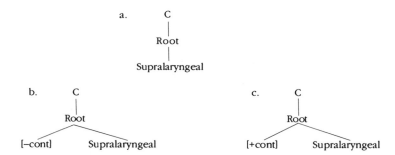

FIG. 7.4. Three-way distinction by means of shadow-specification: A segment radically underspecified for manner (a) is distinct from a segment shadow-specified for manner (b), which in turn is distinct from a segment specified for manner (c).

results in a phonetic distinction that corresponds in number and type with the phonological distinction. The other type of change seems more likely in the historical development of a language. That is, an underlying distinction between a shadow-specified representation and a radically underspecified representation is lost over time, resulting in a merger at both the underlying and the phonetic levels. If it is the radically underspecified category that is lost and the shadow-specified category that is retained, contrastive specification would result. Thus, what appear to be contradictory results from fully developed languages for the different underspecification frameworks can instead be seen as the natural consequence of the coexistence of radical underspecification and contrastive specification, which is created by shadow-specification and which is revealed most notably in developing systems.

2. CONTEXT-SENSITIVE RADICAL UNDERSPECIFICATION VERSUS CONTEXT-FREE RADICAL UNDERSPECIFICATION

There is another class of phenomena that is especially revealing in determining the type of (under)specification required for phonological disorders and for developing systems generally. These phenomena all involve, at one stage of a child's development, the complementary distribution of a pair of sounds that are phonemic (contrastive) in the target system (e.g., Camarata & Gandour, 1984; Gierut, 1986, 1989; Gierut, Cho, & Dinnsen, 1993; Smith, 1973; Williams & Dinnsen, 1987). For example, in English, [f] and [s] are phonemic, contrasting in place of articulation. However, Gierut (1986, 1989) reported a case of a speech disordered child, A. J. (age 4;11), who produced [f] and [s] as his only fricatives, with [f] occurring only in word-initial position and [s] occurring elsewhere. The pattern is illustrated in (4).

(4) A. J. (age 4;11), Pretreatment (from Gierut, 1986, 1989)

    a. [fes]   'face'
        [fu]   'food'
        [faɪn]   'vine'
        [fʌm]   'thumb'
        [fɛm]   'them'

    b. [wʊsi]   'wolf'
        [gusi]   'goofy'
        [tisi]   'TV'
        [wɪs]   'with'
        [gæsi]   'glassy'
        [ɑʊs]   'house'

These data reveal that [f] occurs word-initially for various target sounds (including both /f/ and /s/) and that [s] occurs postvocalically, also for a variety of target sounds (including both /f/ and /s/). Gierut's analysis, formulated in terms of standard generative theory, assumed fully specified matrices and thus represented all fricatives in terms of one phoneme, which was specified as [+coronal]. An allophonic rule was then proposed, which specified fricatives as [−coronal] in word-initial position.

Alternatively, in terms of general underspecification theory, these facts would be accounted for by underspecifying place of articulation for all fricatives, because place is noncontrastive and entirely predictable. The values for place would be filled in by a rule as follows: Fricatives are realized as labial in word-initial position and as coronal elsewhere. This account and this stage of development are straightforward, being equally compatible with either contrastive specification or radical underspecification.

The critical evidence relates, however, to how development proceeds from this stage. More specifically, if this child's system is to conform, ultimately, with the target system, a phonemic split must be effected. That is, the allophones [f] and [s], which are associated with a single phoneme, must reassociate with two different phonemes. In an effort to induce a phonemic split along these lines, Gierut provided minimal pair contrast treatment, teaching the child [f] postvocalically and [s] word-initially. Gierut reported moderate success in effecting the phonemic split. That is, following treatment, some untreated words were consistently realized with [s] word-initially and [f] postvocalically, as exemplified in (5).

(5) A. J. Posttreatment (Gierut, 1986, 1989)

    a. [sop]   'soap'
        [sɪp]   'ship'
        [sɛo]   'shell'
    b. [ifi]   'leafy'

[pæf]   'puff'
[lʌf]   'love'
c. [kɔs]   'cough'
[æsɪŋ]   'laughing'
[fus]   'truth'
[fæsɪŋ]   'splashing'

Although some words changed in this way, as shown in (5a) and (5b), the vast majority of words remained unchanged, as illustrated in (5c), preserving the earlier pattern of distribution with [f] in initial position and [s] postvocalically. The change was not across the board, as might have been expected, especially in view of our earlier discussion. Gradual diffusion of this sort through the lexicon is, however, not uncommon in the historical development of a language (e.g., Chen & Wang, 1975; Wang, 1969) or even in acquisition (e.g., Macken, 1992). Even though only a few words changed, technically a phonemic split was achieved. Both [f] and [s] were used contrastively in word-initial position and in postvocalic position after treatment, although not always appropriately. Accordingly, and as would be required in most frameworks, Gierut noted that the allophonic rule was no longer operative. All occurrences of [f]'s and [s]'s after treatment would then have to be specified for place of articulation as they appeared phonetically. This means, in the framework assuming fully specified matrices, that some fricatives would have had to change their underlying specification from [+coronal] to [−coronal] (i.e., Labial). This would, for example, include just those few cases where [s] changed to [f] postvocalically. But what is more important and, presumably, coincidental is that the many more occurrences of [f]'s in word-initial position that never changed phonetically would have had to change their underlying specification from [+coronal] to [−coronal]. This change in underlying specification where there is no change in the phonetic representation is required theoretically because the allophonic rule is no longer operative. On the other hand, because prior to treatment all fricatives were underlyingly specified as [+coronal], no change after treatment in the underlying specification would be necessary for any occurrence of [s], even though a phonetic change occurred in some items in word-initial position. Thus, the facts regarding phonetic change do not accord well with those regarding underlying change in a framework that assumes fully specified representations.

The characterization of these changes is equally problematic for a theory of contrastive specification. Because the contrastive specification of a feature is determined from the phonemic inventory, at the point at which the phonemic split was effected, all occurrences of [f] and [s] (whether correct or incorrect) would have had to change from being underspecified for Place to being contrastively specified. Thus, even though the phonetic changes did not occur across the board, in this framework all lexical items with fricatives would have had to change from being underspecified to being contrastively specified. These underlying changes would, however, not necessarily result in phonetic changes. Additionally, these underlying changes would result in a place specification for some (in fact, the majority of) fricatives that was not compatible with the facts of the target system. For example, the many phonetically unchanged (and incorrect) [f]'s in word-initial position that corresponded to target coronals would have had to be specified as labial after treatment. Likewise, the phonetically unchanged (and incorrect) [s]'s in postvocalic position that corresponded to target labials would have had to be specified as coronal. According to the Distinctive Feature Hypothesis, however, the contrastive specification of features in this way would contradict the acoustic facts of the target system and thus would be impossible. It appears, then, that the account required by a framework of contrastive specification is once again incompatible with the Distinctive Feature Hypothesis. The Distinctive Feature Hypothesis aside, under a contrastive specification framework it is purely accidental that fricatives changed underlyingly as they did. For example, why did an underspecified fricative in word-initial position change more often than not at the underlying level to a specification of labial? Similarly, why did an underspecified fricative in postvocalic position change more often than not to a specification of coronal? In other words, why did many items preserve the pattern of distribution that had been associated with the original allophonic rule?

An answer to these questions is offered within a framework of radical underspecification that allows what can be termed *context-sensitive radical underspecification* (e.g., Iverson, 1993; cf. Kiparsky, 1984, 1993). Consistent with the general requirements of radical underspecification theory, context-sensitive radical underspecification would allow only one value of a contrastive feature to be specified underlyingly, but only in a given context. This ultimately makes both values of a contrastive feature available for specification at the underlying level, but never in the same context. This seems to be precisely what is called for in the characterization of the changes in A. J.'s system. Recall that prior to any clinical treatment, A. J.'s fricatives were characterized as underspecified for place in all contexts and a fill-in rule supplied the feature labial in initial position and the feature coronal elsewhere. After treatment, a few words were consistently realized with [s] in word-initial position, as in (5a), and with [f] postvocalically, as in (5b). The majority of items remained unchanged and largely incorrect, as in (5c). What seems to be going on here is that just those items in (5a) changed from being underspecified to being specified as coronal. In addition, just those items in (5b) changed from being underspecified to being specified as labial. Finally, the items in (5c) (and, for that matter, all items that did not change phonetically) did not change underlyingly, remaining radically underspecified for place. The original fill-in rule that supplied default values for place to underspecified structures continued to operate on all these underspecified items. The rule was prevented from applying to those forms in (5a) and (5b) because they were specified for place. Thus, although both labial and coronal must be specified underlyingly for some words, both features are not being specified in the same contexts. The few cases where labial must be specified involve postvocalic position, and the few cases where coronal must be specified involve initial position. All other occurrences of labial and coronal fricatives are underspecified and derived by a fill-in rule.

Such an account is not possible within a framework of context-free radical underspecification, primarily because only one place feature can be radically underspecified. The phonemicization of /f/ and /s/ would require either labial or coronal to be specified underlyingly, but not both. Given the presumed default status of coronals, it would most likely be the labials that would be specified, with coronals being radically underspecified. The consequence would be that all labials in word-initial position that did not change after treatment would have had to change from being underspecified to being specified as labial. Just as with contrastive specification, this change would be purely accidental. No connection would be made between the occurrence of labials in initial position before treatment and their occurrence in that same position after treatment.

The characterization of sound change within a framework of context-sensitive radical underspecification ascribes minimal change to the system in accord with the minimal phonetic changes that occurred. What changed was the specification of a few lexical items in well-defined contexts in a way that preserved the radically underspecified character of representations. Additionally, the persistence both of underspecification for so many words and of the fill-in rule explains why so many items remained phonetically unchanged, even after treatment and after the phonemic split had been introduced. It might be expected that as time went on, A. J. would specify place for more and more words, resulting in phonetic changes for those words. As the number of words with specified place features increased, the applicability of the fill-in rule would correspondingly decrease, until some point where the rule would have no discernible function and would be lost. It is conceivable as well that, at the point when the rule was lost, the number of words specified either as labial or as coronal would be sufficiently large to warrant a further change. For example, the need to specify for so many words the feature coronal, a feature that is generally considered to be the default and to be radically underspecified, might be interpreted by the child as calling for contrastive specification. Under this scenario, all remaining structures underspecified for place would then have to change to a specified value. Alternatively, the high degree of specification might induce the system to restructure in order to eliminate all coronal specifications, yielding a simpler, context-free radically underspecified system.

3. CONCLUSION

In sum, the phenomena from disordered systems presented he
argued to require a modified framework of radical underspeci
modification allows shadow-specification as a means for d
phonetically identical segments that act differently in terms of
ceptual abilities, phonological rules, or developmental sound c
modification is possible only within a framework of radical un
tion. Shadow-specification, however, introduces a degree o
specification. This coexistence of radical underspecification an
specification in developing systems is offered as a possible ex
the seemingly conflicting evidence from fully developed langua
ing one or the other framework. The other modification allows context-sensitive radical underspecification as a means for explaining the lexical
diffusion of a particular sound change and the persistence of a phonological
generalization. Together, these phenomena reveal that contrastive specification is neither necessary nor sufficient for the characterization of developing systems. To the extent that contrastive specification is warranted for
fully developed languages, it may evolve from radical underspecification.
Developing sound systems, especially those affected by phonological disorders, provide crucial evidence in this regard and allow this evolution to
be observed.

ACKNOWLEDGMENTS

We are especially grateful to Judith Gierut and Gregory Iverson for their
many helpful comments on various aspects of this chapter and to Jessica
Barlow for her technical assistance. This work was supported in part by a
grant to Indiana University from the National Institutes of Health, DC00260.

CHAPTER EIGHT

Mora Conservation in Second Language Prosody

Ellen Broselow
SUNY at Stony Brook

Hye-Bae Park
Suwon University

Much work in language acquisition has focused on the contribution of innate, universal principles to the language learner's discovery of the structural constraints governing a particular target language. In a parameter-setting model of language acquisition, the first language learner's task is defined as discovering the appropriate settings of the linguistic parameters provided by Universal Grammar. Work such as that of Berwick (1985) and Wexler and Manzini (1987) has provided a model of first language acquisition as movement from an initial state, in which parameters are set at universally defined default values, to a state in which parameters have been reset to be consistent with target language data. The study of second language acquisition in a parameter-setting framework is complicated by the fact that second language learners may conceivably approach the target language either from the default parameter settings of Universal Grammar or from the parameter settings of their native language(s). Thus, any study of second language acquisition must contend with the potential influence of the native language, the target language, and Universal Grammar.

In this chapter, we argue that a particular pattern of second language pronunciation requires reference to all three factors. We present an analysis of vowel insertion in the pronunciation of English words by Korean speakers in which both the native and the target language settings for a given parameter are simultaneously active. We argue that the target language setting governs the analysis of target language forms, whereas the native language setting governs the production of these forms in the interlanguage. We also argue that this pattern reflects an attempt to conserve the moraic structure of the English words (as this structure is perceived by Korean learners); vowel insertion is therefore motivated by the universal principle of mora conservation (Hayes, 1989). We then examine vowel insertion patterns in the speech of Japanese learners and argue that those patterns provide additional evidence for what we call *split parameter setting*: a stage in which analysis of the target language is carried out according to the target language parameter setting, whereas production is still governed by the native language setting.

We begin, in section 1, with a presentation of the vowel epenthesis patterns attested in the speech of many Korean-speaking learners of English. We then argue that the pattern in question is not simply a result of an upper bound on syllable weight (section 1.2) but, rather, results from an attempt to conserve the moraic structure of English words. In section 2 we explore the implications of this analysis for theories of parameter setting in second language acquisition.

1. KOREAN EPENTHESIS

1.1. Data

We begin with a consideration of the Korean treatment of obstruent-final English words. Our data have two sources, the pronunciation of loanwords by Korean speakers, and the pronunciation by Korean students of English as a second language. The loanword examples are taken from Lee (1988) and Kwon and Kim (1990) (both published in Korean). Additional examples are taken from the second author's recording of five native speakers of Korean in intermediate ESL classes at SUNY Stony Brook.

The pattern we are concerned with involves epenthesis of [ɨ] word-finally. As the contrast between (1a) and (1b) illustrates, a vowel is typically inserted followed a syllable containing a long (or tense) vowel, but not following a short (or lax) vowel:[1]

(1) a. bitʰɨ   'beat'
      chipʰɨ   'cheap'
      phikʰɨ   'peak'
      rutʰɨ   'route'
      khotʰɨ   'coat'

---

[1]Thus, Lee (1988) gave the following rules for the adaptation of loanwords (second author's translation): "Do not add a vowel after a word-final voiceless stop when preceded by a short vowel (*book, chip*). . . . Otherwise, insert a vowel after a voiceless consonant (*cape, make*)."

    b. bit   'bit'
        tʰip   'tip'
        pʰik   'pick'
        gut   'good'
        buk   'book'

The English voiced stops are actually replaced by voiceless unaspirated stops in Korean, which has no phonemic voiced stops. However, for clarity of discussion, we use voiced stop symbols to represent the Korean speakers rendition of unaspirated voiced stops—for example, the symbol [b] for the initial sound in Korean speakers' pronunciation of words like *beat* (see Park, 1992, for details). Because voiceless stops are permitted syllable-finally in Korean, the vowel insertion pattern cannot be ascribed to constraints on possible segments in the syllable coda. Such constraints do, in fact, condition epenthesis after other segments that are not permitted in syllable-final position, as shown in (2):

    (2) bəsɨ   'bus'
        midɨ   'mid'

Although the forms in (2) contain short vowel nuclei, they still condition epenthesis, unlike the short-nucleus forms in (1b). The reason for the epenthesis in (2) rests not in the composition of the nucleus but, rather, in that of the coda: In these forms, [ɨ] is inserted after a fricative or a voiced obstruent, neither of which can occur in a Korean coda.

Note that the asymmetry between the forms in (1a) (forms with epenthesis) and (1b) (forms without epenthesis) cannot be attributed to constraints on possible codas, because the same stops occur word-finally in both (1a) and (1b). Nor can this epenthesis pattern be attributed to a constraint on minimal word size (for example, a bisyllabic minimum), because that would not distinguish forms in (1a) and (1b); furthermore, the same pattern is found in bisyllabic words, as shown in (3).

    (3) a. yunikʰɨ   'unique'
         difitʰɨ   'defeat'
       b. omit   'omit'
         gasip   'gossip'

Thus, it seems that the only factor distinguishing the forms in (1a) and (1b) is vowel length: A vowel is inserted after a syllable containing a long vowel but not after one containing a short vowel.

1.2. Analysis of the Korean Asymmetry

2.2.1. The Wrong Analysis: Avoidance of Trimoraic Syllables. Two
possible explanations of the relationship between vowel length and
epenthesis in the Korean data in (1) suggest themselves. The most obvious
explanation, which we outline and then reject, is that Korean prohibits
trimoraic syllables. Within moraic theory (Hayes, 1989; Hyman, 1985;
McCarthy & Prince, 1986), short vowels are associated with one mora, as in
(4a), whereas long vowels are bimoraic, as in (4b). In languages in which
CVC syllables pattern with CVV syllables, as opposed to light CV syllables,
coda consonants are also moraic, as in (4c):

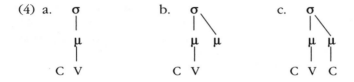

(4) a.   σ   b.   σ   c.   σ

(Onset consonants, which do not figure in syllable weight, are assumed to
attach directly either to the syllable node, or to the first vocalic mora; this
issue is irrelevant to our discussion.) In a language that assigns weight to
consonants in coda position, a syllable containing both a long vowel and
a following consonant (like *beat*) would be trimoraic (assuming no final
consonant extrametricality), as shown in (5):

(5)

Many languages rule out structures such as (5), often simplifying them
to bimoraic syllables by shortening the vowel (for example, Egyptian Arabic,
Broselow, 1992; Yawelmani Yokuts, Archangeli, 1991; Turkish, Clements &
Keyser, 1983). The Korean epenthesis pattern could provide an alternative
means of eliminating trimoraic syllables; in a word like *beat*, a vowel is
inserted, moving the final [t] to onset position, as in (6a).[2] For a word like
bit no such insertion is required, because the form contains no trimoraic
syllables, as shown in (6b):

---

[2]Several Arabic dialects employ epenthesis to eliminate trimoraic syllables (Broselow, 1992).

(6) a.

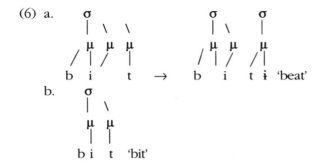

b.

There are several reasons to reject this analysis. First, the recorded forms revealed no perceptible difference in vowel length in the forms in (1a) and (1b). And second, it is not the case that a long vowel followed by a consonant always triggers vowel insertion. As the forms in (7b) illustrate, vowel insertion does not apply after a final sonorant consonant, even one preceded by a long vowel:

(7) a. bin   'bin'
       bin   'bean'
    b. sol   'soul'
       stim   'steam'

To account for the absence of vowel insertion in (7), as opposed to (1a), we would need to assume that although obstruent consonants in coda position are moraic, thereby rendering forms like *beat* trimoraic, sonorant consonants in coda position are not moraic, a contrast shown in (8):

(8) a.   beat   b.   bean

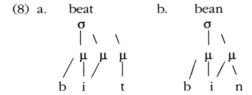

This contrast is not motivated by the facts of Korean. Although the existence of a vowel length distinction in Korean is controversial, it is clear that for dialects that employ long vowels, such vowels can occur before any tauto-syllabic consonant, whether obstruent or sonorant:

(9) a. sok   'sequel, continuation'
       sook   'inside'
    b. il   'one'
       iil   'work'

Thus the elimination of syllables containing long vowel followed by obstruent (but not sonorant) would have to be a feature of Korean speakers' pronunciation of English, but not of Korean. Such a feature cannot be proposed as an effect of universal constraints on syllable structure, because it runs directly contrary to common assumptions concerning the relationship between moraic value and sonority. Zec (1988) argued at length that although certain languages do permit only certain classes of consonants to be moraic in coda position, it is universally the more sonorous consonants that are moraic. Thus, a language may allow all coda consonants to be moraic; in terms of Hayes (1989), such a language employs the rule of Weight by Position, which assigns a mora to a coda consonant. Alternatively, a language may lack the Weight by Position rule, with the result that no coda consonants are moraic. But if a language distinguishes different consonant classes by allowing some consonant types to be mora-bearing in coda position and others to be nonmoraic in that position, it is always the more sonorous consonants that are moraic. We can schematize this distribution as in (10):

(10) *Coda consonant weight parameter settings:*
    a. All coda consonants are moraic (English, Latin, Arabic, Japanese).
    b. Some coda consonants are moraic. Where α = a consonant that may be moraic and β = a consonant that is never moraic, α is more sonorous than β. For instance, all nasals, liquids, and glides are moraic in coda position, but all obstruents are nonmoraic (Kwakwala, Korean).
    c. No coda consonants are moraic (Lardil, Mongolian, Huasteco).

The assumption that Korean speakers insert a vowel in *beat* but not in *bean* because the obstruent coda [t] is moraic whereas the nasal coda [n] is not moraic would violate Zec's otherwise well-supported generalization that if any consonant is moraic in coda position, then all more sonorous consonants are also moraic in that position.

And finally, an additional argument for rejecting the assumption that obstruent consonants are moraic in Korean, whereas sonorant consonants are nonmoraic, comes from the facts of Korean itself. As shown in (11), Korean has underlying geminate sonorants:

(11) innæ   'perseverance'   inæ   'immediately'
       sallim   'livelihood'   sarim   'literacy circles'
       əmma   'mother'   əma   'Dear me!'

Following McCarthy and Prince (1986) and Hayes (1989), we assume that the phonemic contrast between single consonants and geminates is represented as in (12); single consonants are underlyingly moraless, whereas geminates bear a mora in lexical representation:

(12) a. Single consonants   b. Geminates

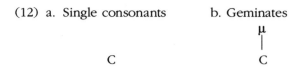

Then the surface representation in which a geminate is doubly linked, as in (13a), is derived by syllabification rules. These rules have two crucial components. First, moraic vowels are assigned to a syllable node. Any postvocalic consonantal mora is also assigned to the syllable dominating the preceding vowel, as in the second step of (13a). Next, any prevocalic consonant is attached to the onset of the following syllable, as in the third steps of (13a) and (13b):

(13) a. innæ

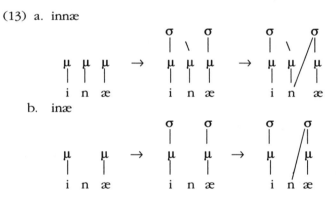

   b. inæ

Geminates, being underlyingly moraic, are linked to both the coda of the preceding syllable and the onset of a following syllable, whereas single consonants before a vowel are linked only to onset position. Thus, because the contrast between single and geminate sonorants is contrastive in Korean, moraic sonorants must be permitted.[3]

As far as obstruents are concerned, we argue that there are no underlying geminate obstruents in Korean. Although it has been claimed (Kim, 1986) that Korean tense stops [p', t', k'] are underlyingly geminate, we reject this claim for the following reason. The distribution of tense stops in Korean differs from the distribution of geminate sonorants: Although geminate sonorants occur only intervocalically, tense stops may occur syllable-initially as well, as shown in (14):

(14) a. k'æ   'sesame'
       t'o   'again'
       p'aŋ   'bread'

---

[3]However, see Selkirk (1990) for an alternative representation of geminate consonants; see Broselow (in press) for an overview of issues concerning representation of geminates.

b. sunk'æ   'pure sesame'
   səkp'aŋ   'release'
   k'olc'i   'the last in a race'

If both sonorant and obstruent consonants may be geminates, there is no explanation for the different restrictions on their distribution. Furthermore, as Hayes (1989) pointed out, the analysis of geminate consonants as consonants linked to two different syllable positions, a moraic coda slot and the onset of a following syllable, predicts that true geminates should occur only in intervocalic position, not in syllable-initial position. Therefore, Korean appears to conform to Zec's generalization: The consonants that can be moraic are the more sonorous ones.

We therefore reject the analysis of the vowel insertion asymmetry in (1) as resulting from a Korean constraint against trimoraic syllables, where word-final obstruents are moraic. We argue instead that this pattern results from the universal principle of mora conservation.

1.2.2. The Right Analysis: Mora Conservation. The analysis we assume of the vowel insertion facts illustrated in (1) is that Korean learners at a certain stage of proficiency learn to recognize a difference in the moraic structure of English long and short vowels. However, the absence of a vowel length distinction in their own dialect prevents them from realizing this difference on the syllable nucleus. Therefore, they preserve the distinction between English monomoraic short vowels, as in *bit*, and bimoraic long vowels, as in *beat*, by producing vowels of the same length, but by adding an additional monomoraic syllable to the English bimoraic form. (15a) shows the lexical representation assigned to *bit* by Korean speakers. The monomoraic vocalic nucleus is assigned to a syllable node, as shown in (15b), and the prevocalic consonant is assigned to syllable onset, as in (15c). The final consonant is then adjoined to the preceding mora, as in (15d). We assume that Korean coda obstruents are nonmoraic, because no grammatical processes of Korean appear to distinguish CV syllables from CVC syllables.

(15) bit

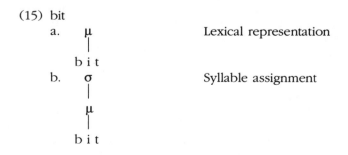

a.   μ   Lexical representation

     b i t

b.   σ   Syllable assignment

     μ

     b i t

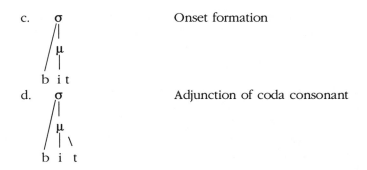

c.   Onset formation

d.   Adjunction of coda consonant

The structure in (15d) is completely well formed according to Korean syllable structure constraints. Assuming that Korean speakers take (15a) as the lexical representation for the English form, (15d) also preserves the underlying moraic structure of the English word. Therefore, epenthesis is motivated neither by the imperative to create well-formed Korean syllables nor by the imperative to preserve the underlying moraic structure of the English form.

The forms in (1a), such as *beat*, have a somewhat different derivation. To account for these forms, we must begin by examining the role of vowel length in Korean. Although many researchers have assumed that Korean employs a vowel length distinction (for example, Kim-Renaud, 1974), Moon (1981) argued that even though some vowels are relatively long, they do not differentiate meaning in speech—that is, that vowel length is not contrastive. And Magen and Blumstein (1991) argued that contrastive vowel length is being lost as a feature of Korean, particularly among younger speakers. The second author's questioning of speakers of her generation revealed that although speakers have been taught in school that certain forms have long vowels, most do not actually produce or even hear a vowel length distinction in these forms. We assume, then, that for speakers who produce the pattern in (1), vowel length is no longer phonemic in Korean; we may represent their grammar as employing setting (a) on the following parameter:

(16) *Nucleus weight parameter:*
    a. Syllable nuclei are maximally monomoraic (Korean).
    b. Syllable nuclei are either monomoraic or bimoraic (English).

This assumption now allows us to account for the vowel epenthesis asymmetries in Korean interlanguage, given the following assumptions: (a) Although Korean speakers do not produce a vowel length distinction in native vocabulary, they nevertheless recognize the difference between *beat* and *bit*, for instance, as a difference in vowel length, or moraic structure; and (b) Korean speakers attempt to preserve the perceived moraic structure of the English words.

To see the implications of these assumptions, we can trace the derivation of the surface form of *beat*. (17a) shows the lexical representation of the English form assigned by Korean learners. Because vowel nuclei are limited to a single mora in Korean, the two vocalic morae of (17a) cannot be assigned to a single syllable node, so one mora is delinked from the vowel, as in (17b). This stranded mora is then assigned to a separate syllable node and its nucleus filled by epenthesis, as in (17c). It surfaces as (17d), a structure that has the same number of morae as the underlying representation in (17a). However, although the English surface form is a bimoraic mono-syllable, the Korean interlanguage surface form is composed of two mono-moraic syllables.

(17) beat

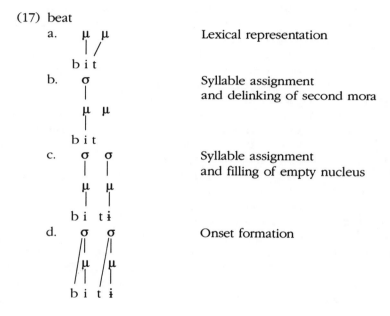

a. Lexical representation

b. Syllable assignment
    and delinking of second mora

c. Syllable assignment
    and filling of empty nucleus

d. Onset formation

Epenthesis of this type is regarded as a result of the Mora Conservation Law given in (18).

(18) *Moraic Conservation* (Hayes, 1989):
Mora count tends to be preserved.

This Korean epenthesis pattern is reminiscent of Hayes' (1989) analysis of compensatory lengthening in Middle English. In Middle English, a stressed penult in an open syllable lengthened just in case a word-final schwa was dropped, as in (19). (19a) shows the structure before schwa drop. The loss of schwa in (19b) leaves a stray mora. Parasitic Delinking, in (19c), deletes syllable structure from syllables whose nuclei are empty. The stray mora is then filled by spreading the vowel melody, as in (19d):

(19) talə > taːl (Modern English 'tale')

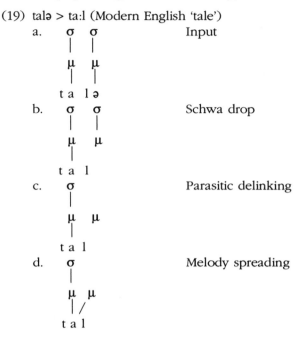

Korean interlanguage epenthesis is the converse of Middle English vowel loss followed by vowel lengthening; the Korean case results from vowel shortening and vowel insertion. Like the Middle English case, the Korean epenthesis is a mechanism to maintain mora count: Speakers hear syllable weights, and they attempt to keep the mora count constant. Because long vowels are not possible segments in Korean, a vowel cannot be linked to two morae. The stray mora cannot be linked to the coda obstruent, because obstruents are nonmoraic. Therefore, the unaffiliated mora is filled by epenthesis to preserve the mora count.

Recall now that epenthesis does not occur after a sonorant, whether the preceding vowel is long or short. For example, the English word *bean* is pronounced not as [biniɨ] but as [bin]. Thus, this pattern suggests that sonorants have a special status in the L2 phonology of Korean speakers. We can explain this by assuming that sonorant consonants, unlike obstruents, can be moraic. This assumption was supported by the occurrence of underlying geminate sonorants, illustrated in (11). We assume that the underlying representation of *bean* is interpreted as in (20a) by Korean learners. As discussed earlier, one mora is delinked because Korean does not allow long vowels, giving the form in (20b). Then, because *n* can be moraic in Korean, *n* is associated with the stray mora, as in (20c).

(20) a.

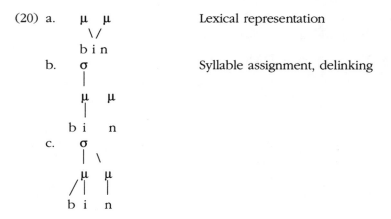

As a result, there is no epenthesis, because the resulting structure both conforms to Korean syllable structure constraints and preserves the underlying mora count.

The assumption that Korean syllable nuclei may not be bimoraic is further supported by the treatment of heterorganic diphthongs in English. As shown in (21), these forms also trigger epenthesis:

(21) a. pʰaipʰɨ   'pipe'
     b. leikɨ   'lake'
     c. pʰolaitʰɨ 'polite'
     d. iskʰeipʰɨ 'escape'

We therefore assume that when Korean speakers identify such diphthongs as bimoraic in English, the constraint against bimoraic nuclei forces them to associate both portions of the diphthong to a single mora. The derivation of the Korean interlanguage pronunciation of *lake* would then be as in (22):

(22) lake

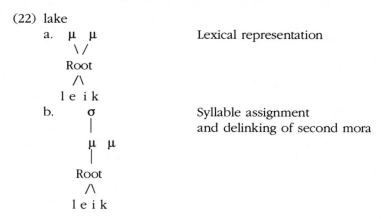

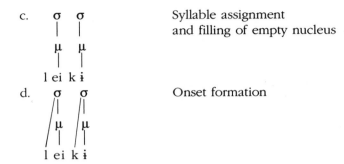

c.   Syllable assignment
     and filling of empty nucleus

d.   Onset formation

The assumption that syllable nuclei, even those containing a sequence of vocalic units, must be monomoraic has consequences for Korean phonology as well. In Korean, the distinction between glides and vowels is unpredictable, as illustrated in (23).

(23) a. iəŋ   'straw thatch'
        yəŋ   'zero'
     b. kiul   'bran'
        kyul   'tangerine'
     c. nui   'sister'
        nwi   'who'

The first member of each pair in (23) has a two-vowel sequence, whereas the second member has a sequence of glide followed by vowel. Following Hayes (1989), we assume that glides have no moraic specification underlyingly, in contrast to vowels. The underlying representations in (24a) will therefore serve to distinguish forms such as *kiul* 'bran' and *kyul* 'tangerine'. Because both vocalic portions of *kiul* are moraic, the prohibition on bimoraic syllable nuclei in Korean prevents them from being assigned to a single syllable, so they are assigned to separate syllables, as shown in (24b). For *kyul*, however, [i] can be assigned to the syllable onset.

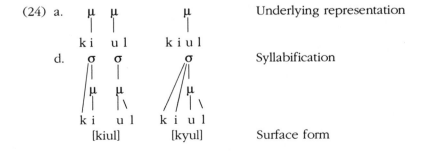

(24) a.   Underlying representation

d.   Syllabification

[kiul]   [kyul]   Surface form

Therefore, the assumption that Korean maintains a monomoraic limit on syllable nuclei is consistent with the facts of both the interlanguage and the native language.

2. SPLIT PARAMETER SETTING

2.1. Korean Epenthesis

We have argued that the Korean epenthesis asymmetry illustrated in (1) is motivated by the recognition that the English forms in (1a) have a bimoraic syllable nucleus, whereas the forms in (1b) have a monomoraic syllable nucleus. Korean speakers are prevented by their own grammar from producing bimoraic syllable nuclei and so choose an alternative route to conserving this difference in moraic structure—namely, insertion of a vowel to produce bimoraic forms.

We now examine this scenario in terms of what it might tell us about parameter setting in second language acquisition. The differences between the English and Korean parameter settings required to account for the production of the Korean learners' forms are set out in (25).

(25)   Korean   English
    a. Coda C weight parameter: μ   μ
                                               │   │
                                            Son   any C

    b. Nucleus weight parameter: μ   μ, μμ

We first consider the settings in (25a) for the coda consonant weight parameter. Recall that in order to explain the presence of sonorant, but not obstruent, geminates in Korean, we assumed that Korean allows sonorant consonants to be moraic in the syllable coda, whereas obstruent consonants are adjoined to the mora of the preceding vowel. The fact that Korean learners tend not to epenthesize a vowel after a sonorant consonant, even when that consonant is preceded by a long vowel, suggests that the native language setting of this parameter is maintained in their interlanguage grammar:

(26) Korean interlanguage
     Coda C weight parameter:

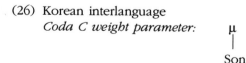

It is not surprising that these speakers do not seem to have reset the coda consonant weight parameter to the English setting, because the evidence for the weight of English coda consonants is fairly subtle. For example, there are numerous surface exceptions to a general pattern of stressing closed syllables in stress-bearing positions (for example, the unstressed penultimate syllable in *calendar* alongside the stressed penult in *agenda*).

The Korean interlanguage setting for the syllable nucleus weight parameter in (25b) is more complex and more interesting. In order for the mora conservation analysis sketched here to work, we assumed both that Korean speakers recognized that English has a contrast between monomoraic short vowel nuclei and bimoraic long vowel nuclei, and that Korean speakers cannot produce bimoraic nuclei but instead insert an additional vowel to preserve a bimoraic pattern. This analysis is therefore not compatible with either the English or the Korean parameter settings for the nucleus weight parameter. We therefore need to assume two different parameter settings, one controlling perception and one controlling production. That is, Korean learners at an intermediate stage recognize that bimoraic nuclei represent a possible option for languages, and that English employs this option: Therefore, they recognize that English sets the nucleus weight parameter to allow bimoraic nuclei. Their own production, however, is controlled by the original Korean setting—they still cannot produce bimoraic nuclei. Note that this is not a simple matter of trying to produce such nuclei but failing to master the production at the level of phonetic implementation. The vowel insertion facts suggest that the Korean speakers are apparently not even trying to produce bimoraic nuclei in the English forms; instead they choose an alternate means—vowel insertion—to preserve the monomoraic/bimoraic distinction:

(27) Korean Interlanguage
Nucleus weight parameter:
perception: μ, $\mu\mu$
production: μ

This analysis suggests a progression in the resetting of phonological parameters: Speakers may go through a stage in which both the native language (NL) and the target language (TL) parameter settings are in some sense active in their interlanguage grammars. The target language parameter settings may control perception and analysis of target language forms, whereas production of interlanguage equivalents is still governed by native language parameter settings. We may describe this progression as in (28):

(28) *Progression of parameter setting:*
Stage 1: NL setting governs perception and production.
Stage 2: TL setting governs perception; NL setting governs production.
Stage 3: TL setting governs production and perception.

Evidence for Stage 1 in Korean interlanguage comes from examination of the production of beginning learners. Such learners are often described as inserting a vowel after any final stop; this is probably due to the interpretation of stop release as vowel insertion. What beginning Korean-speaking learners of English typically do not do is distinguish forms like *bit* and *beat*; vowel insertion applies with the same frequency to both sorts of forms.

2.2. Japanese Epenthesis

Some potential independent support for a stage in which perception and production of interlanguage forms are governed by different parameter settings can be found in the facts of vowel epenthesis among Japanese learners of English. Vowel length also has an impact on the alteration of the L2 syllable by Japanese speakers, though the patterns are quite different from those shown by Korean speakers. In the interlanguage of Japanese speakers at a beginner/intermediate level as well as in the pronunciation of loanwords in Japanese (Lovins, 1975; Otake, 1983), epenthesis is mandatory after a syllable-final obstruent. This epenthesis is motivated by syllable structure constraints: Japanese syllables cannot end in obstruents unless the obstruent is the initial part of a heterosyllabic geminate. Thus, a vowel must be inserted after a word-final obstruent regardless of the length of the preceding vowel, as shown in (29):

(29) a. suteppu   'step'
        katto   'cut'
        setto   'set'
        kikku   'kick'
     b. kooto   'coat'
        reeku   'lake'
        biito   'beat'
        ruuto   'route'

Note that Japanese learners do produce a difference in vowel length that mirrors the English difference; this is as expected, because Japanese employs the same setting of the nucleus weight parameter as English, allowing a contrast between long and short vowels.

However, the forms in (29) illustrate that although vowel length is not related to vowel insertion, it does seem to be related to gemination of the syllable-final consonants: Final consonants are geminated when they follow short vowels, as in (29a). On the other hand, consonants following tense (long) vowels or diphthongs do not geminate, as shown in (29b).

We briefly sketch one possible analysis of these facts that relates them to different settings of the parameter governing the composition of syllable codas in Japanese and English (but see Park, 1992, for an alternative analysis). Coda consonants in Japanese syllables are limited to a nasal or the first part of a geminate. In other words, the coda licenses obstruents only if they are doubly linked (Itô, 1986). We could therefore describe the differences between Japanese and English in terms of (30):

(30) *Obstruent coda parameter:*

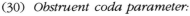
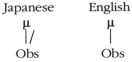

Japanese   English

μ   μ

Obs   Obs

Let us assume that at some stage Japanese speakers recognize that English allows even obstruent codas that are not doubly linked—that is, they perceive a word like *bit* as having the structure shown under the English setting in (30). However, they still prefer to produce such a syllable-final obstruent in accord with the Japanese setting in (30), in which the obstruent is the first part of a geminate cluster. They therefore choose (31a) over (31b) as the pronunciation of *bit*, even though (31b) also satisfies the syllable structure constraints of Japanese:

(31) a. 'bit'   bitto
    b.   *bito
    c. 'beat' *biitto
    d.   biito

Note that (31b) preserves the mora count of the bimoraic English form, whereas (31a) involves addition of a third mora; the principle of mora conservation prevents mora loss but not mora addition. (31c), which also preserves the moraic status of *t*, is presumably ruled out in favor of (31d) because trimoraic syllables like *biit* are generally disfavored in Japanese; they are produced only by certain morphological processes (Itô, 1986; Lovins, 1975). In the terms of Optimality Theory (Prince & Smolensky, 1993), we can assume that the set of constraints governing the surface forms of Japanese includes a constraint against trimoraic syllables. This constraint may be violated if its violation represents the only way to satisfy other, more highly ranked constraints of the language. But in this case, there is no need to violate the constraint against trimoraic syllables, because (31d) satisfies all the relevant constraints.

This account of Japanese is consistent with the postulation of a stage of development of language proficiency in which the target language parameter setting governs perception, while production is still governed by the native language parameter setting. If this account is correct, we would expect speakers of any language with Japanese-type restrictions on coda obstruents to geminate these obstruents in English words, syllable structure constraints permitting.

3. CONCLUSION

We have argued, first, that mora conservation—a resistance to the loss of morae—plays a role in second language acquisition, specifically in explaining vowel insertion in Korean interlanguage forms. This analysis in turn suggests that language learners proceed through a stage in which the native and the target language parameter settings are simultaneously active, with target language settings used for analysis of target language forms, and native language settings used in production: a stage we have called split parameter setting. The account of parameter resetting in second language acquisition presented here is one in which learners begin with the settings of their native language and then proceed through some intermediate stage to the target language setting; in this intermediate stage, their grammar differs from the grammars of speakers of both the native and the target languages. The evidence presented here thus contributes to the growing body of evidence that second language learners tend to start from the parameter settings of their native language (see, for example, White, 1985) and proceed through parameter settings somewhere between the settings of the native and the target languages (see Broselow & Finer, 1991, for this effect in the resetting of multivalued parameters in both phonology and syntax). This work suggests, then, that any understanding of the patterns of second language acquisition must take into account the grammars of both the native and the target language as well as the principles and constraints of Universal Grammar.

CHAPTER NINE

Differentiation, Recognition, and Identification in the Discrimination of Foreign Accents

Thomas Scovel
San Francisco State University

For more than three decades, second language acquisition researchers have been interested in investigating the possibility that children enjoy an innate ability to acquire languages more easily and accurately than adults. Penfield (1963) was the first to publish and popularize this notion; but the idea of a critical period for second language acquisition was most effectively promulgated by Lenneberg (1967), who suggested that there were biological foundations for this inherent superiority of children over adolescents and adults. Since the publication of Lenneberg's work, there have been many studies undertaken that suggest that the critical period for language acquisition is most clearly linked to the emergence of foreign accents at about puberty. Second language acquisition researchers have been able to document the unusual but consistent ability of native speakers to rapidly and accurately identify nonnative speech. Larew (1961), Scovel (1969), Asher and Garcia (1969), Seliger, Krashen, and Ladefoged (1975), and Oyama (1976) all have confirmed that native speakers of a variety of languages (e.g., Spanish, English, and Hebrew) can recognize nonnative speakers of these languages who acquired their second languages after childhood. These early studies continue to be supported by more recent investigations (Levitt, 1992; Major, 1987; Mendes-Figueiredo, 1991; Tahta, Wood, & Lowenthal, 1981; Thompson, 1991), leading one of the most prominent researchers in the field, Long (1990), to argue strongly for the existence of maturational constraints in language learning, not only for phonology but perhaps for morphology and syntax as well. Because there are only a few studies that

169

suggest that the acquisition of morphology and/or syntax in a second language may be adversely affected by increasing age (Coppieters, 1987; Johnson & Newport, 1991; Patkowski, 1980), and because there seems to be contradictory evidence against age constraints on these nonphonological aspects of second language acquisition (Ioup, 1984; Morris & Gerstman, 1986), my own review of the research leads to me to the more traditional and limited claim that there is a critical period for speech, but not for any other aspects of second language acquisition (Scovel, 1988).

With few exceptions then, most researchers believe in the existence of some form of limitation on the ability to sound like a native speaker if a second language is acquired after puberty. Having accepted this, we are now ready to mull over issues that go beyond the question of the existence of a critical period for second language acquisition. The focus of this chapter then is on one such issue—the criteria used by native speakers to identify nonnative speech. If the identification of foreign accent is a relatively straightforward and ubiquitous ability, as the research cited here tends to suggest, what criteria do native speakers use to ferret out nonnative accents so readily? This very broad and general question can be addressed in terms of the three sequential stages that I have adopted for consideration here:

1. *Differentiation:* How do native speakers differentiate among the many acoustic and phonetic features in the speech of a voice they have just heard and, despite the quick and dirty data, almost immediately hone in on the seemingly insignificant cues that can be used for effective accent recognition?

2. *Recognition:* How do native speakers use the paralinguistic and phonetic information about the voice they are hearing to recognize whether or not that voice contains nonnative features of speech?

3. *Identification:* Finally, which are the most important phonological clues in identifying nonnative speakers, mistakes using segmental sounds (e.g., using /i/ instead of /ɪ/), or mistakes employing suprasegmentals or prosodic features (e.g., putting primary stress on the wrong syllable in a word)?

1. DIFFERENTIATION

Linguists, speech scientists, and language teachers are quick to ignore the enormous task that listeners face in screening out irrelevant acoustic information; they usually begin their discussion of listening comprehension by discussing the role of linguistic input and how or if that input begets intake. But by basing their models of how people listen to speech on the process of speech comprehension, they preclude any serious consideration of the equally complex activities of speech differentiation, recognition, and identification. That is, among all the environmental sounds that inundate the human ear during most conversations, how is it possible for people to hone in on, become aware of, and attend to the sound of a human voice (often the voice of one particular individual among several) amid all the competing sounds bombarding the ear—sometimes even sounds with higher amplitudes than the voice being attended to? And after a individual voice has been selected, what acoustic information does a listener choose to reach the rapid but difficult decision about whether or not the voice being listened to is that of a native speaker of the listener's mother tongue?

This initial question of speech differentiation was of great interest to experimentalists in the early years of cognitive psychology, and research by Cherry (1953) and Broadbent (1958) provided some initial answers to the problem of how the human ear could differentiate a particular sound from many. Cherry's work demonstrated that subjects could attend to an individual voice while ignoring equally loud conversations going on simultaneously. This famous "cocktail party" phenomenon led Broadbent to develop his filter metaphor of human attention. Subsequent research and models of selective attention in perception and communication were reviewed by Hilgard (1987) in his historical summary of cognitive psychology. More recently, Schmidt (1990, 1992) provided an excellent discussion of competing psychological models of attention, consciousness, and learning and addressed their relevance to the field of second language acquisition.

Along with the ability to recognize the voice of a specific individual, often in the midst of competing acoustic signals, humans have the ability to recognize certain permanent characteristics of the voices they hear such as those indicating the sex of the speakers (Coleman, 1971), and their age (Ptacek & Sander, 1966). But listeners can also differentiate certain temporary features of these voices as well. For example, Tartter (1980) showed that people can use acoustic information alone in recognizing whether or not speakers are smiling while they are talking. Although these differentiation abilities may seem quite extraordinary at first glance, they each have fairly straightforward acoustic explanations. Identification of sex is largely dependent on the size of the larynx and the vocal tract; because males generally have larger and longer vocal tracts and larger larynxes, their fundamental frequencies tend to be lower (MacKay, 1987). Identification of age depends largely on the physical characteristics of the resonating material because age has a direct effect on the resonance of the larynx and vocal tract. Finally, a temporary feature such as whether or not the speaker is smiling while talking over the telephone depends on the length of the resonating chamber. Because smiling shortens the vocal tract, it is possible for a listener to detect the acoustic consequences of this shortening and assume that the speaker is smiling during a certain span of speech.

This research on the ability of listeners to use acoustic signals from the human voice to differentiate among important identifying features of speakers has even been used (or, more accurately, abused) by various commercial enterprises to market voice detectors to monitor phone calls and to warn business people if their interlocutor is lying during a telephone negotiation! This, of course, is an extreme and unsubstantiated example of the differentiation abilities of the human ear, but it serves to underscore the amazing capacity humans have for making quick and generally accurate judgments about the voices they are attending to, based on relatively sparse and often noisy acoustic information.

Among these differentiation judgments then, is the almost uncanny ability of listeners to recognize whether or not the voice belongs to a native speaker of the their mother tongue. That is, at the same time listeners are making judgments about features like the speaker's age and sex, they are also able to select acoustic cues that can be used to detect whether or not the voice is that of a native speaker. Obviously, the acoustic cues the listener hones in on for this decision are different from the acoustic information just discussed that is used to identify a speaker's sex, age, or degree of smiling. Judgments about foreign accents are made irrespective of the sex, age, or friendliness of the voice being attended to, so the acoustic information a listener selects to ascertain if the speaker has a foreign accent cannot depend on such permanent features as the size of the larynx, the length of the vocal tract, and the physical effects of age on the resonating material of the vocal tract. Nor can it depend on such temporary features as the brief shortening of the vocal tract when the speaker is smiling. It seems evident, therefore, that after these initial differentiation judgments are made, the listener enters a second stage of discrimination and starts to use other acoustic cues that enable the listener to recognize native or nonnative features of the speaker's voice. It is at this second stage that listeners begin to focus in on characteristics of the language being spoken. Specifically, they begin to use acoustic information based on phonetic features to help them make judgments about whether or not the voice belongs to a native speaker.

2. RECOGNITION

What I am calling recognition depends on the more narrow attention of the listener to acoustic cues that are phonetic—sounds that are used as speech signals in human language. This means that after listeners have attended to all the myriad acoustic cues that deal with the differentiation of sounds at the first stage of categorizing human voices, they more selectively attend to sounds that contain linguistic information. There is a rich body of research that shows that humans are innately endowed with this ability to attend to phonetic information, even in very early childhood. Neonatal experiments on high amplitude sucking responses (Morse, 1972), heart rate deceleration (Morse, 1974), and auditorily evoked potentials in the left hemisphere (Molfese, Freeman, & Palermo, 1975), have all shown that young infants have an innate interest in phonetic sounds and contrasts, such as the difference between voiced and voiceless stops, in comparison to nonphonetic environmental sounds. These experiments suggest that humans are not just good at going beyond the differentiation of acoustic stimuli to recognize phonetic stimuli, they are virtually incapable of ignoring phonetic sounds in their environment.

I believe it is useful to divide the phonetic information being processed at this stage into two different categories: phonetic information that is largely paralinguistic in nature (using fundamental pitch, amplitude, voice setting, etc.) and phonetic information that is basically linguistic in nature (using vowel length, voice onset timing, formant frequencies, etc.). Because the first set of phonetic features is closely related to the set of acoustic features that listeners use to make recognition judgments in Stage 1, I discuss these features first and then proceed to a description of the phonetic features that are purely linguistic in nature. Note that this implies, not surprisingly, that there are no abrupt transitions from one stage of listening to another. In addition, because these listening tasks gradually become more and more discriminatory, there is a general progression from low level processing at the beginning stage to high level processing at the more advanced stage. In other words, differentiation involves simpler, broader, and more direct cognitive processing than recognition, and identification demands the narrowest and most complex and indirect cognitive processing of all.

What are the paralinguistic features of speech that are quasi-phonetic and that play a role during the initial stages of recognition of foreign accents? Esling and Wong (1982) discussed characteristics of *voice setting*, associated with certain types of speakers. For example, nasality is used to categorize one speaker as American, or retroflection is used to categorize another as Indian. In my own studies of the ability of native speakers to identify nonnative speakers easily and accurately after listening to only brief samples of speech, I have found some indirect evidence that voice setting may play a role in identifying nonnative speech (Scovel, 1981). The vast majority of the native speakers of American English who served as my judges were able to distinguish correctly between the taped voices of native speakers and those of nonnative speakers more than 95% of the time, even though they heard only a few seconds of speech. On the tape these judges listened to, I had interspersed the voices of 10 speakers of American English with the voices of 10 people who were not native speakers of American English—in fact, the majority of the latter were native speakers of non-English languages (e.g., Arabic, Swedish, Chinese, Romanian). It was of interest that of these

10 nonnative speakers, the person who was almost never identified as a native speaker of American English was a native speaker of South African Indian English. It appeared that the paralinguistic feature of retroflection (especially in his retroflected stops) was such a salient phonetic aspect of his pronunciation and was so clearly not a paralinguistic feature of American English that it served as an immediate signal to the judges that this person was a nonnative. Here is a clear example of voice setting being used in accent recognition.

Slightly less obvious but also indicative, I believe, was the opposite type of evidence, a false positive—the nonnative speaker who was most frequently misidentified by the subjects as a speaker of American English. I had assumed that the few non-Americans who were occasionally misidentified by the judges would be speakers of non-American dialects of English or speakers of Indo-European languages closely related to English. It can already be seen that this presupposition was not supported by the data; the speaker of South African Indian English, even though a native speaker of a dialect of English, was clearly the easiest to identify as a non-American, probably because of the aforementioned paralinguistic feature of heavily retroflected stops. Further corroboration that my presupposition was untenable lay in the fact that the nonnative speaker who received the highest number of false positives spoke Arabic as his mother tongue! Again, I believe that paralinguistic features played a role in this misjudgment. The Arabic speaker had an unusually low voice and because of previous experience in broadcasting, performed very comfortably and capably in the audio laboratory where the tapes were made. It appeared to me that once again, paralinguistic features influenced the recognition task that the judges were asked to make. If they did not have enough phonetic or phonological evidence on which to make a decision about the speaker's native tongue, paralinguistic features either masked or influenced the judges' decisions about whether or not the voice they heard was accented.

A final example of how paralinguistic features may influence this recognition ability is found in the other type of errors the judges in my experiments made. On rare occasions, the judges would select a false negative; that is, they sometimes classified 1 of the 10 native speakers of American English as a speaker with a foreign accent. The native speaker who was most often misidentified as a nonnative speaker was the slowest and most deliberate speaker of the 20 taped voices on the identification tape. Again, it seemed to me that voice setting, in this case the speaker's slow and almost overly precise pronunciation, sometimes misled the judges to conclude that the voice did not belong to a native speaker. In all of these examples, it is instructive to remember that the great majority of the time (about 97%), the speakers of American English who served as judges were able to recognize quickly which of the 20 speakers were, like them, speakers of American

English and which spoke with a foreign accent. That is, the evidence was irrefutable that native speakers could discriminate between native and nonnative voices with statistically significant accuracy, even after listening to the voice on the tape for only a few seconds. Nevertheless, when mistakes were made in recognition, it seemed that paralinguistic features of voice setting played an important role in disrupting the normal ability to make accurate judgments.

In addition to these phonetic features, which are paralinguistic in nature, there also seem to be phonetic features used at this recognition stage that play a more direct, linguistic role in the recognition of foreign accents. I did not examine this use of phonetic information in my own research on accent recognition, but several other investigators have found evidence that phonetic evidence is useful in recognizing nonnative speech. Marks (1980) asked native speakers to assess which phonetic cues were most reliable in helping them recognize nonnative speech, and he concluded from his data that vowel sounds were more effective indicators of accented speech than consonant sounds. This conclusion is not surprising, because vowel sounds provide much more phonetic information than consonants: They are always longer and usually of higher amplitude, they frequently are marked by syllabic stress, and because they are always voiced and are syllabic, they carry the fundamental frequency of the voice and thus contain a great deal of prosodic (suprasegmental) information as well. In fact, given all of these reasons, it is not unreasonable to speculate that at this recognition stage, native speakers use phonetic information from the vowels they hear, because it is so salient and so telling, as the most important criterion in judging whether or not the voice they are listening to belongs to a native speaker of their mother tongue. From this position, it is natural to progress to the third and final stage where native speakers use phonological information from their knowledge of the phonemic structure of the vowels, consonants, and prosodic features of their mother tongue to identify native or nonnative speech.

3. IDENTIFICATION

At this final third stage, native speakers assess the linguistic information they glean from the voices they are attending to, vis-à-vis the phonological knowledge they possess about their mother tongue, to identify whether or not the voices belong to nonnative speakers. Depending on the linguistic experience of the listeners, they are also able to identify the native language of the accented voices. For example, many Americans can identify the voices of strangers seated in an airplane behind them not only as nonnative speakers of English, but as native speakers of Japanese or French. This third stage of discrimination is the narrowest and probably most complex cognitively, because it involves comparisons with the phonological structure of the listener's mother tongue, and it may also involve the listener's overall experience listening to English being spoken by native speakers of a variety of other languages. This phonological information is traditionally divided into two categories: segmental (vowels and consonants) and prosodic or suprasegmental (stress, rhythm, and intonation).

We have already seen that general, phonetic information about vowels is used by listeners to recognize nonnative speech, and there is additional research at the phonological level indicating that phonological or phonemic information about the vowels of the listener's mother tongue is very useful in identifying foreign accents. Encouraged by earlier research by Flege and Eefting (1987), Major (1987) examined the pronunciation of a discrete set of English phonemes by 53 adult Brazilian Portuguese speakers of English. Seven native speakers of American English were used as controls, and tapes of the pronunciation of English phoneme contrasts by the 60 speakers were played to 10 judges who were native speakers of American English. The judges were asked to rate the degree of nativeness of these phonemic contrasts on a scale that was broad enough to represent scores from 0 to 256. Using this scale, the judges gave a mean score of 252 to the 7 native speakers but only a mean of 111 to the 53 nonnative speakers. Even more telling was the fact that the highest score any of the Portuguese speakers received was 225, in contrast to 246, the lowest score that any native speaker received. What is relevant to note for this discussion is that unlike other researchers investigating the identification of foreign accents (e.g., my own research), Major did not ask his judges to react holistically to a taped sequence of phrases—a natural stretch of speech. He requested them to compare contrasts in minimal pairs that involved only the two English vowel phonemes /ε/ (as in *bet*) and /æ/ (as in *bat*). Obviously, irrespective of a persons's ability to use acoustic information and/or phonetic information to determine whether or not a speaker has a foreign accent, phonological knowledge of a very specific and discrete nature is sufficient to allow listeners to make exceedingly accurate judgments about the nativeness of the voice they are attending to. Reviewing the evidence we have mustered so far, it is apparent that listeners have a wide range of cognitive processes available to them in order to make judgments about foreign accents. They can utilize speech characteristics ranging from very broad and general paralinguistic cues such as the speed or the fundamental frequency of the voice they are hearing, to the exceedingly precise phonological parameters that English speakers use to categorize a sound as belonging to one of two contrasting vowel phonemes (e.g., /ε/ vs. /æ/).

Bohn and Flege (1990) examined the role of vowel phonemes in accent identification from a slightly different perspective. They contrasted the pronunciations of two different groups of native speakers of German—those who were experienced in speaking English and those who were not. Unlike Major, they found that for some vowel contrasts, for example, the /ɛ/ versus /æ/ contrast that Major had used, experienced EFL (English as a Foreign Language) speakers identified the vowel stimuli in a manner identical to that of native speakers of English; but for other vowel contrasts, for example, /i/ versus /ɪ/ (as in *beat* vs. *bit*), experienced EFL speakers were neither different nor better in identifying these English vowels than the inexperienced EFL speakers. Bohn and Flege's study suggests several qualifications on any claim that phonological contrasts are simple and salient cues to nonnative speech. It suggests, for one thing, that the phonological structure of the nonnative's mother language influences the overall effect of the foreign accent on the vowel contrast that is being produced in the target language—in this case, English. It also suggests that all things being equal, some English vowels served as more salient signals of nonnative speech than other English vowels. For example, because the /i/ versus /ɪ/ phonemic contrast is lacking in most of the world's languages and is not a natural component of universal phonology, this contrast is more marked and is much more difficult for nonnatives to acquire in English. It is hence much more useful to native speakers in identifying foreign accents than some other phonological contrasts in English.

There is little evidence to suggest that consonant phonemes alone are used or are useful in identifying nonnative speech. Marks (1980) found little evidence that consonants provided his English-speaking judges with much information about the nonnativeness of the speech they were attending to. However, he did find that his judges sometimes detected first language interference in the pronunciation of certain English sonorants, specifically, /l/ and /r/. This slight evidence led Marks to conclude that when consonants are most like vowels (e.g., sonorants like /l/ and /r/ as opposed to obstruents like stops and affricates), consonant phonemes are possibly more useful in identifying foreign accents. In sum, the research to date suggests that for segmental phonemes, vowels are more helpful in identifying nonnative speech than consonants, and that among the English vowels, vowel phonemes that are marked are more useful than unmarked phonemes in identifying nonnative voices.

Finally, what about prosodic features such as stress, rhythm, and intonation? Impressionistically, they strike me as the most salient cues in identifying nonnative speech, especially from my experience with nonnative speakers using tonal languages such as Thai or Mandarin; or with speakers whose mother tongue is English, which is a stress-timed language, speaking Japanese, which is largely syllable-timed. These prosodic contrasts are especially conspicuous in the nonnative speech of inexperienced users of a second language, and they seem to be prevalent even in the discourse of highly proficient nonnative speakers.

Adams (1979) was one of the first to make a detailed study of the rhythmic and stress problems facing foreign learners of English. Not only did she ask native speakers to distinguish nonnative from native speakers based on these prosodic features, she also undertook acoustic analyses of these recorded voices to see if she could find invariant differences in pitch, amplitude, or duration that would serve to distinguish the native from nonnative voices. Finally, she also conducted electromyographic recordings of the thoracic musculature responsible for expiration to see if native speakers used different patterns of muscular movement from nonnative speakers. Not surprisingly, she found that native speakers could quickly and easily identify the nonnative voices on her tapes based on the prosodic information they heard. But she was unable to link this ability to any consistent differences in the acoustic information she recorded about the pitch, amplitude, and duration of these voices; nor did she discover any differences in the electromyographic patterns of the way native and nonnative speakers of English generated chest pulses.

There is recent evidence from an increasingly greater variety of languages that, regardless of the difficulty in defining the specific invariant acoustic parameters that characterize the nonnative prosodic productions that native speakers can so readily identify, suprasegmental features are significant in the identification of foreign accents. Juffs (1990) reported that Chinese learners of English experienced difficulty acquiring nativelike stress and rhythm, even though unlike Japanese, which is a syllable-timed language, Chinese languages use stress-timing in a way similar to English. Levitt (1992) investigated the acquisition of French prosody by speakers of English. She found that her English-speaking learners exhibited consistent difficulty in accurately picking up timing patterns in French, and that this was a prominent indicator of their nonnative speech.

Shen (1990) also described an experiment on how nonnative learners of French, in this case, speakers of Chinese, failed to produce French prosodic patterns natively. In this study, the nonnative speakers were unable to produce completely accurate French intonation patterns, even though they were able to perceive and categorize French intonation patterns accurately on identification tests. This particular study replicates the experience of most pronunciation teachers: Even though foreign language students can recognize a phonological contrast when they hear it, this does not ensure that they can then go on to produce the contrast consistently and accurately. Of course, many students of a foreign language are able to learn to produce many phonological contrasts, either segmental or suprasegmental, with virtual native speaker accuracy, although this does not imply they can speak the target language without a foreign accent. The ability to produce these contrasts does presuppose the ability to recognize the contrasts when they are heard; however, the reverse is not true. The ability to recognize phonological contrasts in a foreign language is a necessary but not a sufficient criterion for successful production.

4. CONCLUSION

I have suggested that there are three stages through which native speakers can progress in assessing whether or not the voice that they hear belongs to a fellow native speaker. At the first stage, listeners differentiate among many competing environmental noises and hone in on relevant acoustic cues that may very indirectly assist them in making judgments about foreign accents. At this initial stage, by differentiating among voices, a listener can filter out irrelevant voices and environmental sounds in order to attend to a particular voice and thus be able to progress to the next stage of accent recognition. At this second stage, native speakers use paralinguistic and phonetic cues so that they can recognize the degree of nativeness of the voice they have selected in Stage 1. Here, they may use a combination of paralinguistic information, such as the speaker's voice setting, and phonetic data, such as the speaker's degree of retroflection, to judge whether they recognize the voice as belonging to a native speaker or to a nonnative. Finally, at Stage 3, listeners resort to the most cognitively complex judgments of all and, based on their native speaker competence, use phonological criteria to identify the voice they are listening to as speaking with or without a foreign accent. Depending on the overall linguistic experience of the listeners, they may identify the native language of the person speaking. As I have already intimated in my previous discussion, the boundaries among these three stages are not discrete, but I believe they are sequential steps in the recognition process. Although evidence has been provided for different types of discriminatory processes at each of the three stages, several issues arise that should be addressed in this concluding summary.

I have suggested that these stages represent a sequencing from simpler, more transparent, and more general cognitive processes to processing that is more complex, abstract, and specific. Does this mean that these stages are also sequenced chronologically? I do not believe so. I do not see any contradiction in conceptualizing them as stages in sequential complexity but, at the same time, not conceiving them as representing chronological stages that listeners go through in making judgments about the voices they hear. In other words, it seems plausible to me that native speakers can resort to any of the information available to them at any moment, so that they can and do use identification judgments without first making recognition decisions. Or, to cite another example, a listener may very well make a judgment based on recognition information without resorting to any information at the differentiation stage. I think native speakers will employ the most salient and most useful information available to them at any moment in the discrimination process, regardless of what sequential stage that processing may require.

Of course this raises the much more complex issue of executive processing. What I have just suggested requires that in discrimination tasks such as recognizing foreign accents, the human brain possesses some sort of top down ability to decide what information is most relevant for any particular context. Hundert (1990) provided an excellent summary of recent neuropsychological research that documents how attention, to use the psychological construct, or the reticular formation, to name the neuroanatomical mechanism, winnows away irrelevant perceptual information so that the mind/brain can attend to information that is relevant to the schemata that are central to cognition at that moment. Given this cognitive ability, it seems likely to me that when native speakers are interested in whether or not the voice being heard belongs to a fellow native speaker, they will instantly employ whatever data most aptly apply to this cognitive decision. In some cases, acoustic information about the speaker's voice may be useful; in other conditions, phonetic qualities of the voice, such as degree of retroflection, may come into play; and in other situations, phonological cues such as prosodic features might be important. But because native speakers can make these judgments so quickly and so accurately, it is unlikely that they progress chronologically through the stages I have described; rather, the processing time is very rapid because executive decisions have already been made for the ear to attend to the first relevant cue that would indicate that the voice being heard can be classified nonnative.

Finally, because judgments about whether or not a person is speaking with a foreign accent do not appear to be based on accretive, linear, step-by-step processing but are more of an all-or-nothing gestalt decision, this cognitive or metalinguistic decision seems to be based on a process called restructuring (McLaughlin, 1990; Schmidt, 1992). Once native speakers have made an executive decision to determine whether the voice being attended to contains a foreign accent, they begin to scan all the information they have available at the acoustic, phonetic, and phonological stages, searching for any data that would disconfirm the assumption that the voice belongs to a fellow native speaker. (It is also possible, although less natural to me, to assume that the listener begins with the opposite presupposition, that the voice belongs to a nonnative speaker and the task is to search for any disconfirming evidence.) If at any moment and if from any source, there is any indication that this presupposition is false and that the voice does indeed contain nonnative qualities, the listener immediately restructures the original premise and concludes that the speaker is a nonnative. Based on the notion of restructuring, we have a reasonable explanation of why native speakers can make judgments so quickly and why they appear to base these judgments on such diverse information.

There is still a great deal we do not understand, however, about this "simple" ability by which all humans can so readily distinguish who shares their mother tongue and who does not. Although I have suggested evidence and explanations for the rapidity with which native speakers can make these judgments, it is still completely unclear how they can make these judgments so accurately, especially given the paucity of acoustic information that is usually available to them. All of this suggests that one does not need to leave the study of sound systems to find mystery in second language acquisition: Phonology alone contains magic enough!

References

Adams, C. (1979). *English speech rhythm and the foreign learner.* The Hague: Mouton.

Allen, G. D., & Hawkins, S. (1980). Phonological rhythm: Definition and development. In G. Yeni-Komshian, J. Kavanagh, & C. A. Ferguson, (Eds.), *Child phonology: Vol. 1. Production* (pp. 227–256). New York: Academic Press.

Anderson, J. M., & Ewen, C. (1987). *Principles of dependency phonology.* Cambridge: Cambridge University Press.

Anttonen, E. C. (1993). *Specification and representation in phonemic acquisition.* Unpublished master's thesis, Indiana University, Bloomington.

Applegate, J. R. (1961). Phonological rules of a subdialect of English. *Word, 17,* 186–193.

Archangeli, D. (1991). Syllabification and prosodic templates in Yawelmani. *Natural Language & Linguistic Theory, 9,* 231–283.

Archangeli, D. (1988). Aspects of underspecification theory. *Phonology, 5,* 183–207.

Archangeli, D. (1985). Yokuts harmony: Evidence for coplanar representation in nonlinear phonology. *Linguistic Inquiry, 16,* 335–372.

Archangeli, D. (1984). *Underspecification in Yawelmani phonology and morphology.* Unpublished doctoral dissertation, MIT, Cambridge, MA.

Archangeli, D., & Pulleyblank, D. (1986). *The content and structure of phonological representations.* Unpublished manuscript, University of Arizona, Tucson, and University of British Columbia, Vancouver.

Archibald, J. (1993a). The acquisition of English metrical parameters by adult speakers of Spanish. *International Review of Applied Linguistics, 30*(1–2), 129–141.

Archibald, J. (1993b). *Language learnability and L2 phonology: The acquisition of metrical parameters.* Dordrecht: Kluwer.

Archibald, J. (1992). Transfer of L1 parameter settings: Some empirical evidence from Polish metrics. *Canadian Journal of Linguistics, 37,* 301–339.

Archibald, J. (1991). *Language learnability and phonology: The acquisition of L2 metrical parameters.* Unpublished doctoral dissertation, University of Toronto.

Asher, J., & Garcia, R. (1969). The optimal age to learn a foreign language. *Modern Language Journal, 38*, 334–341.

Avery, P. (in preparation). Doctoral dissertation, University of Toronto.

Avery, P., & Rice, K. (1989). Segment structure and coronal underspecification. *Phonology, 6*, 179–200.

Avery, P., & Rice, K. (1988). Underspecification theory and the Coronal node. *Toronto Working Papers in Linguistics, 9*, 101–119.

Baker, C. L. (1979). Syntactic theory and the projection problem. *Linguistic Inquiry, 10*, 533–581.

Baker, W. J., & Derwing, B. (1982). Response coincidence analysis as evidence for language acquisition strategies. *Applied Psycholinguistics, 3*, 193–221.

Barton, D. (1976). *The role of perception in the acquisition of phonology.* Unpublished doctoral dissertation, University of London.

Berko, J. (1958). The child's learning of English morphology. *Word, 14*, 150–177.

Bernhardt, B. (1992a). The application of nonlinear phonological theory to intervention with one phonologically disordered child. *Clinical Linguistics & Phonetics, 6*, 283–316.

Bernhardt, B. (1992b). Developmental implications of nonlinear phonological theory. *Clinical Linguistics & Phonetics, 6*, 259–281.

Berwick, R. (1985). *The acquisition of syntactic knowledge.* Cambridge, MA: MIT Press.

Bloch, B. (1941). Phonemic overlapping. *American Speech, 16*, 278–284.

Bohn, O.-S., & Flege, J. (1990). Interlingual identification and the role of foreign language experience in second language vowel perception. *Applied Psycholinguistics, 11*, 303–328.

Borowsky, T. (1987). Antigemination in English phonology. *Linguistic Inquiry, 18*, 671–677.

de Boysson-Bardies, B., & Vihman, M. (1991). Adaptation to language: Evidence from babbling and first words in four languages. *Language, 67*, 297–319.

Braine, M. D. S. (1976). Review of *The acquisition of phonology* by N. V. Smith. *Language, 52*, 489–498.

Brannigan, G. (1976). Syllabic structure and the acquisition of consonants: The great conspiracy. *Journal of Psycholinguistic Research, 15*, 117–133.

Broadbent, D. (1958). *Perception and communication.* London: Pergamon.

Broselow, E. (in press). Skeletal positions and moras. In J. Goldsmith (Ed.), *A handbook of phonological theory.* Oxford: Basil Blackwell.

Broselow, E. (1992). Parametric variation in Arabic dialect phonology. In E. Broselow, M. Eid, & J. McCarthy (Eds.), *Perspectives on Arabic linguistics IV* (pp. 7–45). Amsterdam: John Benjamins.

Broselow, E., & Finer, D. (1991). Parameter setting in second language phonology and syntax. *Second Language Research, 7*, 35–59.

Brown, C., & Matthews, J. (1992, October). *The elaboration of segmental structure in first language acquisition: Evidence from the phonological discrimination of English phonemes.* Paper presented at the 17th Annual Boston University Conference on Language Development, Boston, MA.

Bryan, A., & Howard, D. (1992). Frozen phonology thawed: The analysis and remediation of a developmental disorder to real word phonology. *European Journal of Disorders of Communication, 27*, 343–365.

Camarata, S., & Gandour, J. (1984). On describing idiosyncratic phonologic systems. *Journal of Speech and Hearing Disorders, 49*, 262–266.

Chao, Y. R. (1973). The Cantian idiolect: An analysis of the Chinese spoken by a twenty-eight-month-old child. In C. A. Ferguson & D. I. Slobin (Eds.), *Studies of Child Language Development* (pp. 13–33). New York: Holt, Rinehart & Winston.

Chen, M., & Wang, W. S.-Y. (1975). Sound change: Actuation and implementation. *Language, 51*, 255–281.

Cherry, E. (1953). Some experiments on the recognition of speech, with one and with two ears. *Journal of the Acoustical Society of America, 25*, 975–979.

Chiat, S. (1983). Why Mikey's right and my key's wrong: The significance of stress and word boundaries in a child's output system. *Cognition, 14*, 275–300.

Chimombo, M., & Mtenje, A. (1989). Interaction of tone, syntax and semantics in the acquisition of Chichewa negation. *Studies in African Linguistics, 20*, 103–150.

Chin, S. B. (1993). *The organization and specification of features in functionally disordered phonologies.* Unpublished Doctoral dissertation, Indiana University, Bloomington.

Chin, S. B., & Dinnsen, D. A. (1992). Consonant clusters in disordered speech: Constraints and correspondence patterns. *Journal of Child Language, 19*, 259–285.

Chomsky, N. (1981). *Lectures on government and binding.* Dordrecht: Foris.

Chomsky, N. (1964). *Current issues in linguistic theory.* The Hague: Mouton.

Chomsky, N., & Halle, M. (1968). *The sound pattern of English.* New York: Harper & Row.

Clements, G. N. (1988a). *Sesotho tone.* Paper presented at the 19th Annual Conference on African Linguistics, Boston University, Boston, MA.

Clements, G. N. (1988b). Towards a substantive theory of feature specifications. *Proceedings of NELS, 18*, 79–93.

Clements, G. N. (1985). The geometry of phonological features. *Phonology Yearbook 2*, 225–252.

Clements, G. N., & Ford, K. (1979). Kikuyu tone shift and its synchronic consequences. *Linguistic Inquiry, 10*, 179–210.

Clements, G. N., & Goldsmith, J. (Eds.). (1984). *Autosegmental studies in Bantu tone.* Dordrecht: Foris.

Clements, G. N., & Keyser, S. J. (1983). *CV phonology.* Cambridge, MA: MIT Press.

Clumeck, H. (1980). The acquisition of tone. In G. Yeni-Komshian, J. Kavanagh, & C. A. Ferguson (Eds.), *Child phonology: Vol. 1. Production* (pp. 257–275). New York: Academic Press.

Clumeck, H. (1977). *Studies in the acquisition of Mandarin phonology.* Unpublished doctoral dissertation, University of California, Berkeley.

Coleman, R. (1971). Male and female voice quality and its relationship to vowel formant frequencies. *Journal of Speech and Hearing Research, 14*, 565–577.

Compton, A. J. (1975). Generative studies of children's phonological disorders: A strategy for therapy. In S. Singh (Ed.), *Measurements in hearing, speech, and language* (pp. 55–90). Baltimore, MD: University Park Press.

Coppieters, R. (1987). Competence differences between native and non-native speakers. *Language, 63*, 544–573.

Crystal, D. (1986). Prosodic development. In P. Fletcher & M. Garman, (Eds.), *Language acquisition* (pp. 174–197). Cambridge: Cambridge University Press.

Dalgish, G. (1975). On underlying and superficial constraints in OluTsootsu. *Papers from the Chicago Linguistic Society, 11*, 142–51.

Demirdache, H. (1988). Transparent vowels. In H. van der Hulst & N. Smith (Eds.), *Features, segmental structure, and harmony processes, part II* (pp. 39–76). Dordrecht: Foris.

Demuth, K. (in press). The prosodic structure of early words. In J. Morgan & K. Demuth (Eds.), *Signal to syntax: Bootstrapping from speech to grammar in early acquisition.* Hillsdale, NJ: Lawrence Erlbaum Associates.

Demuth, K. (1993). Issues in the acquisition of the Sesotho tonal system. *Journal of Child Language, 20*, 275–301.

Demuth, K. (1992). Acquisition of Sesotho. In D. Slobin (Ed.), *The cross-linguistic study of language acquisition* (Vol. 3). Hillsdale, NJ: Lawrence Erlbaum Associates.

Demuth, K. (1991). Acquisition of the Sesotho tonal system. *Afrikanistische Arbeitspapiere, 26*, 5–35.

Demuth, K. (1989). Problems in the acquisition of grammatical tone. *Stanford University Papers and Reports on Child Language Development, 28*, 81–88.

den Dikken, M., & van der Hulst, H. (1990). Segmental hierarchitecture. In H. van der Hulst & N. Smith (Eds.), *Features, segmental structure, and harmony processes* (pp. 1–78). Dordrecht: Foris.

Dinnsen, D. A. (in press). Theoretical issues in disordered child phonology. In T. K. Bhatia & W. C. Ritchie (Eds.), *Handbook of language acquisition*. New York: Academic Press.

Dinnsen, D. A. (1993). Underspecification and phonological disorders. In M. Eid & G. Iverson (Eds.), *Principles and prediction: The analysis of natural language* (pp. 287–304). Amsterdam: John Benjamins.

Dinnsen, D. A. (1992). Variation in developing and fully developed phonologies. In C. A. Ferguson, L. Menn, & C. Stoel-Gammon (Eds.), *Phonological development: Theories, research, implications* (pp. 191–210). Timonium, MD: York Press.

Dinnsen, D. A., & Chin, S. B. (1993a). Individual differences in phonological disorders and implications for a theory of acquisition. In F. R. Eckman (Ed.), *Confluence: Linguistics, L2 acquisition, speech pathology* (pp. 137–152). Amsterdam: John Benjamins.

Dinnsen, D. A., & Chin, S. B. (1993b). *Shadow-specification in phonological acquisition*. Unpublished manuscript, Indiana University, Bloomington.

Dinnsen, D. A., & Chin, S. B. (1991, October). *Underspecification and 'shadow-specification' in phonological development*. Paper presented at the 16th Annual Boston University Conference on Language Development, Boston, MA.

Dinnsen, D. A., Chin, S. B., & Elbert, M. (1992). On the lawfulness of change in phonetic inventories. *Lingua, 86*, 207–222.

Dinnsen, D. A., Chin, S. B., Elbert, M., & Powell, T. W. (1990). Some constraints on functionally disordered phonologies: Phonetic inventories and phonotactics. *Journal of Speech and Hearing Research, 33*, 28–37.

Dinnsen, D. A., & Elbert, M. (1984). On the relationship between phonology and learning. In M. Elbert, D. A. Dinnsen, & G. Weismer (Eds.), *Phonological theory and the misarticulating child* (ASHA Monograph No. 22, pp. 59–68). Rockville, MD: American Speech-Language-Hearing Association.

Doke, C. M., & Mofokeng, S. M. (1957). *Textbook of Southern Sotho grammar*. Cape Town: Longman.

Dresher, B. E. (1981a). Abstractness and explanation in phonology. In N. Hornstein & D. Lightfoot (Eds.), *Explanation in linguistics* (pp. 76–115). London: Longman.

Dresher, B. E. (1981b). On the learnability of abstract phonology. In C. L. Baker & J. J. McCarthy (Eds.), *The logical problem of language acquisition* (pp. 188–210). Cambridge, MA: MIT Press.

Dresher, B. E., & Kaye, J. (1990). A computational learning model for metrical phonology. *Cognition, 34*, 137–195.

Echols, C., & Newport, E. (1992). The role of stress and position in determining first words. *Language Acquisition, 2*, 189–220.

Edwards, M. L., & Shriberg, L. D. (1983). *Phonology: Applications in communicative disorders*. San Diego, CA: College-Hill Press.

Elbert, M., Powell, T. W., & Swartzlander, P. (1991). Toward a technology of generalization: How many exemplars are sufficient? *Journal of Speech and Hearing Research, 34*, 81–87.

Esling, J., & Wong, R. (1982). Voice quality settings and teaching of pronunciation. *TESOL Quarterly, 17*, 89–96.

Fee, E. J. (1992a). Exploring the minimal word in early phonological acquisition. In *Proceedings of the 1992 Annual Conference of the Canadian Linguistic Association*. Toronto: Toronto Working Papers in Linguistics.

Fee, E. J. (1992b, October). *Vowel acquisition in Hungarian: Evidence for an order of feature acquisition*. Paper presented at the 17th Annual Boston University Conference on Language Development, Boston, MA.

Fee, E. J. (1991). *Underspecification, parameters, and the acquisition of vowels.* Unpublished doctoral dissertation, University of British Columbia, Vancouver.

Fee, E. J., & Ingram, D. (1982). Reduplication as a strategy of phonological development. *Journal of Child Language, 9,* 41–54.

Ferguson, C. A. (1977). Learning to pronounce: the earliest stages of phonological development in the child. In F. D. Minifie & L. L. Lloyd, (Eds.), *Communication and cognitive abilities: Early behavioral assessment* (pp. 273–297). Cambridge: Cambridge University Press.

Ferguson, C. A., & Farwell, C. B. (1975). Words and sounds in early language acquisition. *Language, 51,* 419–439.

Ferguson, C., Menn, L., & Stoel-Gammon, C. (1992). *Phonological development: Models, research, and implications.* Timonium, MD: York Press.

Fey, M. E. (1989). Describing developing phonological systems: A response to Gierut. *Applied Psycholinguistics, 10,* 455–467.

Fikkert, P. (1992, October). *The acquisition of Dutch stress.* Paper presented at the 17th Annual Boston University Conference on Language Development, Boston, MA.

Flege, J., & Eefting, W. (1987). Cross-language switching in stop consonant perception and production by Dutch speakers of English. *Speech Communication, 6,* 185–202.

Fletcher, P. (1985). *A child's learning of English.* Oxford: Basil Blackwell.

Fodor, J. D. (1989). Learning the periphery. In R. J. Matthews & W. Demopoulos (Eds.), *Learnability and linguistic theory* (pp. 129–154). Dordrecht: Kluwer.

Gierut, J. A. (1992). The conditions and course of clinically-induced phonological change. *Journal of Speech and Hearing Research, 35,* 1049–1063.

Gierut, J. A. (1989). Describing developing phonological systems: A surrebuttal. *Applied Psycholinguistics, 10,* 469–473.

Gierut, J. A. (1986). Sound change: A phonemic split in a misarticulation child. *Applied Psycholinguistics, 7,* 57–68.

Gierut, J. A. (1985). *On the relationship between phonological knowledge and generalization learning in misarticulating children.* Unpublished doctoral dissertation, Indiana University, Bloomington.

Gierut, J. A., Cho, M.-H., & Dinnsen, D. A. (1993). Geometric accounts of consonant/vowel interactions in developing systems. *Clinical Linguistics & Phonetics, 7,* 219–236.

Gierut, J. A., & Dinnsen, D. A. (1986). On word-initial voicing: Converging sources of evidence in phonologically disordered speech. *Language and Speech, 29,* 97–114.

Gierut, J. A., Elbert, M., & Dinnsen, D. A. (1987). Functional analysis of phonological knowledge and generalization learning in misarticulating children. *Journal of Speech and Hearing Research, 30,* 462–479.

Gilbert, Z. (1992). *The representation of consonants in Telugu.* Unpublished master's thesis, University of Toronto.

Gleitman, L., Gleitman, H., Landau, B., & Wanner, E. (1988). Where learning begins: Initial representations for language learning. In F. Newmeyer, (Ed.), *Linguistics: The Cambridge survey* (Vol. 3, pp. 150–193). Cambridge: Cambridge University Press.

Goad, H. (1989). Language acquisition and the Obligatory Contour Principle. *Stanford University Papers and Reports on Child Language Development, 28,* 115–122.

Goad, H., & Ingram, D. (1987). Individual variation and its relevance to a theory of phonological acquisition. *Journal of Child Language, 14,* 419–432.

Goldman, R., & Fristoe, M. (1986). *Goldman–Fristoe Test of Articulation.* Circle Pines, MN: American Guidance Service, Inc.

Goldsmith, J. (1990). *Autosegmental and metrical phonology.* Oxford: Basil Blackwell.

Goldsmith, J. (1979). *Autosegmental phonology.* New York: Garland Press.

Goldsmith, J. (1976). *Autosegmental Phonology.* Unpublished doctoral dissertation, MIT, Cambridge, MA. (Distributed by the Indiana University Linguistics Club)

Grunwell, P. (1982). *Clinical phonology.* London: Croom Helm.

Halle, M., & Vergnaud, J. R. (1987). *An essay on stress*. Cambridge, MA: MIT Press.

Hamilton, P. (1993). On the internal structure of the Coronal node: Evidence from Australian languages. Unpublished manuscript, University of Toronto.

Hammond, M. (1990). Parameters of metrical theory and learnability. In I. Roca (Ed.), *Logical issues in language acquisition*. Dordrecht: Foris.

Harris, J. (1990). Segmental complexity and phonological government. *Phonology, 7*, 255–300.

Harris, J. (1983). *Syllable structure and stress in Spanish: A nonlinear analysis*. Cambridge, MA: MIT Press.

Hayes, B. (1991). *Metrical stress theory: Principles and case studies*. Unpublished manuscript.

Hayes, B. (1989). Compensatory lengthening in moraic phonology. *Linguistic Inquiry, 20*, 253–306.

Hayes, B. (1987). A revised parametric metrical theory. *Proceedings of NELS, 17*, 274–289.

Hayes, B. (1980). *A metrical theory of stress rules*. Unpublished doctoral dissertation, Cambridge, MA: MIT.

Hilgard, E. (1987). *Psychology in America: A historical survey*. San Diego, CA: Harcourt Brace Jovanovich.

Hochberg, J. (1988a). First steps in the acquisition of Spanish stress. *Journal of Child Language, 15*, 273–292.

Hochberg, J. (1988b). Learning Spanish stress: Developmental and theoretical perspectives. *Language, 64*, 683–706.

Hochberg, J. (1987). The acquisition of word stress rules in Spanish. *Papers and Reports on Child Language Development, 26*, 56–63.

Hodson, B. W., & Paden, E. P. (1983). *Targeting intelligible speech*. Austin, TX: Pro-Ed.

Hoffman, P. R., & Damico, S. K. (1988). Cluster reducing children's identification and production of /sk/ clusters. *Clinical Linguistics & Phonetics, 2*, 17–27.

Hooper, J. B. (1976). *An introduction to natural generative phonology*. New York: Academic Press.

Hulst, H. van der. (in press). Radical CV phonology: The categorial gesture. In F. Katamba & J. Durand (Eds.), *New frontiers in phonology*. London: Longman.

Hulst, H. van der. (1993). *Radical CV phonology*. Unpublished manuscript, Department of Linguistics, Leiden University, The Netherlands.

Hulst, H. van der. (1989). Atoms of segmental structure: Components, gestures and dependency. *Phonology, 6*, 253–284.

Hulst, H. van der. (1987). A lexical-autosegmental analysis of vowel harmony in Hungarian. In W. Dressler, V. Luschützky, H. Pfeiffer, E. Oskar, & J. R. Rennison (Eds.), *Phonologica 1984* (pp. 103–108). London: Cambridge University Press.

Hundert, E. (1990). *Philosophy, psychiatry, and neuroscience: Three approaches to the mind*. Oxford: Clarendon Press.

Hyams, N. (1986). *Language acquisition and the theory of parameters*. Dordrecht: Reidel.

Hyman, L. (1985). *A theory of phonological weight*. Dordrecht: Foris.

Hyman, L. (1970). How concrete is phonology? *Language, 46*, 58–76.

Idsardi, W. (1992). *The computation of prosody*. Unpublished doctoral dissertation, MIT, Cambridge, MA.

Ingram, D. (1992). Early phonological acquisition: A crosslinguistic perspective. In C. Ferguson, L. Menn, & C. Stoel-Gammon (Eds.), *Phonological development*. Yorkton, MD: York Press.

Ingram, D. (1991). Toward a theory of phonological acquisition. In J. Miller (Ed.), *Research perspectives on language disorders* (pp. 55–72). Boston: College Hill Press.

Ingram, D. (1989a). *First language acquisition: Method, description and explanation*. Cambridge: Cambridge University Press.

Ingram, D. (1989b). *Phonological disability in children* (2nd ed.). London: Cole & Whurr.

Ingram, D. (1989c). Underspecification and phonological acquisition. Unpublished manuscript, University of British Columbia, Vancouver.

Ingram, D. (1988). Jakobson revisited: Some evidence from the acquisition of Polish phonology. *Lingua, 75,* 55–82.

Ingram, D. (1986). Phonological development: Production. In P. Fletcher & M. Garman (Eds.), *Language acquisition* (pp. 223–239). Cambridge: Cambridge University Press.

Ingram, D. (1981). *Procedures for the phonological analysis of children's language.* Baltimore, MD: University Park Press.

Ingram, D. (1978). The role of the syllable in phonological development. In A. Bell & J. B. Hooper (Eds.), *Syllables and segments* (pp. 143–155). New York: North-Holland.

Ingram, D. (1976). *Phonological disability in children.* London: Edward Arnold.

Ingram, D. (1974). Phonological rules in young children. *Journal of Child Language, 1,* 49–64.

Ioup, G. (1984). Is there a structural foreign accent?: A comparison of syntactic and phonological errors in second language acquisition. *Language Learning, 34,* 1–17.

Itô, J. (1986). *Syllable theory in prosodic phonology.* Unpublished doctoral dissertation, University of Massachusetts, Amherst.

Iverson, G. K. (1993). (Post)Lexical rule application. In S. Hargus & E. Kaisse (Eds.), *Phonetics and phonology (Vol. 4): Studies in lexical phonology* (pp. 255–275). San Diego, CA: Academic Press.

Iverson, G., & Wheeler, D. (1987). Hierarchical structures in child phonology. *Lingua, 23,* 243–257.

Jakobson, R. (1968). *Child language, aphasia and phonological universals.* The Hague: Mouton. (Original work published 1941)

Jakobson R., & Halle, M. (1956). *Fundamentals of language.* The Hague: Mouton.

James, A. (1988). The acquisition of a second language phonology. Tübingen, Germany: Gunter Narr Verlag.

Johnson, J., & Newport, E. (1991). Critical period effects on universal properties of language: The status of subjacency in the acquisition of a second language. *Cognition, 39,* 215–218.

Juffs, A. (1990). Tone, syllable structure and interlanguage phonology. *IRAL, 28,* 99–117.

Kahn, D. (1976). *Syllable-based generalizations in English phonology.* Unpublished doctoral dissertation, MIT, Cambridge, MA. (Distributed by the Indiana University Linguistics Club)

Kaye, J. (1988). *Phonology: A cognitive view.* Hillsdale, NJ: Lawrence Erlbaum Associates.

Kaye, J., Lowenstamm, J., & Vergnaud, J.-R. (1985). The internal structure of phonological elements: A theory of charm and government. *Phonology Yearbook, 2,* 305–328.

Keating, P. A. (1988). Underspecification in phonetics. *Phonology, 5,* 275–292.

Khoali, B. (1991). *A grammar of Sesotho tone.* Unpublished doctoral dissertation, University of Illinois, Urbana.

Kim, C. M. (1986). *Phonology and syntax of Korean morphology.* Unpublished doctoral dissertation, University of Southern California, Los Angeles.

Kim-Renaud, Y. K. (1974). *Korean consonantal phonology.* Honolulu: University of Hawaii Press.

Kiparsky, P. (1993). Blocking in nonderived environments. In S. Hargus & E. Kaisse (Eds.), *Phonetics and phonology (Vol. 4): Studies in lexical phonology* (pp. 277–313). San Diego, CA: Academic Press.

Kiparsky, P. (1984). On the lexical phonology of Icelandic. In C.-C. Elert, I. Johansson, & E. Strangert (Eds.), *Nordic phonology III: Papers from a symposium* (pp. 135–164). Stockholm: University of Umeå/Almqvist & Wiksell.

Kiparsky, P. (1982a). How abstract is phonology? In P. Kiparsky, *Explanation in phonology* (pp. 119–163). Dordrecht: Foris. (Original work published 1968)

Kiparsky, P. (1982b). Lexical morphology and phonology. In The Linguistic Society of Korea (Ed.), *Linguistics in the morning calm* (pp. 1–91). Seoul, Korea: Hanshin.

Kiparsky, P., & Menn, L. (1977). On the acquisition of phonology. In J. Macnamara (Ed.), *Language learning and thought.* New York: Academic Press.

Kirk, L. (1973). An analysis of speech imitations by Gã children. *Anthropological Linguistics, 15,* 267–275.

Kisseberth, C., & Mmusi, S. (1989). *The Obligatory Contour Principle and the tone of the object prefix in Setswana.* Paper presented at the 20th Annual Conference on African Linguistics, University of Illinois, Urbana.

Klein, H. (1984). Learning to stress: A case study. *Journal of Child Language, 11,* 375–390.

Köhler, O. (1956). Das Tonsystem des Verbum im Südsotho [The tone system of the verb in southern Sesotho]. *Mitteilungen des Instituts für Orientforschung* (pp. 435–474).

Kunene, D. (1961). *A study of Sesotho tone.* Unpublished doctoral dissertation, University of Cape Town, South Africa.

Kunene, D. (1972). *A preliminary study of downstepping in Southern Sotho.* African Studies, *31,* 11–24.

Kwon, Y. S., & Kim, M. (1990). *New standard Korean spelling dictionary.* Seoul: Chiphyun-Jun.

Larew, L. (1961). The optimal age for beginning a foreign language. *Modern Language Journal, 45,* 203–206.

Leben, W. (1978). The representation of tone. In V. Fromkin (Ed.), *Tone: A linguistic survey* (pp. 177–190). New York: Academic Press.

Leben, W. (1973). *Suprasegmental phonology.* Unpublished doctoral dissertation, MIT, Cambridge, MA. (Distributed by the Indiana University Linguistics Club)

Lee, E. J. (1988). *Explanation of 'Standard Korean'.* Seoul: Dae Jae Kak.

Lenneberg, E. (1967). *Biological foundations of language.* New York: Wiley.

Leopold, W. (1947). *Speech development of a bilingual child: A linguist's record, Vol. 2: Sound learning in the first two years.* Evanston, IL: Northwestern University Press.

Letele, G. L. (1955). *The role of tone in the Southern Sotho language.* Unpublished doctoral dissertation, University College of Fort Hare, South Africa.

Levelt, C. (in press). Consonant harmony: A reanalysis in terms of vowel-consonant interaction. *The Amsterdam Series in Child Language Development.*

Levin, J. (1985). A metrical theory of syllabicity. Unpublished doctoral dissertation, MIT, Cambridge, MA.

Levitt, A. (1992). Reiterant speech as a test of non-native speakers' mastery of the timing of French. *Haskins Laboratories Status Report on Speech Research, 109–110,* Janlune, pp. 59–72.

Li, C., & Thompson, S. (1977). The acquisition of tone in Mandarin-speaking children. *Journal of Child Language, 4,* 185–199.

Lightfoot, D. (1989). The child's trigger experience: Degree-0 learnability. *Behavioral and Brain Sciences, 12,* 321–375.

Lindblom, B. (1988). Role of input in children's early vocal behavior. Discussant's comments in *Symposium on Neurobiology of Early Infant Behavior* (pp. 303–307). Stockholm: Gren Center.

Locke, J. (1983). *Phonological acquisition and change.* New York: Academic Press.

Locke, J. (1980). The inference of speech perception in the phonologically disordered child. Part II: Some clinically novel procedures, their use, some findings. *Journal of Speech and Hearing Disorders, 45,* 445–468.

Lombardi, L. (1991). *Laryngeal features and laryngeal neutralization.* Unpublished doctoral dissertation, University of Massachusetts, Amherst.

Long, M. (1990). Maturational constraints on language development. *Studies in Second Language Acquisition, 12*(3), 251–286.

Lovins, J. (1975). *Loanwords and the phonological structure of Japanese.* (Distributed by the Indiana University Linguistics Club)

MacKay, I. (1987). *Phonetics: The science of speech production.* Boston: Little, Brown.

Macken, M. (1979). Developmental reorganization of phonology: A hierarchy of basic units of acquisition. *Lingua, 49,* 11–49.

Macken, M. (1980). Aspects of the acquisition of stop systems: A cross-linguistic perspective. In G. Yeni-Komshian, J. Kavanagh, & C. A. Ferguson (Eds.), *Child phonology: vol. 1. Production* (pp. 143–168). New York: Academic Press.

Macken, M. (1992). Where's phonology? In C. A. Ferguson, L. Menn, & C. Stoel-Gammon (Eds.), *Phonological development: Models, research, implications* (pp. 249–269). Timonium, MD: York Press.

Macken, M. (1986). Phonological development: A crosslinguistic perspective. In P. Fletcher & M. Garman (Eds.), *Language acquisition* (pp. 251–268). Cambridge: Cambridge University Press.

Macken, M., & Ferguson, C. (1983). Cognitive aspects of phonological development: Model, evidence and issues. In K. Nelson (Ed.), *Children's language, 5* (pp. 255–282). Hillsdale, NJ.: Lawrence Erlbaum Associates.

Maddieson, I. (1984). *Patterns of sounds.* Cambridge: Cambridge University Press.

Magen, H., & Blumstein, S. (1991). Effects of speaking rate on the vowel length distinction in Korean. Unpublished manuscript, Brown University, Providence, RI.

Mairs, J. L. (1989). Stress assignment in interlanguage phonology: An analysis of the stress system of Spanish speakers learning English. In S. Gass & J. Schachter (Eds.), *Linguistic perspectives on second language acquisition* (pp. 260–284). New York: Cambridge University Press.

Major, R. (1987). Phonological similarity, markedness, and rate of second language acquisition. *Studies in Second Language Acquisition, 9,* 63–82.

Marks, J. (1980). *Foreign accent and the interlanguage hypothesis.* Unpublished master's thesis, University of Toronto.

Maxwell, E. M. (1979). Competing analyses of a deviant phonology. *Glossa, 13,* 181–214.

Maxwell, E. M. (1982). *A study of misarticulation from a linguistic perspective.* Unpublished doctoral dissertation, Indiana University, Bloomington.

McCarthy, J. (1991). *The phonology of semitic pharyngeals.* Unpublished manuscript, University of Massachusetts, Amherst.

McCarthy, J. (1988). Feature geometry and dependency. *Phonetica, 43,* 84–108.

McCarthy, J. (1986). OCP effects: Gemination and antigemination. *Linguistic Inquiry, 17,* 207–263.

McCarthy, J., & Prince, A. (1990). Foot and word in prosodic morphology: The Arabic broken plurals. *National Language & Linguistic Theory, 8,* 209–283.

McCarthy, J., & Prince, A. (1986). *Prosodic morphology.* Unpublished manuscript, University of Massachusetts, Amherst, and Brandeis University.

McCawley, J. (1977). Accent in Japanese. In L. Hyman (Ed.), *Studies in stress and accent.* Los Angeles: University of Southern California, Department of Linguistics.

McLaughlin, B. (1990). Restructuring. *Applied Linguistics, 11,* 129–158.

Mehler, J., Jusczyk, P. W., Lambertz, G., Halstead, N., Bertoncini, J., & Amiel-Tison, C. (1988). A precursor of language acquisition in young infants. *Cognition, 29,* 143–178.

Mendes-Figueiredo, M. (1991, December). Acquisition of second language pronunciation: The critical period. *CTJ Journal,* 41–47.

Menn, L. (1983). Development of articulatory, phonetic, and phonological capabilities. In B. Butterworth (Ed.), *Language production: Development, writing and other language processes* (Vol. 2, pp. 3–50). New York: Academic Press.

Menn, L. (1980). Phonological theory and child phonology. In G. Yeni-Komshian, J. Kavanagh, & C. A. Ferguson (Eds.), *Child Phonology* (Vol. 1, pp. 23–41). New York: Academic Press.

Menn, L. (1978). Phonological units in beginning speech. In A. Bell & J. B. Hooper (Eds.), *Syllables and segments,* (pp. 157–171). Amsterdam: North-Holland.

Menn, L. (1977). Phonotactic rules in beginning speech. *Lingua, 26,* 225–251.

Menn, L., & Matthei, E. (1990). The "two-lexicon" account of child phonology: Looking back, looking ahead. In C. Ferguson, L. Menn, & C. Stoel-Gammon, (Eds.), *Phonological development: Models, reseach, implications.* Timonium, MD: York Press.

Mester, R.-A., & Itô, J. (1989). Feature predictability and underspecification: Palatal prosody in Japanese mimetics. *Language, 65,* 258–293.

Mmusi, S. (1991). *OCP effects and violations—The case of Setswana verbal tone.* Unpublished doctoral dissertation, University of Illinois, Urbana.

Molfese, D., Freeman, R., & Palermo, D. (1975). The ontogeny of brain lateralization for speech and nonspeech stimuli. *Brain and Language, 2,* 356–368.

Montés Giraldo, J. J. (1976). El sistema, la norma y el aprendizaje de la lengua. *Thesaurus: Boletín del instituto Caro y Cuervo, 31,* 14–40.

Montés Giraldo, J. J. (1971). Acerca de la apropriación por el niño del sistema fonológico español [On the child language acquisition of the Spanish phonological system]. *Thesaurus: Boletín del instituto Caro y Cuervo, 26,* 322–346.

Moon, K.-H. (1981). Korean P-irregular verbs revisited. *Linguistic Analysis, 8,* 377–402.

Morris, B., & Gerstman, L. (1986). Age contrasts in the learning of language-relevant materials. *Language Learning, 36,* 311–352.

Morse, P. (1974). Infant speech perception: A preliminary model and review of the literature. In R. Schiefelbusch & L. Lloyd (Eds.), *Language perspectives: Acquisition retardation and intervention* (pp. 19–53). Baltimore, MD: University Park Press.

Morse, P. (1972). The discrimination of speech and nonspeech stimuli in early infancy. *Journal of Experimental Child Psychology, 14,* 477–492.

Moskowitz, A. (1970). The two-year-old stage in the acquisition of English phonology. *Language, 46,* 426–441.

Moto, F. (1988). *The acquisition of Chichewa tone.* Paper presented at the 19th Conference on African Linguistics, Boston University, Boston, MA.

Nittrouer, S. (1992). Age-related differences in perceptual effects of formant transitions within syllable and across syllable boundaries. *Journal of Phonetics, 20,* 351–382.

Nittrouer, S., & Studdert-Kennedy, M. (1987). The role of coarticulatory effects in the perception of fricatives by children and adults. *Journal of Speech and Hearing Research, 30,* 319–329.

Odden, D. (1988). Anti antigemination and the OCP. *Linguistic Inquiry, 19,* 451–475.

Odden, D. (1986). On the role of the Obligatory Contour Principle in phonological theory. *Language, 62,* 353–383.

Otake, T. (1983). *Sequential voicing in Japanese and English loanwords in Japanese.* Unpublished master's thesis, University of Texas, Austin.

Oyama, S. (1976). A sensitive period for the acquisition of a non-native phonological system. *Journal of Psycholinguistic Research, 5,* 261–283.

Paradis, C., & Prunet, J.-F. (Eds.). (1991). *Phonetics and phonology 2. The special status of coronals. Internal and external evidence.* New York: Academic Press.

Park, H.-B. (1992). *External evidence for representations, rules, and constraints in Korean and Japanese.* Unpublished doctoral dissertation, SUNY, Stony Brook.

Pater, J. (1991, October). *Parameter resetting in second language metrical phonology.* Paper presented at the Michigan State Conference on Theory Construction and Methodology in Second Language Research.

Patkowski, M. (1980). The sensitive period for the acquisition of syntax in a second language. *Language Learning, 30,* 449–472.

Penfield, W. (1963). *The second career.* Boston: Little, Brown.

Piggott, G. (1992). Variability in feature dependency: The case of nasality. *Natural Language & Linguistic Theory, 10,* 33–77.

Piggott, G. (1990). The parameters of nasalization. In H. van der Hulst & N. Smith (Eds.), *Features, segmental structure and harmony processes* (pp. 132–167). Dordrecht: Foris.

Pinker, S. (1984). *Language learnability and language development*. Cambridge, MA: Harvard University Press.

Prince, A. (1983). Relating to the grid. *Linguistic Inquiry, 14*, 19–100.

Prince, A., & Smolensky, P. (1993). *Optimality theory*. Unpublished manuscript, Rutgers University.

Ptacek, P., & Sander, E. (1966). Age recognition from voice. *Journal of Speech and Hearing Research, 9*, 273–277.

Pye, C., Ingram, D., & List, H. (1987). A comparison of initial consonant acquisition in English and Quiché. In K. Nelson & A. van Kleek (Eds.), *Children's language* (Vol. 6, pp. 175–190). Hillsdale, NJ: Lawrence Erlbaum Associates.

Rice, K. (1993a). Default variability: The coronal-velar relationship. *Toronto Working Papers in Linguistics, 12*(2), 97–130).

Rice, K. (1993b). A reexamination of the feature [sonorant]: The status of 'sonorant obstruents.' *Language, 69*(2), 308–344.

Rice, K. (1991, January). *Variability in default interpretation*. Paper presented at the Montreal-Ottawa-Toronto Workshop on Phonology.

Rice, K., & Avery, P. (1993). Segmental complexity and the structure of inventories. *Toronto Working Papers in Linguistics, 12*(2), 97–130.

Rice, K., & Avery, P. (1991a, October). *A learning path for phonology: A theory of segmental elaboration*. Paper presented at the 16th Annual Boston University Conference on Language Development, Boston, MA.

Rice, K., & Avery, P. (1991b). On the relationship between laterality and coronality. In C. Paradis & J.-F. Prunet (Eds.), *Phonetics and phonology 2. The special status of coronals. Internal and external evidence* (pp. 101–124). New York: Academic Press.

Rice, K., & Avery, P. (1990). On the representation of voice. *Proceedings of NELS, 20*,

Sagey, E. (1986). *The representation of features and relations in nonlinear phonology*. Unpublished doctoral dissertation, MIT, Cambridge, MA.

Sandler, W. (1993). *Suboral articulators*. Unpublished manuscript, University of Haifa, Israel.

Schmidt, R. (1992). Psychological mechanisms underlying second language fluency. *Studies in Second Language Acquisition, 14*, 357–385.

Schmidt, R. (1990). The role of consciousness in language learning. *Applied Linguistics, 11*, 129–158.

Schwartz, R. G., & Leonard, L. B. (1982). Do children pick and choose? An examination of phonological selection and avoidance in early lexical acquisition. *Journal of Child Language, 9*, 319–336.

Scobbie, J. M. (1992). *Attribute value phonology*. Unpublished doctoral dissertation, University of Edinburgh, Scotland.

Scovel, T. (1988). *A time to speak: A psycholinguistic inquiry into the critical period for human speech*. Boston: Heinle & Heinle.

Scovel, T. (1981). The recognition of foreign accents in English and its implications for psycholinguistic theories of language acquisition. In *Proceedings of the 5th International Assoiation of Applied Linguistics* (pp. 389–401). Montreal: Laval University Press.

Scovel, T. (1969). Foreign accents, language acquisition, and cerebral dominance. *Language Learning, 19*, 245–253.

Seliger, H., Krashen, S., & Ladefoged, P. (1975). Maturational constraints in the acquisition of second language accent. *Language Sciences, 36*, 20–22.

Selkirk, E. (1990). A two-root theory of length. *UMass Occasional Papers, 14*, 123–171.

Selkirk, E. (1982). The syllable. In H. van der Hulst & N. Smith (Eds.), *The structure of phonological representations* (Vol. 2, pp. 337–384). Dordrecht: Foris.

Shen, X. (1990). Ability of learning the prosody of an intonational language by speakers of a tonal language: Chinese speakers learning French prosody. *IRAL, 28*, 119–134.

Shriberg, L., & Kwiatkowski, J. (1986). *Natural Process Analysis (NPA): A procedure for phonological analysis of continuous speech samples*. New York: MacMillan.

Slobin, D. (Ed.). (1985). *The crosslinguistic study of language acquisition: Vol. 1. The data*. Hillsdale, NJ: Lawrence Erlbaum Associates.

Smith, N. V. (1973). *The acquisition of phonology: A case study*. Cambridge: Cambridge University Press.

Spencer, A. (1988). A phonological theory of phonological development. In M. J. Ball (Ed.), *Theoretical linguistics and disordered language* (pp. 115–151). San Diego, CA: College-Hill Press.

Spencer, A. (1986). Toward a theory of phonological development. *Lingua, 68*, 3–38.

Stampe, D. (1972). *A dissertation on natural phonology*. Unpublished doctoral dissertation, University of Chicago.

Stampe, D. (1969). The acquisition of phonemic representation. In *Proceedings of the Fifth Regional Meeting of the Chicago Linguistic Society* (pp. 433–444). Chicago: Chicago Linguistic Society.

Steriade, D. (1987). Redundant values. In A. Bosch, B. Need, & E. Schiller (Eds.), *Parasession on autosegmental and metrical phonology* (pp. 339–362). Chicago: Chicago Linguistic Society.

Steriade, D. (1982). *Greek prosodies and the nature of syllabification*. Unpublished doctoral dissertation, MIT, Cambridge, MA.

Stoel-Gammon, C. (1985). Phonetic inventories, 15–24 months: A longitudinal study. *Journal of Speech and Hearing Research, 28*, 505–512.

Stoel-Gammon, C., & Cooper, J. (1984). Patterns of early lexical and phonological development. *Journal of Child Language, 11*, 247–271.

Strange, W., & Broen, P. A. (1980). Perception and production of approximant consonants by 3-year-olds: A first study. In G. Yeni-Komshian, J. Kavanagh, & C. A. Ferguson (Eds.), *Child phonology. Vol. 2: Perception* (pp. 117–154). New York: Academic Press.

Stemberger, P., & Stoel-Gammon, C. (1991). The underspecification of coronals: Evidence from language acquisition and performance errors. In C. Paradis & J.-F. Prunet (Eds.), *Special status of coronal: Internal and external evidence* (pp. 181–199). San Diego, CA: Academic Press.

Suzman, S. (1991). *Language acquisition in Zulu*. Unpublished doctoral dissertation, Witwatersrand University, South Africa.

Tahta, S., Wood, M., & Lowenthal, K. (1981). Foreign accents: Factors relating to transfer of accent from the first language to a second language. *Language and Speech, 24*, 265–272.

Tartter, V. (1980). Happy talk: The perceptual and acoustic effects of smiling on speech. *Perception and Psychophysics, 27*, 24–27.

Templin, M. (1957). *Certain language skills in children: Their development and interrelationships*. Minneapolis: University of Minnesota Press.

Thompson, I. (1991). Foreign accents revisited: The English pronunciation of Russian immigrants. *Language Learning, 41*, 177–204.

Tse, J. K. P. (1978). Tone acquisition in Cantonese: A longitudinal case study. *Journal of Child Language, 5*, 191–204.

Tuaycharoen, P. (1977). *The phonetic and phonological development of a Thai baby: From early communicative interaction to speech*. Unpublished doctoral dissertation, University of London.

Tucker, A. (1969). *The comparative phonetics of the Suto-Chuana group of Bantu languages*. London: Gregg International Publishers Ltd. (Original work published 1929)

Tyler, A. A., & Figurski, G. R. (1994). Phonetic inventory changes after treating distinctions along an implicational hierarchy. *Clinical Linguistics and Phonetics, 8*, 91–107.

Vennemann, T. (1973). Phonological concreteness in natural generative grammar. In R. Shuy & C. J. Bailey, (Eds.), *Toward tomorrow's linguistics* (pp. 202–219). Washington, D.C.: Georgetown University Press.

Vihman, M. (1982). A note on children's lexical representations. *Journal of Child Language, 9*, 249–253.

Vihman, M. (1978). Consonant harmony: Its scope and function in child language. In J. H. Greenberg (Ed.), *Universals of human language 2* (pp. 282–334). Stanford: Stanford University Press.

Vihman, M., Ferguson, C., & Elbert, M. (1986). Phonological development from babbling to speech: Common tendencies and individual differences. *Applied Psycholinguistics, 7*, 3–40.

Wang, W. S.-Y. (1969). Competing sound changes as a result of residue. *Language, 45*, 9–25.

Waterson, N. (1987). *Prosodic phonology: The theory and its application to language acquisition and speech processing.* Tübingen: Gunter Narr Verlag.

Waterson, N. (1971). Child phonology: A prosodic view. *Journal of Linguistics, 7*, 179–211.

Weismer, G., Dinnsen, D. A., & Elbert, M. (1981). A study of the voicing distinction associated with omitted, word-final stops. *Journal of Speech and Hearing Disorders, 40*, 320–328.

Wexler, K., & Manzini, M. R. (1987). Parameters and learnability in binding theory. In T. Roeper and E. Williams (Eds.), *Parameter setting* (pp. 41–76). Dordrecht: Reidel.

White, L. (1985). The acquisition of parametrized grammars: Subjacency in second language acquisition. *Second Language Research, 1*, 1–17.

Williams, A. L, & Dinnsen, D. A. (1987). A problem of allophonic variation in a speech disordered child. *Innovations in Linguistics Education, 5*, 85–90.

Williams, E. (1976). Underlying tone in Margi and Igbo. *Linguistic Inquiry, 7*, 463–484.

Winitz, H., & Irwin, O. C. (1958). Syllabic and phonetic structure of infants' early words. *Journal of Speech and Hearing Research, 1*, 250–256.

Yip, M. (1990). *Two cases of double-dependency in feature geometry.* Unpublished manuscript, University of California at Irvine.

Yip, M. (1988). The Obligatory Contour Principle and phonological rules: A loss of identity. *Linguistic Inquiry, 19*, 65–100.

Youssef, A., & Mazurkewich, I. (1993, January). *The acquisition of English metrical parameters and syllable structure by adult Cairene Arabic speakers.* Paper presented at the MIT Workshop on Recent Advances in Second Language Acquisition, Cambridge, MA.

Zec, D. (1988). *Sonority constraints on prosodic structure.* Unpublished doctoral dissertation, Stanford University, Stanford, CA.

Author Index

197

Subject Index